# Let's Review Regents:

# English Revised Edition

Carol Chaitkin, M.S.
*Former Director of American Studies*
*Lycée Français de New York*
*New York, New York*

*Former English Department Head*
*Great Neck North High School*
*Great Neck, New York*

# Acknowledgments

Page 75: "Pitcher" from *The Orb Weaver* by Robert Francis © 1960, by Robert Francis and reprinted by permission of Wesleyan University Press.

Page 79: "Old Photograph of the Future" by Robert Penn Warren © 1985. Reprinted by permission of Random House, Inc.

Page 81: "Child on Top of a Greenhouse," copyright © 1946 by Editorial Publications, Inc.; from COLLECTED POEMS by Theodore Roethke. Used by permission of Doubleday, an imprint of Knopf Doubleday Publishing Group, a division of Random House LLC. All rights reserved.

Page 81: "The Sleeping Giant" from OLD AND NEW POEMS by Donald Hall. Copyright © 1990 by Donald Hall. Reprinted by permission of Houghton Mifflin Harcourt Publishing Company. All rights reserved.

Published by Kaplan North America, LLC, dba Barron's Educational Series
1515 West Cypress Creek Road
Fort Lauderdale, FL 33309
www.barronseduc.com

ISBN: 978-1-5062-6481-3

10 9 8 7 6 5

Kaplan North America, LLC, d/b/a Barron's Educational Series print books are available at special quantity discounts to use for sales promotions, employee premiums, or educational purposes. For more information or to purchase books, please call the Simon & Schuster special sales department at 866-506-1949.

# TABLE OF CONTENTS

**INTRODUCTION** — **1**

A Guide to the New York State Standards in
Literacy (ELA) — 1

Terms to Help You Understand the
State Standards — 2

The Regents ELA (Common Core) Exam — 3

Ways to Use *Let's Review: English* — 4

**CHAPTER 1**    **READING COMPREHENSION** — **5**

Close Reading — 5

Questions to Keep in Mind As You Read — 6

Reading Comprehenshion Passages and
Questions for Review — 7

**CHAPTER 2**    **WRITING FROM SOURCES** — **23**

Step One—Reading for Information and
Understanding — 23

Looking at the Texts — 30

Step Two—Composing a Source-based Argument — 31

Planning the Essay — 32

Looking at a Variety of Effective Claims — 32

**CHAPTER 3**    **READING AND WRITING TO
ANALYZE TEXT** — **35**

Text Analysis: Exposition — 35

Sample Text and Expository Response — 35

Additional Texts for Analysis and Review — 38

**CHAPTER 4**    **READING PROSE** — **45**

What Writers Do: A List of Useful Terms — 45

Reading Fiction — 46

Reading Nonfiction — 53

A Glossary of Literary Terms and Techniques — 66

**CHAPTER 5**  **READING POETRY**                                    **75**

Introduction                                                         75
Structure and Language in Poetry                                     78
Theme in Poetry                                                      83
Tone                                                                 86
Writing About Poetry/Explication                                     86
Poetry on Examinations                                               87
A Handful of Poems for Further Reading                               87
A Glossary of Poetic Terms and Techniques                            94

**CHAPTER 6**  **WRITING ABOUT LITERATURE:**
               **A GENERAL REVIEW**                                  **101**

Topics for Literary Essays                                           101
Topic and Focus                                                      102
Selection of Significant Details                                     102
Developing the Topic                                                 102
Looking at Key Terms in Literature Questions                         104
Using Fluent and Precise Language                                    104
Choosing Your Own Topic: Representative
  Literary Subjects and Themes                                       105
Audience and Literature Essays                                       108
A Note on Conclusions                                                108

**CHAPTER 7**  **WRITING ON DEMAND**                                 **109**

Writing to Inform or Persuade                                        109
Writing from a Prompt                                                115
Evaluating Composition                                               118
Preparing for Essay Exams                                            119
Writing on Timed Examinations                                        119
Using Synonymies to Enhance Your Writing                             121
A Glossary of Terms for Writing                                      124

**CHAPTER 8**  **VOCABULARY**                                        **127**

Academic Language                                                    128
Unfamiliar and Archaic Language                                      133
Studying New Words                                                   135

Roots and Prefixes from Latin and Greek 136
A Note on Synonyms and Using a Thesaurus 142
Organizing Vocabulary Study 143
Vocabulary for Study 149

**CHAPTER 9 GRAMMAR AND USAGE FOR THE CAREFUL WRITER: A GUIDE TO STANDARD WRITTEN ENGLISH 161**

Reviewing the Fundamentals 161
Avoiding Common Errors in Writing 165
Expressions Often Confused, Misused, and Overused 174

**CHAPTER 10 PUNCTUATION: GUIDELINES AND REMINDERS 183**

End Punctuation 183
Internal Punctuation 187
Titles of Works of Literature 196
A Final Note on Punctuation 196

**CHAPTER 11 SPELLING 197**

Spelling on Writing Exams 197
Spelling Rules and Patterns 197
Words Commonly Confused 206
Words Commonly Misspelled 207

**RECOMMENDED READING 215**

Novels 215
Autobiography, Essays, and Other Nonfiction 217
Poetry 218
Short Stories 220
Plays 220

**APPENDICES: THE NEW YORK STATE COMMON CORE LEARNING STANDARDS FOR ENGLISH LANGUAGE ARTS 223**

# REGENTS ELA (COMMON CORE) EXAMINATIONS

June 2019 Examination .......... 233

## INDEX .......... 261

# INTRODUCTION

*Let's Review* is designed as a handbook for high school English courses, including those aligned with the new Common Core Standards, and as a review book for students preparing to take the Regents Exam in English Language Arts (Common Core). Because the English Regents Exam is not a test of specific curriculum but an assessment of skills in reading comprehension, literary analysis, and composition, *Let's Review* offers a comprehensive guide to essential language, literature, and critical reading and writing skills all high school students should seek to demonstrate as they prepare for college and the workplace.

## A GUIDE TO THE NEW YORK STATE STANDARDS IN LITERACY (ELA)

Most middle school and high school students in New York State should already be familiar with some key shifts in curriculum and instruction in their English courses. These shifts in emphasis include the following:

- Students will read more informational texts and perhaps fewer literary texts than in the past. Alignment with the Common Core requires a balancing of the two.
- In all academic subjects, students will be expected to build their knowledge primarily through engaging directly with text.
- Throughout secondary school, students will read texts of increasing complexity and will be expected to develop skills in **close reading** in all academic subjects.
- Students will be expected to engage in rich and rigorous **evidence-based** conversations/class discussions about text.
- Student writing will emphasize **use of evidence** from sources to express their understanding and to form and develop argument.
- Students will acquire the **academic vocabulary** they need to comprehend and respond to grade level complex texts. This vocabulary is often relevant to more than one subject.

# TERMS TO HELP YOU UNDERSTAND THE STATE STANDARDS

- **ELA/LITERACY**—**English Language Arts** refers to skills in reading, writing, speaking, and listening. Courses and exams once identified as English may also be identified as ELA. **Literacy** refers to the ability to read and write and to use language proficiently. The term also identifies the quality of being knowledgeable in a particular subject or field. For example, we often refer to "digital" or "computer literacy."
- **COMMON CORE LEARNING STANDARDS (CCLS)\***—These are the learning standards in ELA and math, also known as **CCSS** (Common Core State Standards), developed and adopted by a consortium of over 40 states. New York State adopted the CCLS in 2010 and continues to implement them in curriculum and assessments (testing).
- **CCR**—The phrase **"college and career ready"** is widely used in discussion of new curriculum and assessments. This refers to the fundamental principle of the Common Core Standards: to reflect the knowledge and skills that all students need for success in college and careers.
- **ASSESSMENT**—You may hear teachers and other educators using the term **assessment** instead of test or examination. An **assessment** is more than a simple test (in vocabulary, say) because it seeks to measure a number of skills at one time. Although we continue to refer to the English Regents as an exam or test, its goal is to be a valid **assessment** of a broad range of reading, thinking, language, and writing skills outlined in the Standards.
- **TEXT**—Broadly, the term text refers to any written material. The Common Core standards use the term to refer to the great variety of material students are expected to be able to read, understand, analyze, and write about. Texts may include **literary** works of fiction, drama, and poetry; and **informational**, or nonfiction, including essays, memoirs, speeches, and scientific and historical documents. The Common Core also emphasizes the use of **authentic texts;** that is, students will read actual historical documents or scientific essays rather than simply read articles about them.
- **CLOSE READING**—Skill in close, analytic reading is fundamental to the CCLS and to the new Regents exam. The Common Core curriculum focuses student attention on the text itself in order to understand not only what the text says and means but also how that meaning is constructed and revealed. Close reading enables students to understand central ideas and key supporting details. It also enables students to reflect on the meanings of individual words and sentences, the order in which sentences unfold, and the development of ideas over the course

of the text, which ultimately leads students to arrive at an understanding of the text as a whole.

- **ARGUMENT**—What is an argument? In academic writing, an argument is usually a central idea, often called a **claim** or **thesis statement,** which is backed up with evidence that supports the idea. Much of the writing high school students do in their English courses constitutes essays of argument, in addition to personal essays, descriptive pieces, and works of imagination.
- **SOURCE-BASED/EVIDENCE-BASED**—The ability to compose sound arguments using relevant and specific evidence from a given text is central to the expectations of the Common Core Standards.
- **WRITING STRATEGY**—This is the general term for a literary element, literary technique, or rhetorical device. Examples include characterization, conflict, denotation/connotation, metaphor, simile, irony, language use, point of view, setting, structure, symbolism, theme, and tone. In class discussions and on examinations, students are expected to understand and explain how literary elements and writing strategies contribute to the meaning of a text.

*The Anchor (Common Core) Standards for Grades 11–12 Reading, Writing, and Language are found in the Appendices, pages 223–227.

# THE REGENTS ELA (COMMON CORE) EXAM

This 3-hour examination requires students to read, analyze, and write about both literary and informational texts.

## PART I—READING COMPREHENSION

This part requires close reading of three texts and will contain at least one literature text, one poem, and one informational text, followed by 24 multiple-choice questions.

## PART II—WRITING FROM SOURCES: ARGUMENT

This part includes close reading of four informational texts and may contain some information in graphics; students will compose an essay of argument with a claim based on the sources.

## PART III—TEXT ANALYSIS: EXPOSITION

Students will perform a close reading of one informational or one literature text and write a two to three paragraph expository response that identifies a central idea in the text and analyzes how the author's use of one writing strategy develops that central idea.

*Note:* The ACT and the new SAT (2015) include similar assessments of close reading, text analysis, the rhetoric of arguments, and the use of academic vocabulary.

# WAYS TO USE *LET'S REVIEW: ENGLISH*

As a handbook for literature study in high school and college courses, see especially

Chapter 4—Reading Prose
Chapter 5—Reading Poetry
Chapter 6—Writing About Literature: A General Review

As a handbook for reading comprehension and language skills, see especially

Chapter 1—Reading Comprehension
Chapter 3—Reading and Writing to Analyze Text
Chapter 4—Reading Prose
Chapter 5—Reading Poetry
Chapter 8—Vocabulary

As a handbook for writing and proofreading, see especially

Chapter 2—Writing from Sources
Chapter 3—Reading and Writing to Analyze Text
Chapter 6—Writing About Literature: A General Review
Chapter 9—Grammar and Usage for the Careful Writer
Chapter 10—Punctuation: Guidelines and Reminders

As a review text for the ELA (Common Core) Regents exam, the SAT, and the ACT, see especially

Chapter 1—Reading Comprehension
Chapter 2—Writing from Sources
Chapter 3—Reading and Writing to Analyze Text
Chapter 8—Vocabulary
Appendices—The New York State Common Core Learning Standards for English Language Arts

# Chapter 1

# READING COMPREHENSION

Throughout your schooling, you have been developing skills in the ability to read and comprehend works of literature as well as informational texts in nearly every subject, including history and social studies, science, and technical studies. Because the ability to understand, interpret, and make use of a wide range of texts is central to learning, it is a skill students are regularly asked to demonstrate. Assessment of students' reading comprehension skills may be informal or indirect, as in a class discussion or short quiz, or through formal testing.

Students at Regents level—11th and 12th grades—are expected to have the ability to understand and interpret both literary and informational texts of significant complexity: that is, Regents-level students understand literary texts with multiple levels of meaning, with structures that may be complex or unconventional, and with elements of figurative or deliberately ambiguous language that are integral to its meaning. The expectations for reading informational texts include the ability to interpret and analyze personal essays, speeches, opinion pieces, and memoir and autobiographical works as well as official documents and historical, scientific, and technical material for subject courses other than English. This increased emphasis on a wide range of informational texts is one of the key shifts in high school curriculum and should already be familiar to most students. It is also helpful to know that both the ACT and new SAT (2015) exams include a similar variety of texts and primary source documents.

## CLOSE READING

One useful way to think about what we mean by "close reading" is to think about what you are doing when you can annotate something you are reading; that is, what do you underline? circle? check in the margins? You are probably checking off main ideas and conclusions, underlining the most important details, and circling significant or unfamiliar words. Whether or not you actually mark up a text, that process of checking, underlining, and circling is the thinking process of close reading.

In-class discussions of literary works are often exercises in what is meant by close reading—Where are we? Which details give us an image of the setting? What just happened? What is this character thinking now? What does the story lead us to expect? What is surprising? How were we prepared? How does the author/narrator guide our understanding of characters and their actions? Why is this incident important in the plot? What does this character's remark really mean? Was the ending convincing?

The most satisfying "close reading," however, is what we are doing when our imaginations are fully engaged in a story, a play, a poem, or a film(!) Then it is not an academic exercise or assessment but the pleasure of experiencing a good story.

Reading for information in history, social studies, or science requires careful attention to the sequence of ideas, to how general statements are supported with relevant details. This kind of reading may also require familiarity with specialized language. (See Academic Language in Chapter 8 — Vocabulary.)

On exams, you will exercise this same kind of thinking and engagement with the text on your own. The multiple-choice questions are designed to assess your close reading skills and the depth of your understanding.

## QUESTIONS TO KEEP IN MIND AS YOU READ

*If you are reading a literary passage*, ask yourself

What is this piece about? What is the narrative point of view?
What do we understand about the setting?
What do we understand about the narrator? Other characters?

*In reading a poem*, consider

What experience, memory, or dramatic situation is the poem about?
Who and where is the narrator/speaker?
How does the organization of lines and stanzas affect the meaning?
How are language and imagery used?

*In passages of memoir and personal essay*, ask

What experience is meant to be shared and understood?
What does the author say? Describe? Suggest? Reveal?

*If you are reading an informational text*, ask yourself

What is the subject? What do I already know about this subject?
What main idea or theme is being developed? What phrases or terms
  signal that?
What is the purpose? To inform? To persuade? To celebrate? To guide? To
  show a process? To introduce a new or unfamiliar subject?

# READING COMPREHENSION PASSAGES AND QUESTIONS FOR REVIEW

The following passages and questions are from actual tasks on Regents ELA exams.

## PASSAGE ONE—LITERATURE

This passage is from a classic Sherlock Holmes story by Sir Arthur Conan Doyle. Many of the expressions are unfamiliar but can be understood in context. High school students may already be familiar with the character of Sherlock Holmes, both through reading of the original stories and through modern retelling in popular American and British television series. On the Regents ELA exam, you are expected to read and analyze texts from works of American literature as well as works from British and world literatures.

It was upon the 4th of March, as I have good reason to remember, that I rose somewhat earlier than usual, and found that Sherlock Holmes had not yet finished his breakfast. The landlady had become so accustomed to my late habits that my place had not been laid nor my coffee prepared. With the unreasonable petulance[1] of
(5)  mankind I rang the bell and gave a curt intimation that I was ready. Then I picked up a magazine from the table and attempted to while away the time with it, while my companion munched silently at his toast. One of the articles had a pencil-mark at the heading, and I naturally began to run my eye through it. ...

"From a drop of water," said the writer, "a logician could infer the possibility
(10)  of an Atlantic or a Niagara without having seen or heard of one or the other. So all life is a great chain, the nature of which is known whenever we are shown a single link of it. Like all other arts, the Science of Deduction and Analysis is one which can only be acquired by long and patient study, nor is life long enough to allow any mortal to attain the highest possible perfection in it. Before turning to those
(15)  moral and mental aspects of the matter which present the greatest difficulties, let the inquirer begin by mastering more elementary problems. Let him, on meeting a fellow-mortal, learn at a glance to distinguish the history of the man and the trade or profession to which he belongs. Puerile[2] as such an exercise may seem, it sharpens the faculties of observation and teaches one where to look and what to look for. By
(20)  a man's fingernails, by his coat-sleeve, by his boot, by his trouser-knees, by the callosities of his forefinger and thumb, by his expression, by his shirt-cuffs—by each of these things a man's calling is plainly revealed. That all united should fail to enlighten the competent inquirer in any case is almost inconceivable."

---

[1]petulance — a quality or state of being rude
[2]puerile — childish

(25) "What ineffable twaddle!" I cried, slapping the magazine down on the table; "I never read such rubbish in my life."

"What is it?" asked Sherlock Holmes.

"Why, this article," I said, pointing at it with my egg-spoon as I sat down to my breakfast. "I see that you have read it, since you have marked it. I don't deny that it is smartly written. It irritates me, though. It is evidently the theory of some arm-
(30) chair lounger who evolves all these neat little paradoxes in the seclusion of his own study. It is not practical. I should like to see him clapped down in a third-class carriage on the Underground and asked to give the trades of all his fellow-travellers. I would lay a thousand to one against him."

"You would lose your money," Sherlock Holmes remarked, calmly. "As for the
(35) article, I wrote it myself."

"You?"

"Yes, I have a turn both for observation and for deduction. The theories which I have expressed there, and which appear to you to be so chimerical, are really extremely practical—so practical that I depend upon them for my bread-and-
(40) cheese."

"And how?" I asked, involuntarily.

"Well, I have a trade of my own. I suppose I am the only one in the world. I'm a consulting detective, if you can understand what that is. Here in London we have lots of government detectives and lots of private ones. When these fellows are at
(45) fault they come to me, and I manage to put them on the right scent. They lay all the evidence before me, and I am generally able, by the help of my knowledge of the history of crime, to set them straight. There is a strong family resemblance about misdeeds, and if you have all the details of a thousand at your finger-ends, it is odd if you can't unravel the thousand and first. Lestrade is a well-known detective. He
(50) got himself into a fog recently over a forgery case, and that was what brought him here."

"And these other people?"

"They are mostly sent out by private inquiry agencies. They are all people who are in trouble about something, and want a little enlightening. I listen to their story,
(55) they listen to my comments, and then I pocket my fee."

"But do you mean to say," I said, "that without leaving your room you can unravel some knot which other men can make nothing of, although they have seen every detail for themselves?"

"Quite so. I have a kind of intuition that way. Now and again a case turns up
(60) which is a little more complex. Then I have to bustle about and see things with my own eyes. You see, I have a lot of special knowledge which I apply to the problem, and which facilitates matters wonderfully. Those rules of deduction laid down in that article which aroused your scorn are invaluable to me in practical work. Obser-

vation with me is second nature. You appeared to be surprised when I told you, on
(65)  our first meeting, that you had come from Afghanistan."

"You were told, no doubt."

"Nothing of the sort. I *knew* you came from Afghanistan. From long habit the
train of thought ran so swiftly through my mind that I arrived at the conclusion
without being conscious of intermediate steps. There were such steps, however. The
(70)  train of reasoning ran: 'Here is a gentleman of a medical type, but with the air of a
military man. Clearly an army doctor, then. He has just come from the tropics, for
his face is dark, and that is not the natural tint of his skin, for his wrists are fair. He
has undergone hardship and sickness, as his haggard face says clearly. His left arm
has been injured. He holds it in a stiff and unnatural manner. Where in the tropics
(75)  could an English army doctor have seen much hardship and got his arm wounded?
Clearly in Afghanistan.' The whole train of thought did not occupy a second. I then
remarked that you came from Afghanistan, and you were astonished." ...

I was still annoyed at his bumptious style of conversation. I thought it best to
change the topic.
(80)  "I wonder what that fellow is looking for?" I asked, pointing to a stalwart,
plainly dressed individual who was walking slowly down the other side of the street,
looking anxiously at the numbers. He had a large, blue envelope in his hand, and
was evidently the bearer of a message.

"You mean the retired sergeant of marines," said Sherlock Holmes.
(85)  "Brag and bounce!" thought I to myself. "He knows that I cannot verify his
guess." The thought had hardly passed through my mind when the man whom we
were watching caught sight of the number on our door, and ran rapidly across the
roadway. We heard a loud knock, a deep voice below, and heavy steps ascending
the stair.
(90)  "For Mr. Sherlock Holmes," he said, stepping into the room and handing my
friend the letter.

Here was an opportunity of taking the conceit out of him. He little thought of
this when he made that random shot. "May I ask, my lad," I said, blandly, "what
your trade may be?"
(95)  "Commissionnaire, sir," he said, gruffly. "Uniform away for repairs."

"And you were?" I asked, with a slightly malicious glance at my companion. "A
sergeant, sir, Royal Marine Light Infantry, sir. No answer? Right, sir." He clicked
his heels together, raised his hand in a salute, and was gone.

—A. Conan Doyle
excerpted from *A Study in Scarlet*, 1904
Harper & Brothers Publishers

## Questions for Comprehension

This passage, narrated by the character of Dr. Watson, reveals the differences in character and personality of the two men. The discussion of the magazine article leads to a dramatic demonstration of Holmes's powers of observation and deduction. At the end, Watson's doubts are erased, and he is left speechless.

1 The phrase "with the unreasonable petulance of mankind" (lines 4–5) emphasizes the narrator's

    (1) frustration with himself for missing sleep
    (2) irritation about not finding his breakfast ready
    (3) concern regarding the pencil-mark on the newspaper
    (4) impatience with Sherlock Holmes's silence      1____

2 How do the words "logician" (line 9), "deduction" (lines 12, 37, and 62), and "analysis" (line 12) advance the author's purpose?

    (1) by indicating the relationship between science and art
    (2) by suggesting the reasons why private inquiry agencies seek outside help
    (3) by highlighting the complexity of the crimes encountered by Sherlock Holmes
    (4) by emphasizing the systematic nature of Sherlock Holmes's approach to solving crimes      2____

3 What is the effect of withholding the identity of Sherlock Holmes as the author of the article (lines 9 through 35)?

    (1) It creates a somber mood.
    (2) It foreshadows an unwelcome turn of events.
    (3) It allows the reader to learn the narrator's true feelings.
    (4) It leads the reader to misunderstand who the writer is.      3____

4 In this passage, the conversation between Holmes and the narrator (lines 24 through 40) serves to

(1) reinforce the narrator's appreciation for deduction
(2) establish a friendship between the narrator and Holmes
(3) reveal how Holmes makes his living
(4) expose some of Holmes's misdeeds                4____

5 As used in line 38, the word "chimerical" most nearly means

(1) unfair              (3) aggravating
(2) unrealistic         (4) contradictory          5____

6 Which analysis is best supported by the details in lines 45 through 58 of the text?

(1) Private detectives base their analyses on an understanding of human nature.
(2) Sherlock Holmes's association with other well-known detectives improves his crime-solving abilities.
(3) Government detectives are mostly ineffective at solving complicated crimes.
(4) Sherlock Holmes's intuition relies on his ability to detect similarities among various crimes.          6____

## Looking at the Questions and the Standards

- Questions 1, 2, and 5 ask you to determine the meaning of words and phrases as they are used in context and to understand how they contribute to the meaning of the text.
- Question 3 asks you to recognize how the author uses one element or detail to structure the plot. Holmes deliberately allows Watson to think someone else wrote the article, which then creates the situation in which he can show how skilled and clever he is.
- Questions 4 and 6 ask you to recognize how specific details contribute to character development and plot structure.

### Answers

(1) **2**   (2) **4**   (3) **3**   (4) **3**   (5) **2**   (6) **4**

(See Chapter 4—Reading Prose for a detailed review of the elements of fiction.)

### PASSAGE TWO—POEM

#### Money Musk

Listen, you upstate hillsides (nothing
Like the herb-strewn fields of Provence[1])
Which I have loved
So loyally, your wood lots
*(5)*   And trailers and old farmhouses,
Your satellite dishes—

Haven't I driven
Past the strip malls and country airports,
The National Guard armories and even
*(10)*   That abandoned missile depot
Clutched in the lake's fingers
Past the tattered billboards.
The barns spray-painted with praise,

―――――――――
[1]Provence—a region of southern France

Past the farm tools, fiddles,
(15) And fishing lures, the sprung bellows
Of accordions on the tables of flea markets,
Just to catch a glimpse of you as you once were,
Like the brass showing, raw and dull,
Where the silver plate has worn off
(20) The frame around this mirror, and the silver
Gone too, the only reflection as faint

As light on dusty glass,
And beyond it, tarnished, dim, the rafters
And beams of the attic where I climbed
(25) To take out my grandmother's mandolin
And play on the three or four unbroken strings
With a penny for a pick.
                                        Listen,
Wasn't that offering enough, a life
(30) Of playing half-badly on an antique instrument,
Trying to catch a tune you'd long ago
Forgotten even the name of, *Money Musk*
Or *Petronella*.² Wasn't it enough
To take my vows of poverty of spirit
(35) Before the plain geometry of a 19th-century
Farmhouse, and praise no other goods
Than this rectitude,³ this stillness,
This clarity you have spurned now, oh
Landscape I have sung
(40) Despite my voice, despite the stubborn
Silence behind your tawdry,⁴ best intentions.

—Jordan Smith
from *The Cortland Review*
Issue Eight, August 1999

---

²Money Musk or Petronella—classic old American dances
³rectitude—honesty
⁴tawdry—cheap

# Questions for Comprehension

The opening line establishes the dramatic situation and the speaker in this poem: we hear the voice of someone who once lived in the area he is now driving through and who now regrets the changes he sees. The poem is a song to the landscape he has loved and been loyal to.

1 The details presented in lines 4 through 13 emphasize the landscape's

(1) historical significance
(2) beauty
(3) economic possibilities
(4) transformation                                            1____

2 What shift in focus occurs from lines 7 through 27?

(1) from social conflict to personal conflict
(2) from external description to childhood memory
(3) from the narrator's feelings to his family's feelings
(4) from the narrator's thoughts to the narrator's
    actions                                                  2____

3 What is the effect of the simile used in lines 21 and 22?

(1) It suggests how the narrator has changed.
(2) It conveys the narrator's lack of awareness.
(3) It indicates the darkness of the setting.
(4) It emphasizes the diminishing of the past.               3____

4 Which word best describes the narrator's tone in lines 28 through 38 of the poem?

(1) frustrated          (3) contentment
(2) embarrassed         (4) respectful                        4____

5  Lines 33 through 37 contribute to a central theme in the
   poem by describing the narrator's

   (1) wish to live in a suburban setting
   (2) obligation to continue a past tradition
   (2) commitment to the values of a past era
   (4) reluctance to accept different points of view          5____

## Looking at the Questions and the Standards

- Questions 1 and 3 focus on the significance of key details. The importance of the landscape to the narrator is the central theme of the poem.
  The simile in these lines reflects the changes in the landscape the narrator so regrets.
- Question 4 asks you to recognize how the meaning of a word or phrase
  establishes tone, that is, the attitude of the narrator is revealed throughout the poem.
- Questions 2 and 5 ask you to recognize key elements in the structure of
  the poem, through a shift in focus and in the narrator's final address to
  the landscape.

**Answers**

(1) **4**   (2) **2**   (3) **4**   (4) **1**   (5) **3**

(See Chapter 5—Reading Poetry for a detailed review of the elements of
poetry.)

## PASSAGE THREE — INFORMATIONAL

This passage is an engaging and effective presentation for a general reader of a challenging question in modern physics and cosmology: Is there "a theory of everything"? Readers familiar with the highly successful film *The Theory of Everything* (2014) will recognize some of the ideas explored in the article.

A few years ago the City Council of Monza, Italy, barred pet owners from keeping goldfish in curved fishbowls. The sponsors of the measure explained that it is cruel to keep a fish in a bowl because the curved sides give the fish a distorted view of reality. Aside from the measure's significance to the poor goldfish, the story raises
(5)  an interesting philosophical question: How do we know that the reality we perceive is true?

The goldfish is seeing a version of reality that is different from ours, but can we be sure it is any less real? For all we know, we, too, may spend our entire lives staring out at the world through a distorting lens.

(10)  In physics, the question is not academic. Indeed, physicists and cosmologists are finding themselves in a similar predicament to the goldfish's. For decades we have strived to come up with an ultimate theory of everything—one complete and consistent set of fundamental laws of nature that explain every aspect of reality. It now appears that this quest may yield not a single theory but a family of intercon-
(15)  nected theories, each describing its own version of reality, as if it viewed the universe through its own fishbowl.

This notion may be difficult for many people, including some working scientists, to accept. Most people believe that there is an objective reality out there and that our senses and our science directly convey information about the material world.
(20)  Classical science is based on the belief that an external world exists whose properties are definite and independent of the observer who perceives them. In philosophy, that belief is called realism.

### Do Not Attempt to Adjust the Picture

The idea of alternative realities is a mainstay of today's popular culture. For example, in the science-fiction film *The Matrix* the human race is unknowingly liv-
(25)  ing in a simulated virtual reality created by intelligent computers to keep them pacified and content while the computers suck their bioelectrical energy (whatever that is). How do we know we are not just computer-generated characters living in a Matrix-like world? If we lived in a synthetic, imaginary world, events would not necessarily have any logic or consistency or obey any laws. The aliens in control
(30)  might find it more interesting or amusing to see our reactions, for example, if everyone in the world suddenly decided that chocolate was repulsive or that war was not

an option, but that has never happened. If the aliens did enforce consistent laws, we would have no way to tell that another reality stood behind the simulated one. It is easy to call the world the aliens live in the "real" one and the computer-generated
(35) world a false one. But if—like us—the beings in the simulated world could not gaze into their universe from the outside, they would have no reason to doubt their own pictures of reality.

The goldfish are in a similar situation. Their view is not the same as ours from outside their curved bowl, but they could still formulate scientific laws governing
(40) the motion of the objects they observe on the outside. For instance, because light bends as it travels from air to water, a freely moving object that we would observe to move in a straight line would be observed by the goldfish to move along a curved path. The goldfish could formulate scientific laws from their distorted frame of reference that would always hold true and that would enable them to make predictions
(45) about the future motion of objects outside the bowl. Their laws would be more complicated than the laws in our frame, but simplicity is a matter of taste. If the goldfish formulated such a theory, we would have to admit the goldfish's view as a valid picture of reality.

### Glimpses of the Deep Theory

In the quest to discover the ultimate laws of physics, no approach has raised
(50) higher hopes—or more controversy—than string theory. String theory was first proposed in the 1970s as an attempt to unify all the forces of nature into one coherent framework and, in particular, to bring the force of gravity into the domain of quantum[1] physics. By the early 1990s, however, physicists discovered that string theory suffers from an awkward issue: there are five different string theories. For
(55) those advocating that string theory was the unique theory of everything, this was quite an embarrassment. In the mid-1990s researchers started discovering that these different theories—and yet another theory called supergravity—actually describe the same phenomena, giving them some hope that they would amount eventually to a unified theory. The theories are indeed related by what physicists call duali-
(60) ties, which are a kind of mathematical dictionaries for translating concepts back and forth. But, alas, each theory is a good description of phenomena only under a certain range of conditions—for example at low energies. None can describe every aspect of the universe.

String theorists are now convinced that the five different string theories are just
(65) different approximations to a more fundamental theory called M-theory. (No one seems to know what the "M" stands for. It may be "master," "miracle" or "mystery," or all three.) People are still trying to decipher the nature of M-theory, but it seems that the traditional expectation of a single theory of nature may be untenable[2]

---

[1]quantum—a small, indivisible unit of energy
[2]untenable—indefensible

(70) and that to describe the universe we must employ different theories in different situations. Thus, M-theory is not a theory in the usual sense but a network of theories. It is a bit like a map. To faithfully represent the entire Earth on a flat surface, one has to use a collection of maps, each of which covers a limited region. The maps overlap one another, and where they do, they show the same landscape. Similarly, the different theories in the M-theory family may look very different, but they can all be
(75) regarded as versions of the same underlying theory, and they all predict the same phenomena where they overlap, but none works well in all situations.

Whenever we develop a model of the world and find it to be successful, we tend to attribute to the model the quality of reality or absolute truth. But M-theory, like the goldfish example, shows that the same physical situation can be modeled
(80) in different ways, each employing different fundamental elements and concepts. It might be that to describe the universe we have to employ different theories in different situations. Each theory may have its own version of reality, but according to model-dependent realism, that diversity is acceptable, and none of the versions can be said to be more real than any other. It is not the physicist's traditional expecta-
(85) tion for a theory of nature, nor does it correspond to our everyday idea of reality. But it might be the way of the universe.

—Stephen Hawking and Leonard Mlodinow
excerpted from "The (Elusive) Theory of Everything,"
*Scientific American*, October 2010

## Questions for Comprehension

The topic is highly complex, but the narrative of description and explanation is composed in language that is highly readable and developed through a series of vivid images and analogies, beginning with the anecdote about goldfish in curved bowls.

1 The authors' anecdote about pet owners in Monza, Italy, serves to introduce a

   (1) proof of a universal world view
   (2) measure that is objectionable to scientists
   (3) central question about the way we see
   (4) philosophical question about what we value      1____

2 The primary purpose of lines 10 through 16 is to clarify the

    (1) need for a single theory
    (2) role of the senses in understanding
    (3) possibility of other life in the universe
    (4) origin of alternative theories        2____

3 How do lines 17 through 22 develop a claim?

    (1) by providing details about a philosophical challenge faced by scientists
    (2) by showing how scientists should handle alternate realities
    (3) by arguing for an approach that scientists have always followed
    (4) by explaining how scientists should view a philosophical approach        3____

4 The reference to *The Matrix* in lines 24 through 28 is used to emphasize the questioning of our

    (1) virtues
    (2) perception
    (3) education
    (4) ideals        4____

5 The references to goldfish in lines 39 through 49 contribute to the authors' purpose by suggesting that

    (1) people's theories are influenced by their viewpoints
    (2) nature's mysteries are best left undiscovered
    (3) reality can only be determined by an outside perspective
    (4) light must be viewed under similar circumstances        5____

6 As used in lines 51 and 52 of the text, what does the word "coherent" mean?

    (1) balanced
    (2) indisputable
    (3) popular
    (4) understandable        6____

7 The authors' reference to "a collection of maps" (line 72) is used to help clarify

    (1) a complex theory
    (2) a historical concept
    (3) the representation of space
    (4) the limitations of previous theories     7____

8 The function of lines 77 through 84 is to

    (1) argue for a specific theory
    (2) suggest that theories relate to expectations
    (3) describe the way differing theories should co-exist
    (4) evaluate theories based on specific needs     8____

9 With which statement would the authors most likely agree?

    (1) The perception of the universe can never be questioned.
    (2) There is a single, agreed upon theory of reality.
    (3) There are multiple realities that are possible to prove.
    (4) The understanding of the universe continues to change.     9____

10 The authors attempt to engage the audience through the use of

    (1) absolute statements
    (2) real-world examples
    (3) detailed descriptions
    (4) simple questions     10____

# Looking at the Questions and the Standards

- Questions 1 and 10 call your attention to how rhetorical elements are part of the structure.
  The anecdote at the beginning and the real-world examples used throughout the article help the reader understand key ideas.
- Question 6 is an example of determining the meaning of a term in context, and question 7 calls attention to how a specific image clarifies the meaning of a central idea.
- Questions 2–5 and 7–9 focus on the need to determine the central ideas and analyze how they are developed over the course of a text.

**Answers**

| | | | |
|---|---|---|---|
| (1) **3** | (4) **2** | (7) **1** | (10) **2** |
| (2) **4** | (5) **1** | (8) **3** | |
| (3) **1** | (6) **4** | (9) **4** | |

(See Chapter 4—Reading Prose for a detailed review of elements of nonfiction.)

## Chapter 2

# WRITING FROM SOURCES

Most high school students already have experienced writing essays of opinion and personal experience; these are likely to have been on topics the writer was interested in. The shift in the new standards is to source-based argument, where the writer must first do research to understand a topic before trying to develop an opinion.

In the second part of the Regents ELA exam, you will demonstrate your ability to comprehend and analyze several documents on a substantive, even controversial topic. The topics raise questions that have a variety of legitimate answers or present problems with alternative solutions. You then must take a position on that topic and develop a coherent essay of argument, which is supported by specific evidence in the texts; the final essay must include references to at least three of the sources. These are, in fact, the skills you use when you do any kind of research and writing project.

Close reading in this part means first reading to understand the issue and then to analyze the information in the texts to understand how they support various points of view. As you read the following documents, keep in mind the process of annotation: note central ideas and themes, key details, and important terms and phrases. On an actual exam, you are permitted to take notes in the margins, and you will have scrap paper to plan your essay.

## STEP ONE—READING FOR INFORMATION AND UNDERSTANDING

Here are the texts from a recent Regents ELA Exam.

**Topic:** Should companies be allowed to track consumers' shopping or other preferences without their permission?

23

## Text 1

### Cell Phone Carrier Marketing Techniques:
### An Invasion of Privacy?

BOSTON (CBS) – Your cell phone may be spying on you.

Every time you download an app, search for a website, send a text, snap a QR code or drive by a store with your GPS on, you are being tracked by your cell phone company.

(5)     "They know you were playing Angry Birds. They know that you drove by Sears. They know you drove by Domino's Pizza. They can take that and take a very unique algorithm[1] that can focus on your behavior," explained marketing expert Mark Johnson. "It's very impactful."

According to Johnson, your data trail is worth big money to the cell phone com-
(10)   panies.

Details about your habits, your age and gender are compiled and can be sold to third parties. The information is predominantly used as a marketing tool so adver-tisers can target you with products or services that you are more likely to use or want.

(15)   The idea does not sit well with smartphone user Harrine Freeman. "It does seem creepy that companies are collecting all this information about consumers," she said.

Freeman is so uneasy; she turns off her GPS when she is not using it. She also clears her browser history.

(20)   "I think it is an invasion of privacy," she said.

All of the major cell phone carriers admit to collecting information about its customers. Some in the industry argue it benefits consumers because they get ads that are relevant to them. Cell phone companies do notify customers about the data they collect, but critics say the notices are often hard to understand and written in
(25)   fine print.

Rainey Reitman of the Electronic Frontier Foundation doesn't like the fact that those who don't want to be tracked have to go out of their way to get the company to stop.

"This is something that consumers are automatically opted into," Reitman said.

(30)   To find out how your cell phone company might be monitoring you, be sure to carefully read the privacy policy.

---

[1]algorithm — process or set of rules followed in calculations

Also, make sure you read all of the updates your carrier might send you because this tracking technology keeps changing.

—Paula Ebben
*http://boston.cbslocal.com*, January 16, 2012

## Text 2

### EyeSee You and the Internet of Things: Watching You While You Shop

...Even the store mannequins have gotten in on the gig. According to the *Washington Post*, mannequins in some high-end boutiques are now being outfitted with cameras that utilize facial recognition technology. A small camera embedded in the eye of an otherwise normal looking mannequin allows storekeepers to keep
(5)   track of the age, gender and race of all their customers. This information is then used to personally tailor the shopping experience to those coming in and out of their stores. As the *Washington Post* report notes, "a clothier introduced a children's line after the dummy showed that kids made up more than half its mid-afternoon traffic... Another store found that a third of visitors using one of its
(10)  doors after 4 p.m. were Asian, prompting it to place Chinese-speaking staff members by the entrance."

At $5,072 a pop, these EyeSee mannequins come with a steep price tag, but for store owners who want to know more—*a lot more*—about their customers, they're the perfect tool, able to sit innocently at store entrances and windows, leaving
(15)  shoppers oblivious to their hidden cameras. Itaian mannequin maker Almax SpA, manufacturer of the EyeSee mannequins, is currently working on adding ears to the mannequins, allowing them to record people's comments in order to further tailor the shopping experience. ...

It's astounding the amount of information—from the trivial to the highly per-
(20)  sonal—about individual consumers being passed around from corporation to corporation, all in an effort to market and corral potential customers. Data mining companies collect this wealth of information and sell it to retailers who use it to gauge your interests and tailor marketing to your perceived desires.

All of the websites you visit collect some amount of information about you,
(25)  whether it is your name or what other sites you have visited recently. Most of the time, we're being tracked without knowing it. For example, most websites now include Facebook and Twitter buttons so you can "like" the page you are viewing or "Tweet" about it. Whether or not you click the buttons, however, the companies can still determine which pages you've visited and file that information away for
(30)  later use. ...

As the EyeSee mannequins show, you no longer even have to be in front of your computer to have your consumer data accessed, uploaded, stored and tracked. In August 2012, for example, data mining agency Redpepper began testing a service known as Facedeals in the Nashville, Tennessee area. Facial recognition cameras set (35) at the entrances of businesses snap photos of people walking in, and if you've signed up to have a Facedeals account via your Facebook, you receive instant coupons sent to your smartphone. Similarly, a small coffee chain in San Francisco, Philz Coffee, has installed sensors at the front door of their stores in order to capture the Wi-Fi signal of any smartphone within 60 yards. Jacob Jaber, president of Philz Coffee, (40) uses the information gleaned from these sensors to structure his stores according to the in-store behavior of customers. ...

Not even politicians are immune to the lure of data mining. In the run-up to the 2012 presidential election, the Romney and Obama campaigns followed voters across the web by installing cookies on their computers and observing the (45) websites they visited in an attempt to gather information on their personal views. CampaignGrid, a Republican affiliated firm, and Precision Network, a Democratic affiliated firm, both worked to collect data on 150 million American Internet users, or 80% of the registered voting population. ...

—John W. Whitehead
excerpted *https://www.rutherford.org*, December 17, 2012

## Text 3

## Where Will Consumers Find Privacy Protection from RFIDs?: A Case for Federal Legislation

### What Are RFIDs? How Do RFIDs Work?

...RFID [Radio Frequency Information Device] technology is an automatic identification system that identifies objects, collects data, and transmits information about the object through a "tag." A device called a reader extracts and processes the information on the tag. Experts characterize RFIDs as devices "that can be sensed (5) at a distance by radio frequencies with few problems of obstruction or misorientation."[1] In essence, RFIDs are wireless barcodes. However, unlike typical barcodes, which are identical for all common products, each RFID has a unique identification. Therefore, every individually tagged item has a different barcode sequence.

---

[1] KATHERINE ALBRECHT & LIZ MCINTRYE, SPYCHIPS 13 (Nelson Current 2005) quoting Raghu Das, *RFID Explained: An Introduction to RFID and Tagging Technologies*, ID TECHEX (2003).
[2] *Id.*

(10)   Typical barcodes also require unobstructed paths for scanning, whereas RFIDs can be scanned through solid objects.[2] RFIDs have communication signals that facilitate data storage on RFID tags and enable the stored information to be gathered electronically—hypothetically permitting, for example, Coca-Cola to have a database storing information about the life cycle of a Coke can. The database would contain tracking details from the moment the can is manufactured through its processing at a

(15)   garbage dump—since RFID readers can be attached to garbage trucks. Between the birth and death of a customer's Coke can, the RFID tags would tell the Coca-Cola Company where and when the Coke was purchased, what credit card the Coke was purchased with, and, in turn, the identity of the purchaser. Even if the customer did not purchase the Coke with a credit card, state issued ID cards equipped with RFID

(20)   technology could relay the customer's identity to RFID readers as he or she leaves the store. Coca-Cola's final product of the RFIDs' communications is a database of the life cycles of individual cans of Coke and personal information about their purchasers. With this myriad of information, Coca-Cola has the ability to individually market to each of the 1.3 billion daily Coca-Cola consumers. ...

## How Are RFIDs Used?

(25)   RFIDs are currently used in many ways, including, "livestock management[,] 24 hour patient monitoring[,] authentication of pharmaceuticals[,] tracking consignments in a supply chain[,] remote monitoring of critical components in aircraft [, and] monitoring the safety of perishable food."[3] Advocates of RFID technology, including retailers and manufacturers, praise the increased functionality and effi-

(30)   ciency that will likely ensue from using RFIDs. Once all products are individually tagged, shoppers are expected to be able to purchase items without checking-out. This should be possible since RFID readers will be able to scan every item as the customer exits the store and charge an RFID credit card, thereby simultaneously increasing efficiency and possibly reducing shoplifting. Other RFID uses include

(35)   easy monitoring of product recalls, tracking lobsters for conservation purposes, and purchasing products with transaction-free payment systems.[4] Additionally, in October 2003, the Department of Defense set standards mandating suppliers to place RFID tags on all packaging for the Department of Defense.[5] Thus, RFIDs can be used to increase efficiency and safety. ...

---

[2]*Id.*

[3]Viviane Reding, Member of the European Commission responsible for Information Society and Media, Address at EU RFID 2006 Conference: Heading for the Future, RFID: WHY WE NEED A EUROPEAN POLICY, 1,3 (Oct. 16, 2006).

[4]David Flint, *Everything with Chips!*, BUS. L. REV., Mar. 2006, 73, 73.

[5]PRESS RELEASE, US DEP. OF DEFENSE, DOD ANNOUNCES RADIO FREQUENCY IDENTIFICATION POLICY, UNITED STATES DEPARTMENT OF DEFENSE NEWS RELEASE (Oct. 23, 2003).

# Do Consumers Have a Right to Privacy
## from RFIDs under Tort Law?[6]

(40)     ...In the context of RFIDs, there are some situations where gathering information from RFID tags violates consumers' privacy expectations. For example, a consumer does not have a reasonable expectation of privacy when carrying RFID equipped items in a transparent shopping cart. However, once the items are placed in an opaque bag, a right to privacy immediately arises. If a business or third-party

(45)     gathers data about the items once the items are no longer visible to the naked eye, there is an objective invasion of privacy. Gathering information stored in the RFID tag in a winter jacket worn in public is also not an invasion of privacy, yet pulling data off undergarments is intrusive. However, since the home is always considered a private place, once an active RFID tag enters the home, any information gathered,

(50)     including information from the winter jacket, immediately offends the principles of privacy. Protecting consumers from unreasonably intrusive actions of businesses requires that RFID tags become unreadable once they enter private places. However, the fundamental nature of the technology does not harmonize with this privacy goal because RFID readers do not scrutinize whether the information is

(55)     considered private before it gathers data from the tag. ...

With new technologies come new methods of consumer tracking and changing parameters for what may be considered highly offensive. These new methods of tracking are not considered intrusive simply because the nature of the technology requires consumer purchases to be recorded. If individuals make active decisions to

(60)     use a credit card instead of cash—a voluntary act—their purchases can be tracked. Similarly, the gathering of information stored on RFID technology in consumer goods may not be deemed highly offensive depending on changing consumer expectations. ...

—Serena G. Stein excerpted and adapted
*Duke Law & Technology Review*, 2007, No.3

---

[6]Tort Law — covers civil wrongs resulting in an injury or harm constituting the basis for a claim by the injured person

## Text 4

### RFID Consumer Applications and Benefits

...One of the first consumer applications of RFID was automated toll collection systems, which were introduced in the late 1980s and caught on in the 1990s. An active transponder is typically placed on a car's or truck's windshield. When the car reaches the tollbooth, a reader at the booth sends out a signal that wakes up the
(5)  transponder on the windshield, which then reflects back a unique ID to the reader at the booth. The ID is associated with an account opened by the car owner, who is billed by the toll authority. Consumers spend less time fumbling for change or waiting on lines to pay their toll fee.

In the late 1990s, ExxonMobil (then just Mobil) introduced Speedpass, an RFID
(10)  system that allows drivers who have opened an account to pay for gas automatically. Drivers are given a small, passive 13.56 MHz transponder in a small wand or fob that can be put on a key chain. To pay for gas, they just wave the key fob by a reader built into the gas pump. Seven million people in the United States use the system, and it has increased the number of cars each gas station can serve during
(15)  rush periods. ...

RFID has other consumer applications, besides being a convenient payment system. One is the recovery of lost or stolen items. A company called Snagg in Palo Alto, Calif., has created an electronic registry for musical instruments. It provides an RFID tag that can be affixed to a classic guitar or priceless violin and keeps a
(20)  record of the serial number in the tag. If the instrument is recovered by the police after being lost or stolen, they can call Snagg, which can look up the rightful owner. ...

Merloni Elettrodomestici, an Italian appliance maker, has created a smart washing machine. When you drop your clothes in the machine, an RFID reader in the
(25)  appliance can read the tags in the clothes (if your clothes have tags) and wash the clothes based on instructions written to the tag.

Whether smart appliances with RFID readers catch on depends on how long it takes for RFID tags to become cheap enough to be put into packaging for items. It also depends on whether consumers find RFID-enabled products convenient
(30)  enough to accept the potential invasion of privacy that comes with having RFID tags in products. But RFID will certainly have a positive impact on people's lives in less direct ways.

One area of importance is product recalls. Today, companies often need to recall all tires, meat or drugs if there is a problem to ensure people's safety. But
(35)  they can never be sure they recovered all the bad goods that were released into the supply chain. With RFID, companies will be able to know exactly which items are bad and trace those through to stores. Customers that register their products

(40) could be contacted individually to ensure they know something they bought has been recalled. ...

And RFID should enable consumers to get more information about the products they want to purchase, such as when the items were made, where, whether they are under warrantee and so on. When RFID tags are eventually put on the packaging of individual products, consumers will be able to read the tag with a reader embedded in a cell phone or connected to a computer and download data

(45) from a Web site. They'll be able to learn, for example, whether the steak they are about to buy is from an animal that was raised organically in the United States. Some companies will be reluctant to share this information, but smart companies will provide it to their customers to build trust and loyalty.

RFID could also have an [sic] positive impact on our environment by greatly

(50) reducing waste. The main reason many companies want to use RFID is to better match supply and demand and to make sure that products are where they are supposed to be. If successful, there should be fewer products that are thrown away because no one wants to buy them or they pass their sell-by date (it's estimated that 50 percent of all food harvested in the United States is never eaten).

(55) RFID tags could also help improve our environment by identifying hazardous materials that should not be dumped in landfills. One day, robots at landfills might be equipped with RFID tags, and they might be able to quickly sort through garbage to locate batteries and other items that contain toxic materials. ...

—Bob Violino

excerpted *http://www.rfidjournal.com*, January 16, 2005

## LOOKING AT THE TEXTS

Text 1—*Cell Phone Carrier Marketing Techniques: An Invasion of Privacy?*

This document opens with a dramatic assertion: "Your cell phone may be spying on you." The rest of the short article, from a television news report, gives a general description of data collection by cell phone companies and provides a useful introduction to the issue.

Text 2—*EyeSee You and the Internet of Things: Watching You While You Shop*

This article, from a website devoted to issues of civil liberties, presents several detailed examples of how retailers, Internet providers, and political campaigns make use of data mining. This text is an excellent source of material to support an argument opposed to tracking consumers' behavior without their permission.

Text 3—*Where Will Consumers Find Privacy Protection from RFIDs?: A Case for Federal Legislation*

This article, from a university law review, is the most challenging: The article offers a detailed technical description of what RFIDs are and how they operate. It also offers an analysis of the complex legal issues they raise. Finally, the last paragraph seems to suggest that if consumers are aware of this new technology, its use might not be considered intrusive.

Text 4—*RFID Consumer Applications and Benefits*

The title of this document, from a journal that promotes development and use of RFIDs, is a clear statement of the content and point of view. What follows is a list of various applications of RFID technology in language that is technical but readily understood, and the examples are presented as only beneficial for consumers.

## STEP TWO—COMPOSING A SOURCE-BASED ARGUMENT

Because the issues presented for argument will be relevant and may already be familiar to high school students, you should be able to choose a position (claim) that you can make convincing. Here are the Guidelines for Part 2 of the Regents ELA (Common Core) Exam:

### BE SURE TO:

- Establish your claim regarding companies being allowed to track consumers' shopping or other preferences without their permission
- Distinguish your claim from alternate or opposing claims
- Use specific, relevant, and sufficient evidence from at least **three** of the texts to develop your argument
- Identify each source that you reference by text number and line number(s) or graphic (for example: Text 1, line 4 or Text 2, graphic)
- Organize your ideas in a cohesive and coherent manner
- Maintain a formal style of writing
- Follow the conventions of standard written English

# PLANNING THE ESSAY

First, consider **who your audience is**. You should assume a reader who is interested in the subject but who has not yet formed a strong opinion about the issue. Your reader is interested in what you have to say and can be convinced by a sound and well-documented argument.

**Establishing a claim and distinguishing it** from an alternate or opposing claim means that you are taking a particular position on the issue, you are not just offering a description or explanation of the subject. In each of the following examples, there is a reference to at least one of the issues the topic raises, and there is an indication of how the writer's argument is going to be developed.

Supporting the claim with specific and relevant evidence is part of any effective argument; supporting the claim with **sufficient** evidence means the writer has included not only several examples from different sources but has also used analysis of the texts to determine which evidence **best supports** the argument. Remember, too, that showing faulty or weak reasoning in examples from documents with opposing views is one of the most effective strategies in argument. Identifying references is, of course, part of any source-based writing.

The organization (structure) of the essay should be determined by the logic of the argument. An effective essay moves from establishing the claim through a series of examples (evidence) to a persuasive conclusion. In a **coherent** essay, the reader should understand how each new section extends the ideas that have come before and leads to the ideas that follow and to a convincing conclusion. **Cohesive** writing means that the connection of your ideas within each sentence and at the paragraph level is clear and that the writing follows the conventions of standard written English.

# LOOKING AT A VARIETY OF EFFECTIVE CLAIMS

Here are several examples of how students established effective claims for arguments on the topic of data mining and consumer privacy:

> *Technology is changing, allowing companies and other interests . . . to track our location any given time and collect information about what we buy, all without our consent. There should be a limit to what these entities can gather on us . . .*

*Companies should be permitted to have access to consumers'
spending habits without their permission. The companies may
seem like they are invading our privacy, but they are simply
finding better and more efficient ways to help their customers and
profit their businesses.*

*Under most circumstances, consumers should not be tracked
without permission for sole benefit of companies. However, if the
consumer does authorize its use by way of contract, companies
should have right to track them.*

*Companies should not be permitted to track consumers' shop-
ping and other activities without their consent. Without inform-
ing people of new tracking devices and methods and letting them
decide, companies invade people's personal privacy . . .*

*Technology has made major improvements all over the world;
however, these improvements have made it much easier for companies to track consumers without their permission. I support the
view that the tracking of a customer's habits and preferences is an
invasion of privacy.*

*New innovations in technology have enabled companies to
monitor cell phone usage, the goods bought by consumers, or the
places that people travel. In some cases, this is seen as an invasion of privacy. However, for the majority of the time, this new
technology should be seen as a benefit to both consumers and the
companies involved.*

(See also Chapter 7—Writing on Demand for more discussion.)

# Chapter 3

# READING AND WRITING TO ANALYZE TEXT

## TEXT ANALYSIS: EXPOSITION

Text analysis requires first doing a close reading of a passage to identify a central idea and then analyzing how the author develops that central idea. This means understanding the author's purpose and seeing how the author's choice of literary techniques or a specific rhetorical strategy serves that purpose. In this part of the Regents ELA exam, you may read a literary passage of autobiography or memoir, a speech of historical significance, or a personal essay on a historical or scientific subject or on a philosophical idea.

## SAMPLE TEXT AND EXPOSITORY RESPONSE

...It turned out to be true. The face of the water [Mississippi River], in time, became a wonderful book—a book that was a dead language to the uneducated passenger, but which told its mind to me without reserve, delivering its most cher-ished secrets as clearly as if it uttered them with a voice. And it was not a book to be
(5)   read once and thrown aside, for it had a new story to tell every day. Throughout the long twelve hundred miles there was never a page that was void of interest, never one that you could leave unread without loss, never one that you would want to skip, thinking you could find higher enjoyment in some other thing. There never was so wonderful a book written by man; never one whose interest was
(10)  so absorbing, so unflagging, so sparklingly renewed with every reperusal. The pas-senger who could not read it was charmed with a peculiar sort of faint dimple on its surface (on the rare occasions when he did not overlook it altogether); but to the pilot that was an *italicized* passage; indeed, it was more than that, it was a legend of the largest capitals, with a string of shouting exclamation points at
(15)  the end of it, for it meant that a wreck or a rock was buried there that could tear the life out of the strongest vessel that ever floated. It is the faintest and simplest expression the water ever makes, and the most hideous to a pilot's eye. In truth, the passenger who could not read this book saw nothing but all manner of pretty pictures in it, painted by the sun and shaded by the clouds, whereas to the trained

(20)  eye these were not pictures at all, but the grimmest and most dead-earnest of
reading matter.

Now when I had mastered the language of this water, and had come to know
every trifling feature that bordered the great river as familiarly as I knew the letters
of the alphabet, I had made a valuable acquisition. But I had lost something, too. I
(25)  had lost something which could never be restored to me while I lived. All the grace,
the beauty, the poetry, had gone out of the majestic river! I still kept in mind a
certain wonderful sunset which I witnessed when steamboating was new to me. A
broad expanse of the river was turned to blood; in the middle distance the red hue
brightened into gold, through which a solitary log came floating, black and
(30)  conspicuous; one place a long, slanting mark lay sparkling upon the water; in
another the surface was broken by boiling, tumbling rings, that were as many-
tinted as an opal; where the ruddy flush was faintest, was a smooth spot that was
covered with graceful circles and radiating lines, ever so delicately traced; the shore
on our left was densely wooded, and the sombre shadow that fell from this forest
(35)  was broken in one place by a long, ruffled trail that shone like silver; and high above
the forest wall a clean-stemmed dead tree waved a single leafy bough that glowed
like a flame in the unobstructed splendor that was flowing from the sun. There were
graceful curves, reflected images, woody heights, soft distances; and over the whole
scene, far and near, the dissolving lights drifted steadily, enriching it every passing
(40)  moment with new marvels of coloring.

I stood like one bewitched. I drank it in, in a speechless rapture. The world was
new to me, and I had never seen any thing like this at home. But as I have said,
a day came when I began to cease from noting the glories and the charms which
the moon and the sun and the twilight wrought upon the river's face; another
(45)  day came when I ceased altogether to note them. Then, if that sunset scene had
been repeated, I should have looked upon it without rapture, and should have
commented upon it, inwardly, after this fashion: "This sun means that we are going
to have wind to-morrow; that floating log means that the river is rising, small
thanks to it; that slanting mark on the water refers to a bluff reef which is going to
(50)  kill somebody's steamboat one of these nights, if it keeps on stretching out like that;
those tumbling 'boils' show a dissolving bar and a changing channel there; the lines
and circles in the slick water over yonder are a warning that that troublesome
place is shoaling up dangerously; that silver streak in the shadow of the forest is
the 'break' from a new snag, and he has located himself in the very best place he could
(55)  have found to fish for steamboats; that tall dead tree, with a single living branch, is
not going to last long, and then how is a body ever going to get through this blind
place at night without the friendly old landmark?"

No, the romance and the beauty were all gone from the river. All the value any
feature of it had for me now was the amount of usefulness it could furnish toward
(60)  compassing the safe piloting of a steamboat. Since those days, I have pitied doc-

tors from my heart. What does the lovely flush in a beauty's cheek mean to a doctor but a "break" that ripples above some deadly disease? Are not all her visible charms sown thick with what are to him the signs and symbols of hidden decay? Does he ever see her beauty at all, or doesn't he simply view her professionally, and comment (65) upon her unwholesome condition all to himself? And doesn't he sometimes wonder whether he has gained most or lost most by learning his trade?

—Mark Twain
excerpted and adapted from *Life on the Mississippi*, 1901
Harper & Brothers Publishers

## RESPONSE

In this excerpt, Twain introduces the central idea as a metaphor: "The face of the water {Mississippi River}...became a wonderful book."

Throughout the passage he uses vivid imagery to convey the beauty of the river and to convey how the acquisition of knowledge means losing that beauty. Before the author learned to see the signs of danger in navigating the river, he saw only beauty. When Twain was new to steam boating, he witnessed a particularly magnificent sunset. The sky was red, which reflected on the water and slowly transitioned to gold. He noticed delicate rings growing from a spot in the water. He noticed a dead tree rising above the wall of forest, with a bough of leaves that shone with brightness of flames. He was in a state of "speechless rapture."

Later on, the beauty faded as he learned the signals behind what he saw. Twain tells us that the river was a "wonderful book"; but it was also "the grimmest and most dead-earnest of reading matter." That beautiful red hue in his surroundings would mean wind the next day. The growing ripples marked a dangerous obstacle that could kill a steamboat. The dead tree, whose leaves were like fire, was a "friendly landmark" and would be lost after it fell. In learning to read the book of the river, Twain loses forever the ability to see the beauty and grace of the Mississippi and regrets what he has lost in learning his trade: "No, the romance and beauty were all gone from the river... all it had for me now was the amount of usefulness it could furnish...."

This is an excellent example of an expository response: In the opening sentence, this writer expresses the central idea of the passage and identifies Twain's use of vivid imagery as key to understanding its meaning. The analysis is developed in two paragraphs, each of which cites several specific and relevant examples from the text. In the first paragraph, the images recall Twain's delight in the beauty of the river; in the second, these images become examples of how the knowledge Twain acquires destroys his ability to see beauty in them. This organization in parallel details is both sophisticated and effective. The incorporation of quoted phrases enhances development of the central idea and meets the requirement for an evidence-based analysis.

# ADDITIONAL TEXTS FOR ANALYSIS AND REVIEW

## PASSAGE ONE

*This passage is an excerpt from a speech given by Red Jacket, Chief of the Seneca Nation, to the United States acting secretary of war in Washington, D.C., on February 10, 1801.*

...Brother, the business on which we are now come is to restore the friendship that has existed between the United States and the Six Nations, agreeably to the direction of the commissioner from the fifteen fires[1] of the United States. He assured us that whensoever, by any grievances, the chain of friendship should

(5) become rusty, we might have it brightened by calling on you. We dispense with the usual formality of having your speech again read, as we fully comprehended it yesterday, and it would therefore be useless to waste time in a repetition of it.

Brother, yesterday you wiped the tears from our eyes, that we might see clearly; you unstopped our ears that we might hear; and removed the obstructions

(10) from our throats that we might speak distinctly. You offered to join with us in tearing up the largest pine-tree in our forests, and under it to bury the tomahawk. We gladly join with you, brother, in this work, and let us heap rocks and stones on the root of this tree that the tomahawk may never again be found. ...

---

[1]fires—fires refers to states

(15) Brother, we observe that the men now in office are new men, and, we fear, not fully informed of all that has befallen us. In 1791 a treaty was held by the commissioners of Congress with us at Tioga Point, on a similar occasion. We have lost seven of our warriors, murdered in cold blood by white men, since the conclusion of the war. We are tired of this mighty grievance and wish some general arrangement to prevent it in future. The first of these was murdered on the banks of (20) the Ohio, near Fort Pitt. Shortly after two men belonging to our first families were murdered at Pine Creek; then one at Fort Franklin; another at Tioga Point; and now the two that occasion this visit, on the Big Beaver. These last two had families. The one was a Seneca; the other a Tuscarora. Their families are now destitute of support, and we think that the United States should do something toward (25) their support, as it is to the United States they owe the loss of their heads.

Brother, these offences are always committed in one place on the frontier of Pennsylvania. In the Genesee country we live happy and no one molests us. I must therefore beg that the President will exert all his influence with all officers, civil and military, in that quarter, to remedy this grievance, and (30) trust that he will thus prevent a repetition of it and save our blood from being spilled in future.

Brother, let me call to mind the treaty between the United States and the Six Nations, concluded at Canandaigua. At that treaty Colonel Pickering, who was commissioner on behalf of the United States, agreed that the United States should (35) pay to the Six Nations four thousand five hundred dollars per annum, and that this should pass through the hands of the superintendent of the United States, to be appointed for that purpose. This treaty was made in the name of the President of the United States, who was then General Washington; and, as he is now no more, perhaps the present President would wish to renew the treaty. But if he should (40) think the old one valid and is willing to let it remain in force we are also willing. The sum above mentioned we wish to have part of in money, to expend in more agricultural tools and in purchasing a team, as we have some horses that will do for the purpose. We also wish to build a sawmill on the Buffalo creek. If the President, however, thinks proper to have it continue as heretofore, we shall not be very (45) uneasy. Whatever he may do we agree to; we only suggest this for his consideration.

Brother, I hand you the above-mentioned treaty, made by Colonel Pickering, in the name of General Washington, and the belt that accompanied it; as he is now dead we know not if it is still valid. If not, we wish it renewed—if it is, we wish it copied on clean parchment. Our money got loose in our trunk and tore it. We also (50) show you the belt which is the path of peace between our Six Nations and the United States. ...

Brother, the business that has caused this our long journey was occasioned by some of your bad men; the expense of it has been heavy on us. We beg that as so

great a breach has been made on your part, the President will judge it proper that
(55) the United States should bear our expenses to and from home and whilst here.

Brother, three horses belonging to the Tuscarora Nation were killed by some men
under the command of Major Rivardi, on the plains of Niagara. They have made
application to the superintendent and to Major Rivardi, but get no redress. You
make us pay for our breaches of the peace, why should you not pay also? A white
(60) man has told us the horses were killed by Major Rivardi's orders, who said they
should not be permitted to come there, although it was an open common on
which they were killed. Mr. Chapin has the papers respecting these horses, which
we request you to take into consideration.

—Red Jacket
excerpted from *Orations from Homer to William McKinley*,
Vol. VII, 1902
P.F. Collier and Son

## Looking at the Text

The repetition of "Brother, . . ." at the beginning of each point is the most
obvious rhetorical element in this speech. Careful analysis will show how
that not only establishes the speaker's attitude toward his audience (the tone
of the speech) but also structures the various examples as reminders of past
history and treaty obligations and establishes the legitimacy of the Chief's
demands for compensation and justice.

### PASSAGE TWO

Here is an example of a classic essay form, in which a specific aspect
of human nature or conduct is explored. First made popular by the French
writer Michel de Montaigne in the 16th century, this kind of essay is relatively brief, offers intellectual insight, and often includes anecdotes or analogies as illustrations. In "Of Suspicion," Sir Francis Bacon, a contemporary of
Shakespeare, first offers his observations on how suspicion clouds the mind
and then suggests ways to avoid its corrosive effects.

40

# Of Suspicion

SUSPICIONS amongst thoughts are like bats amongst birds, they ever fly by twilight. Certainly they are to be repressed, or at least well guarded: for they cloud the mind; they leese [lose] friends; and they check with [hinder, restrain] business, whereby business cannot go on currently and constantly. They dispose [lead]
(5) kings to tyranny, husbands to jealousy, wise men to irresolution [indecisiveness] and melancholy. They are defects, not in the heart, but in the brain; for they take place in the stoutest [bravest] natures; as in the example of Henry the Seventh of England. There was not a more suspicious man, nor a more stout. And in such a composition they do small hurt. For commonly they are not admitted, but [unless]
(10) with examination, whether they be likely or no. But in fearful natures they gain ground too fast. There is nothing makes a man suspect much, more than to know little; and therefore men should remedy suspicion by procuring to know more, and not to keep their suspicions in smother [suppressed]. What would men have? Do they think those they employ and deal with are saints? Do they not think they will
(15) have their own ends, and be truer to themselves than to them? Therefore there is no better way to moderate suspicions, than to account upon such suspicions as true and yet to bridle them as false. For so far a man ought to make use of suspicions, as to provide, as if that should be true that he suspects, yet it may do him no hurt. Suspicions that the mind of itself gathers are but buzzes; but suspicions that are
(20) artificially nourished, and put into men's heads by the tales and whisperings of others, have stings. Certainly, the best mean [strategy] to clear the way in this same wood of suspicions is frankly to communicate them with the party that he suspects; for thereby he shall be sure to know more of the truth of them than he did before; and withal shall make that party more circumspect not to give further cause of sus-
(25) picion. But this would not be done to men of base [dishonorable, corrupt] natures; for they, if they find themselves once suspected, will never be true. . . . (c 1625)

## Looking at the Text

This is a passage that requires careful, slow reading. The essay begins with a simile that establishes the tone of what is to follow: suspicions are creatures of twilight; they are elusive, ambiguous, and potentially dangerous. Bacon then insists that suspicions must be kept under control and offers guidance on how best to "clear the way in…the wood of suspicions." Note how condensed the development of ideas is and how each sentence balances two or three assertions. The meanings of some unfamiliar terms have been inserted here, but the language of Bacon is also the language of Shakespeare and should be accessible to high school students at Regents level.

(There is a list of Archaic and Unfamiliar terms in Chapter 8—Vocabulary.)

## PASSAGE THREE

In 1858, Abraham Lincoln and Stephen Douglas were campaigning in Illinois for the U.S. Senate seat then held by Douglas. They held a series of debates throughout the state, which were widely and often raucously attended. Douglas argued that it was an absolute right of self-government for residents of a territory to permit or to prohibit slavery. Here is a passage from an eyewitness account of the seventh and final of the Lincoln-Douglas debates.

. . . Douglas had been theatrical and scholarly, but this tall, homely man [Lincoln] was creating by his very looks what the brilliant lawyer and experienced Senator had failed to make people see and feel. The Little Giant [Douglas] had assumed striking attitudes, played tricks with his flowing white hair, mimicking

(5) the airs of authority, with patronizing allusions; but these affectations, usually so effective when he addressed an audience alone, went for nothing when brought face to face with realities. Lincoln had no genius for gesture and no desire to produce a sensation. The failure of Senator Douglas to bring conviction to critical minds was caused by three things: a lack of logical sequence in argument, a lack of

(10) intuitional judgment, and a vanity that was caused by too much intellect and too little heart. Douglas had been arrogant and vehement, Lincoln was now logical and penetrating. . . .

The enthusiasm created by Douglas was wrought out of smart epigram thrusts and a facile, superficial eloquence. . . . His weight in the political balance was

(15) purely materialistic; his scales of justice tipped to the side of cotton, slavery, and popular passions, while the man who faced him now brought to the assembly cold logic in place of wit, frankness in place of cunning, reasoned will and judgment in place of chicanery and sophistry. . . . His looks, his words, his voice, his attitude, were like a magical essence dropped into the seething cauldron of politics, reacting

(20) against the foam, calming the surface and letting the people see to the bottom. It did not take him long:

> *"Is it not a false statesmanship," he asked, "that undertakes to build*
> *up a system of policy upon the basis of caring nothing about the very*
> *thing that everybody does care the most about? Judge Douglas may say*
> (25) *he cares not whether slavery is voted up or down, but he must have a*
> *choice between a right thing and a wrong thing. He contends that what-*
> *ever community wants slaves has a right to have them. So they have, if*
> *it is not a wrong; but if it is a wrong he cannot say people have a right*
> *to do wrong. He says that upon the score of equality slaves should be*
> (30) *allowed to go into a new Territory like other property. This is strictly*
> *logical if there is no difference between it [slaves] and other property.*

*If it and other property are equal his argument is entirely logical; but if
you insist that one is wrong and the other right there is no use to insti-
tute a comparison between right and wrong."*

This was the broadside. The great duel on the high seas of politics was over.
(35)     The Douglas ship of State Sovereignty was sinking. The debate was a triumph
that would send Lincoln to Washington as President in a little more than two years
from that date.

—Francis Grierson, *The Valley of Shadows*

## Looking at the Text

In this passage, the observer uses various rhetorical elements to recreate
the experience of hearing the two famous men, and within this account, we
are shown how Lincoln himself revealed the morally flawed logic in Douglas's position on slavery.

The observer sets the stage with a series of balanced and contrasting
images: Douglas is theatrical and vain, a man of "too much intellect and too
little heart." Lincoln "had no genius for gesture" or sensational language;
Lincoln was ". . . now logical and penetrating." He introduces Lincoln's
words with a vivid image of an alchemist calming intense passions—the
seething cauldron of politics—with the "magical essence" of clear, moral
argument.

Lincoln attacks Douglas for "caring nothing about" slavery, that is, for
being neutral on the issue, when it is the issue the nation most cares about.
Douglas contends that slavery is an issue of property and rights of States,
but Lincoln says that is a logical fallacy: the issue is not about property,
it is about right and wrong; " . . . *he cannot say people have a right to do
wrong.*" The passage ends with another strong metaphor: Douglas's ship of
State Sovereignty has been sunk in a battle on the [political] high seas by the
cannon shot of Lincoln's words.

(The Lincoln-Douglas Debates, Twain's memoir, and Red Jacket's speech
are examples of what is meant by "seminal U.S. texts" in the State Standards.
Analyzing and evaluating the reasoning in these and other "foundational
U.S. documents of historical and literary significance" can be expected on
the Regents ELA exam and on the new SAT (2015). See the Appendices,
pages 223–227, to review the standards.)

# Chapter 4

# READING PROSE

One of the characters in Moliere's satire *Le Bourgeois Gentilhomme* (*The Bourgeois Gentleman*) makes an astonishing discovery: "For over forty years I have been speaking prose without knowing it!" Prose writing is composed in the rhythms and patterns of spoken discourse. When we read novels and short stories, essays and reports, journals and letters, we are usually reading prose. In our daily lives and as students, we read prose that varies widely in purpose, in method of development, and in tone. Prose serves the purposes of personal expression, persuasion, literary effect, and information.

## WHAT WRITERS DO:
## A LIST OF USEFUL TERMS

A group of high school juniors recently was asked to list all the verbs they could think of to denote what writers *do*. Here is the list they came up with:

| | | | |
|---|---|---|---|
| address | declare | imply | refine |
| affirm | defend | infer | reflect |
| alert | define | influence | refute |
| amuse | delineate | inform | remind |
| analyze | depict | inspire | reveal |
| appraise | describe | interpret | revise |
| argue | discern | invent | scrutinize |
| assert | discover | judge | see |
| assess | dramatize | note | select |
| capture | edit | observe | shock |
| caution | emphasize | offer | show |
| censure | enhance | persuade | suggest |
| cite | enrich | play | summarize |
| clarify | establish | ponder | support |
| classify | evaluate | portray | symbolize |
| comment | examine | present | teach |
| conclude | explain | probe | theorize |
| condemn | explore | produce | uncover |
| conjecture | expose | propose | view |
| convey | expound | provoke | work(!) |
| create | forewarn | question | |
| create images | formulate | reassure | |
| criticize | illustrate | recreate | |

45

As you consider these terms, you will note that they are not separated by categories; many of them denote both purpose and tone, and many suggest a method of development as well. While this list may not include everything writers "do," it is a useful reminder of the great variety in written expression. (Because command of this vocabulary will also help you to express your understanding and appreciation of what you read, you will find examples showing how many of these words are applied to discussions of nonfiction and, in Chapter 6, writing about literature. Note also that most of these terms are part of the vocabulary that is considered Academic Language. (See Chapter 8—Vocabulary.)

To read well you must be listening actively to the narrator's voice, thinking with the author. If you are reading a piece for information or direction, ask questions; expect them to be answered. If you are reading a work of argument or persuasion, question it; actively agree or disagree; follow how the argument is developed. If you are reading a piece of personal expression, try to imagine, even share, the experience. If you are reading a piece of vivid description, recreate the images and feelings for yourself. Reading well offers us the entire range of human history and experience expressed in language.

Works of fiction are usually narrative in form. They tell us stories of what *happened* in the lives of the characters and, more important, *why it happened*. Nonfiction takes many forms, and its subjects touch on nearly everything in the human and natural worlds.

# READING FICTION

When we speak of fiction, we are generally referring to narrative works—works in which events are recounted, are *told*, and have been imagined and structured by the author. (Although not narrative in form, drama shares many of the essential characteristics of fiction.) The subjects of fiction, however, are no less real than those of history or of what we call the actual or real world. In *Aspects of the Novel*, E. M. Forster shows how "fiction is truer than history." He reminds us that only in narrative fiction and drama can we truly know what is in a character's heart or mind; that is, only in a novel, short story, or play can we fully understand the motives, desires, and reasons for characters' actions. The historian draws conclusions from records of the past; the psychologist interprets interviews and tests; a jury weighs evidence and testimony; and our experience indicates that these are highly reliable ways to understand people and their lives. But only the author of a fictional work can offer an absolutely reliable account of what a character feels, believes, and desires, of why things happen as they do.

# Plot and Story

The primary pleasure for most readers of narrative fiction is the story. The reason we become involved in a novel or short story is that we want to know how it turns out; we want to know what is going to happen to those characters. An author creates a **plot*** when he or she gives order and structure to the action: in a plot, the incidents, or episodes, of the story have meaningful relationships to one another. A story becomes a plot when we understand not only *what happened* but also *why*. In good fiction we are *convinced* of the causal relationship among incidents, and we are convinced by the relationship of characters' motives and feelings to the action.

For most readers of fiction, the first response is to keep track of the plot. We do this spontaneously. If you are preparing a novel or story for class discussion, one of the first things your instructor will expect you to know is, "What happens in . . . ?" This is not a trivial question, because you cannot fully understand the significance of character, theme, or structure if you do not first understand the action as it is presented. Understanding plot, of course, requires memory, and remembering the major incidents of a plot is usually a natural and relatively easy response. The more extensively you read, however, the more skilled you become in remembering and relating the key incidents in a complex plot and in recalling details when their full significance becomes evident—sometimes well after the incidents themselves occur. Keeping notes on the development of a complex plot is very useful, especially for students whose reading of a novel is broken up over days or weeks.

For a class, or as part of your preparation for the Regents exam questions on literature, practice summarizing the plots of works you know or are reading. Be able to tell the story of a novel or play to someone who does not know it in a narrative of your own words, including all the major incidents and their consequences. Be able to tell the story in the same way you would retell a familiar children's story or narrate a significant experience of your own.

# Plot and Conflict

At the end of any meaningful story, something has *happened;* something is significantly different in the world and lives of the characters from what it was at the beginning. **Conflict** in the most general sense refers to the forces that move the action in a plot. Conflict in plot may be generated from a search or pursuit, from a discovery, from a deception or misunderstanding, from opportunities to make significant choices, or from unexpected consequences of an action. Although the term *conflict* connotes an active struggle

---

*Terms in bold are featured in A Glossary of Literary Terms and Techniques at the end of the chapter.

between opposing or hostile forces, conflict in fiction may refer to any progression, change, or discovery. The resolution of conflict in a plot may be subtle and confined to the inner life of a character or it may be dramatic and involve irreversible change, violent destruction, or death.

This term may identify an actual struggle between characters, anything from dominance or revenge to simple recognition or understanding. A plot may also focus on conflict between characters and the forces of nature or society. These are essentially **external conflicts**. A work may also center on **internal conflicts**, characters' struggle to know or change themselves and their lives. Most works of fiction and drama contain more than one aspect of conflict.

In Shakespeare's *Romeo and Juliet*, the most dramatic conflicts are external, vivid, and literal: the street brawls between followers of the rival Capulets and Montagues, the fatal fight with Tybalt that leads to Romeo's banishment, and the tragic deaths of the young lovers. In *Macbeth*, however, the primary interest is in the internal conflict between Macbeth's ambitious desires and his understanding of the moral consequences of the actions he takes to achieve those desires. The action in Edith Wharton's most famous story, "Roman Fever," is ironically serene and pleasant: two middle-aged women, longtime friends now both widowed, sit on a terrace overlooking the splendors of Rome and reflect on their common experiences and lifelong friendship. At the end of the conversation—and the story—their actual feelings of rivalry have surfaced, and one of the two learns something that reveals how little she truly knew her husband or understood her marriage or the life of her friend. The conflict between the two women emerges almost imperceptibly, and its meaning is fully understood only in the completely unexpected revelation of the last line.

## Plot and Chronology

Narrative is not necessarily presented in chronological order, but it does have a chronology. In other words, incidents may be presented out of the order in which they actually occurred, but by the end of the work the reader understands their order and relationship and appreciates why the story was structured as it was. Plots that are narrated in flashback or from different points of view are common examples.

*The Great Gatsby*, by F. Scott Fitzgerald, and *Ethan Frome*, by Edith Wharton, are novels in which the narrators first introduce themselves and their interest in the story, then tell the story in a narrative flashback whose full significance to the narrator (and reader) is revealed only at the end. Tennessee Williams's play *The Glass Menagerie* has a similar structure, in which the character of Tom serves both as a narrator in the present and as a principal character in the series of memory scenes that make up the drama. The memory scenes in Arthur Miller's play *Death of a Salesman*, however, are not flashbacks in the same way. Willy Loman relives incidents from the past while the other characters and the action of the play continue in the present. As the play progresses, the shifts in time occur only within Willy's mind.

Shakespeare's tragedies are dramas in which normal chronology is preserved, as it is in such familiar novels as William Golding's *Lord of the Flies* and Mark Twain's *Huckleberry Finn*.

## Plot and Time

Related to understanding of chronology is appreciation of how an author creates understanding of *elapsed time*. In the several hours required to read a novel, the two to three hours for a full-length play, and the half-hour to an hour for a one-act play or short story, how much time in the lives of the characters has been accounted for? In one-act plays and many short stories, the time covered by the action is equal to the time to read them. In Wharton's "Roman Fever," for example, the action of the story is contained in a few hours of one afternoon—little more time than it takes to read the story. That conversation, however, completely transforms the women's, and the reader's, understanding of their lives over twenty-five years. The time required for the action in Shirley Jackson's widely read story "The Lottery" is also roughly equal to the time required to read it, yet the plot accounts indirectly for events that have taken place for longer than anyone in the story can even remember. Miller's play *Death of a Salesman* takes place over a period of only twenty-four hours, but the plot and Willy's memories tell us the story of an entire lifetime. Awareness of how an author uses and accounts for time adds considerably to the reader's appreciation of a work.

## Narrative Point of View

The **narrator** of a work is the character or author's **persona** that tells a story. **Point of view** is the standpoint, perspective, and degree of understanding from which the narrator speaks. For many students and scholars, how a story is told is one of the most interesting questions. What is the narrative point of view? Is the narration **omniscient**, essentially the point of view of the author? If not, who is the narrator? What is the narrator's relationship to the story? What is the narrator's understanding of the story? How much does the narrator really know? Appreciating how, or by whom, a story is told is often essential to understanding its meaning.

One of the most easily discerned narrative points of view is the first person (*I*), in which either the central character or another directly involved in the action tells the story. J. D. Salinger's novel *The Catcher in the Rye* is a vivid and popular example of such narration. Fitzgerald's *The Great Gatsby* is also told in the first person. In each of these works, the fundamental meaning of the novel becomes apparent only when the reader understands the character of the narrator. In each of these works, what the narrator experiences and what he learns about himself and the world are the novel's most important themes.

In first-person narration, the incidents of the plot are limited to those that the narrator himself experiences. First-person narrators can, however, report what they learn from others. In Wharton's *Ethan Frome*, the engineer who narrates tells us that he has "pieced together the story" from the little he has been able to learn in the town of Starkfield, from his limited conversations with Frome himself, and from his brief visit to the Frome house. Wharton's method, of course, dramatizes Frome's inability to express or fulfill the desires of his heart and reveals the reluctance of the people of Starkfield to fully understand the lives of those around them.

Authors may also use first-person narration to achieve an ironic or satiric effect. In Ring Lardner's well-known story "Haircut," a barber in a small midwestern town narrates a story about a local fellow who kept the town entertained with his practical jokes on people. As the story progresses, the reader understands how cruel and destructive the fellow's pranks were, but the barber does not. The narrative method in this story reveals, indirectly, a story of painful ignorance and insensitivity in the "decent" citizens of a small town. Mark Twain's masterpiece, *Huckleberry Finn*, is told by Huck himself. Through the morally naive observations of Huck, Twain satirizes the evils of slavery, fraud, hypocrisy, and virtually every other kind of corrupt human behavior. Edgar Allan Poe's story "The Tell-Tale Heart" is the confession of a cunning madman.

In third-person narration (*he, she, it, they*) a story is reported. The narrative voice may be *omniscient* and, therefore, able to report everything from everywhere in the story; this voice can also report on the innermost thoughts and feelings of the characters themselves. In many novels of the eighteenth and nineteenth centuries, the omniscient narrator even speaks directly to the reader, as if taking him or her into the storyteller's confidence. In Nathaniel Hawthorne's *The Scarlet Letter*, the narrator pauses from time to time to share personal feelings with the reader, as does Nick Carraway, the narrator of *The Great Gatsby*.

A widely used narrative method is the **limited omniscient** point of view. The narrative is in the third person but is focused on and even may represent the point of view of a central character. The actions and feelings of other characters are presented from the perspective of that character. Hawthorne's short story "Young Goodman Brown" is an excellent example.

Some third-person narration is dramatically **objective** and detached; it simply reports the incidents of the plot as they unfold. This narrative method, too, can be used for intensely **ironic** effect. Jackson's "The Lottery" is one of the best examples. The real horror of the story is achieved through the utterly detached, nonjudgmental unfolding of the plot.

In some plays, too, there is a character who serves a narrative role: the Chorus in Shakespeare's *Henry V*, the character of Tom in Williams's *The Glass Menagerie*, and the Stage Manager in Thornton Wilder's *Our Town* are familiar examples.

In each of the works discussed here, the narrative method is not simply a literary device; it is an intrinsic part of the meaning of the work.

## Setting

The setting of a work includes the time and places in which the action is played out; setting may also include a significant historical context. In drama, setting may be presented directly in the set, costumes, and lighting. In narrative fiction, it is usually presented directly through description. In some works, the physical setting is central to the plot and developed in great detail; in other works, only those details necessary to anchor the plot in a time or place will be developed. Regardless of detail, responsive readers recreate images of setting as they read.

In addition to the physical and natural details of the fictional world, setting also includes mood and **atmosphere**. In some works, social or political realities constitute part of the setting. *The Scarlet Letter* is not only set in Puritan Boston, it is also *about* that society; and *The Great Gatsby* presents a vivid picture of life in New York during Prohibition and the roaring twenties.

For some works, the author may create specific details of setting to highlight a theme. In Golding's novel *Lord of the Flies*, the island on which the story takes place has everything essential for basic survival: food and water are available, and the climate is temperate. In order to explore the moral questions of the boys' regression into savagery, Golding carefully establishes a setting in which survival itself is not a primary issue. In *Ethan Frome*, details of the harsh winter and of the isolation of a town "bypassed by the railroad" intensify the story of a man's desperately cold and isolated life.

## Character

We understand characters in fiction and drama, as we do the people in our own lives, by what they say and do and by what others say about them. Because characters are imagined and created by an author, we can even understand them more reliably and fully than we can many of the people around us. Many students find their greatest satisfaction in reading works about characters to whom they can relate, characters whose struggles are recognizable and whose feelings are familiar.

Understanding character in fiction means understanding a person's values and **motivation**, beliefs and principles, moral qualities, strengths and weaknesses, and degree of self-knowledge and understanding. To fully appreciate a work, the reader must understand what characters are searching for and devoting their lives to.

Literature also seeks to account for the forces outside individuals that influence the directions and outcomes of their lives. These "forces" range from those of nature and history to the demands of family, community, and society. The response of characters to inner and outer forces is what literature depicts and makes comprehensible.

Any meaningful or convincing plot stems from human thought, motive, and action. Depending on the narrative point of view (see page 49), a character's thoughts and feelings may be presented directly through omniscient narrative or first-person commentary. In "Young Goodman Brown," the narrator tells us directly what the title character is thinking and feeling; in "Roman Fever," the reader discovers the most important revelations of character simultaneously with the two central characters. Character in drama is revealed directly in dialogue and action, but it may be expanded through soliloquies and asides. In Shakespeare's *Othello*, for example, the full extent of Iago's evil is revealed through the variety of methods Iago uses to manipulate different characters and through his **soliloquies**.

In some works, the author's primary purpose is to reveal character gradually through plot; in others, the author establishes understanding of character from the beginning in order to account for what happens. In the opening pages of *The Great Gatsby*, the narrator, Nick, who is also a character in the novel, introduces himself and declares his judgment of the moral quality of the people and events he is about to narrate. With Nick's own character and motives clearly established, the reader then shares his *gradual* discovery of the truth about Gatsby and his life.

# Theme

The subjects of literature may come from any aspect of human experience: love, friendship, growing up, ambition, family relationships, conflicts with society, survival, war, evil, death, and so on. **Theme** in a work of literature is the understanding, insight, observation, and presentation of such subjects. Theme is what a work *says about* a subject. Themes are the central ideas of literary works.

One way to think about theme is to consider it roughly analogous to the topic or thesis of an expository essay. If the author of a novel, story, or play had chosen to examine the subjects of the work in an essay, what might be the topic assertions of such an essay? The student is cautioned, however, not to overinterpret the analogy. Themes in literature are rarely "morals," such as those found at the end of a fable, but neither are they "hidden meanings." Although scholars and critics often express thematic ideas in phrases, students are often required to state themes in full sentences. In the next paragraph are some examples of statements about theme.

*Macbeth* is a play about the temptation to embrace evil forces and about the power of ambition to corrupt; Macbeth himself makes one of the most important statements of theme in the play when he says, "I do all that becomes a man/who does more is none." *Ethan Frome* and Lardner's "Haircut" both illustrate that people in small towns may not truly understand the innermost needs and desires of other people they *think* they know. William Golding's novel *Lord of the Flies* illustrates the bleak view that supposedly "civilized" people will become savage and brutal without external forces of authority, that human beings are not civilized in their fundamental natures. In contrast, in *Adventures of Huckleberry Finn,* Twain presents civilization as the source of corruption and finds truly moral behavior only in the runaway slave, Jim, and the ignorant boy, Huck.

In Chapter 6 you will find an extensive list of literature topics, many of which are expressed in terms of theme.

# READING NONFICTION

Fiction and nonfiction share many common elements; they also make similar demands and offer comparable rewards to the thoughtful reader. In broad contrast to fiction, where characters and plot are imaginative creations of the author, nonfiction is about actual persons, experiences, and phenomena. The texts reviewed in Chapter 3 are good examples of how nonfiction speculates on abstract and philosophical questions of history and politics, ethics and religion, culture and society, as well as the natural world. In biography and autobiography, the writer focuses on what is meaningful and interesting in the life of an individual. The purpose of this section is to review some of the distinctive features of formal and informal essays and to illustrate some of the methods authors use to develop arguments in persuasive writing. The glossary at the end of the chapter also features extended definitions and examples of many important terms.

## Questions for the Critical Reader

Here again are the questions you are urged to keep in mind as you prepare for the reading comprehension and text analysis sections of the Regents ELA exam:

What is the purpose of this piece? Its tone or mood? Its overall effect?

What does the author say? believe? recall? value? assert?

What does the author mean? imply? suggest? agree with? disagree with?

How are language and imagery used?

What conclusions or inferences is the reader led to?

What experience is meant to be shared and understood?

# Purpose

In speaking of fiction, the central ideas of a work are identified as its themes. In essays, purpose refers both to the central ideas and to their intended effect on the reader. For example, many authors of essays develop a thesis with a view to influencing opinion or urging action. We encounter such writing daily on the editorial and Op-Ed pages of a newspaper. Many of the verbs on the list of "what writers do" (page 45) identify such purposes: *affirm, alert, argue, assert, caution, censure, condemn, criticize, declare, defend, evaluate, expose, forewarn, imply, inspire, judge, persuade, propose, provoke, reveal, scrutinize, support.*

Much nonfiction, of course, has as its purpose to explain and inform. The verbs used to identify informative writing include *analyze, assess, clarify, define, describe, explore, formulate, illustrate, interpret, recreate, summarize.*

Other purposes may be likened to conversations between the author and the reader; these "conversations" may be about anything from the most personal experiences to reflections on the nature of life and the universe. Some useful verbs here might be *address, amuse, capture, comment, conjecture, depict, discover, enhance, enrich, examine, explore, invent, observe, offer, ponder, probe, propose, question, recreate, reflect, shock.*

# Methods of Development and Patterns of Organization

The ability to use a variety of methods to organize and express ideas is one of the most important skills a student writer learns, and the thoughtful reader should also be able to appreciate how a writer develops material. Informational texts are part of the reading comprehension and text analysis parts of the Regents ELA exam and the new SAT (2015); reviewing the following methods of organization is also useful preparation for composing essays of argument.

## FROM ABSTRACT TO CONCRETE/FROM GENERAL TO SPECIFIC

Going from the general to the specific is the most common and natural pattern for explanation, illustration, and reasoning. A passage by author and playwright Sandy Asher is an especially good example:

> **As a child, I sensed there was something I desperately needed from books. As a writer for young readers, I've tried to figure out what that something was. It turned out to be a combination of three things: companionship, a sense of control, and magic.**

In her essay, Asher goes on to develop a paragraph about each of the three things that make up the "something" she is explaining.

Here is how journalist Ernie Pyle begins his explanation of what "The awful waste and destruction of war" really means:

> **I walked for a mile and a half along the water's edge of our many-miled invasion beach. I walked slowly, for the detail on the beach was infinite.**
>
> **The wreckage was vast and startling. The awful waste and destruction of war, even aside from the loss of human life, has always been one of its outstanding features to those who are in it. Anything and everything is expendable. And we did expend on our beachhead in Normandy during those first few hours.**
>
> **For a mile out from the beach there were scores of tanks and trucks and boats that were not visible, for they were at the bottom of the water—swamped by overloading, or hit by shells, or sunk by mines.**

His description of a Normandy beach following the D-Day invasion in 1944 is developed in a series of vivid images and poignant details that make the waste and destruction of war comprehensible to those who have not experienced it.

## FROM CONCRETE TO ABSTRACT/FROM SPECIFIC TO GENERAL

Reversing the more common pattern, going from the specific to the general can also be a very effective way to develop understanding of a general concept. This is the pattern author William Kittredge uses in the **anecdote** about his boyhood encounter with a sage grouse. The passage recounts a specific experience, which leads to the closing general observation:

> **For that childhood moment I believed the world to be absolutely inhabited by an otherness which was utterly demonic and natural, not of my own making. But soon as that bird was enclosed in a story which defined it as a common-place prairie chicken, I was no longer frightened. It is a skill we learn early, the art of inventing stories to explain away the fearful sacred strangeness of the world. Storytelling and make-believe, like war and agriculture, are among the arts of self-defense, and all of them are ways of enclosing otherness and claiming ownership.**

Here is how the passage by Stephen Hawking in Chapter 1 (page 16) begins:

> **A few years ago the City Council of Monza, Italy, barred pet owners from keeping goldfish in curved fishbowls. The sponsors of the measure explained that it is cruel to keep a fish in a bowl because the curved sides give the fish a distorted view of reality. Aside from the measure's significance to the poor goldfish, the story raises an interesting philosophical question: How do we know that the reality we perceive is true?**
>
> **The goldfish is seeing a version of reality that is different from ours, but can we be sure it is any less real? For all we know, we, too, may spend our entire lives staring out at the world through a distorting lens.**

## FROM QUESTION TO ANSWER

Another method of developing **argument** and explanation is to pose a question, which the paragraph or essay then answers. Here is an example from the conclusion of Thoreau's *Walden:*

> **Why should we be in such desperate haste to succeed, in such desperate enterprises? If a man does not keep pace with his companions, perhaps it is because**

he hears a different drummer. Let him step to the
music which he hears, however measured or far away.

And here is a passage from "The Almost Perfect State," an essay by Don
Marquis:

You have seen the tall towers of Manhattan, wonderful under the stars. How did it come about that
such growths come from such soil—that a breed
lawless and prosaic has written such a mighty hiero-
glyphic against the sky? How is it that this hideous,
half-brute city is also beautiful and a fit habitation for
demi-gods? How come? . . . It comes about because
the wise and subtle deities permit nothing worthy
to be lost. It was with no thought of beauty that the
builders labored . . . the baffled dreams and broken
visions and the ruined hopes and the secret desires
of each one labored with him . . . the rejected beauty,
the strangled appreciation, the inchoate art, the sub-
merged spirit—these groped and found each other
and gathered themselves together and worked themselves into the tiles and mortar of the edifice and
made a town that is a worthy fellow of the sunrise and
the sea winds.

This passage by Sandy Asher is also an example of this method; the final
paragraph reveals that the essay is an answer to the question, "Why do I
write for children?"

Magic, companionship, a sense of control. The
wonder of ourselves, of each other, and of life—this
is the true subject matter of all novels. The best children's literature speaks not only to children but to the
human condition. Writing for children simply means
writing for human beings in the beginning, when you
can still take part in creation, before habit, cynicism
and despair have set in, and while there is still hope
and energy, a willingness to learn, and a healthy sense
of humor. These qualities I find irresistible in the
young people I write about and for, qualities I want

to hang onto and to cultivate in myself. So I write for children, not just for their sakes—but for my own.

## CHRONOLOGICAL ORDER/NARRATION

Although narration is the primary mode of development for fiction, it is also widely used in **exposition** and argument. The historian uses narration and chronology in recounting significant events; the scientific writer may use narration to explain a process. Narration is also an essential part of biography and the personal essay. The passage from *Life on the Mississippi* (page 60) is a classic example of personal narrative. Here, author Annie Dillard, in a passage that appeared on a past Regents exam, uses narration to explain what she means by the "unwrapped gifts and free surprises" of Nature.

I walked up to a tree, an Osage orange, and a hundred birds flew away. They simply materialized out of the tree. I saw a tree, then a whisk of color, then a tree again. I walked closer and another hundred blackbirds took flight. Not a branch, not a twig budged: the birds were apparently weightless as well as invisible. Or, it was as if the leaves of the Osage orange had been freed from a spell in the form of red-winged blackbirds; they flew from the tree, caught my eye in the sky, and vanished. When I looked again at the tree, the leaves had reassembled as if nothing had happened. Finally I walked directly to the trunk of the tree and a final hundred, the real diehards, appeared, spread, and vanished. How could so many hide in the tree without my seeing them? The Osage orange, unruffled, looked just as it had looked from the house, when three hundred red-winged blackbirds cried from its crown. I looked upstream where they flew, and they were gone. Searching, I couldn't spot one. I wandered upstream to force them to play their hand, but they'd crossed the creek and scattered. One show to customer. These appearances catch at my throat; they are the free gifts, the bright coppers at the roots of trees.

## CAUSE AND EFFECT

Formal development of cause and effect arguments is essential to the historian, the scientist, and the lawyer. It also serves as a basic method for much of the expository writing students do. This paragraph from a speech by former governor Madeleine Kunin offers a good example of explanation through cause and effect:

> **In my own case, most essential to my political evolution was a strong desire to have an effect on events around me, whether that was a flashing red light at the railroad crossing in my neighborhood, to protect my children on their way to school, or whether it was a new environmental law for the state of Vermont. The fact that I succeeded in obtaining the flashing red light, as a private citizen, enabled me to change the environmental laws as governor. Each step builds a new self-image, enabling us to move from the passive to the active voice.**

Here is a brief example from the Text on RFID technology (page 26) in Chapter 2:

> **All of the websites you visit collect some amount of information about you, whether it is your name or what other sites you have visited recently. Most of the time, we're being tracked without knowing it. For example, most websites now include Facebook and Twitter buttons so you can "like" the page you are viewing or "Tweet" about it. Whether or not you click the buttons, however, the companies can still determine which pages you've visited and file that information away for later use. . . .**

## COMPARISON AND CONTRAST

In these paragraphs, historian Bruce Catton in "Lee and Grant: A Study in Constrasts," brings to a close his extended discussion of the contrasts between Ulysses S. Grant and Robert E. Lee and introduces the discussion of how the two men were alike:

So Grant and Lee were in complete contrast, representing two diametrically opposed elements in American life. Grant was the modern man emerging; beyond him, ready to come on the stage, was the great age of steel and machinery, of crowded cities and a restless burgeoning vitality. Lee might have ridden down from the old age of chivalry, lance in hand, silken banner fluttering over his head. Each man was the perfect champion of his cause, drawing both his strengths and his weaknesses from the people he led.

Yet it was not all contrast, after all. Different as they were—in background, in personality, in underlying aspiration—these two great soldiers had much in common. Under everything else, they were marvelous fighters. Furthermore, their fighting qualities were really very much alike.

Here, from *Life on the Mississippi* (1883), is Mark Twain's comparison of how the North and South treated the Civil War as a topic of conversation, years after it ended:

In the North one hears the war mentioned, in social conversations, once a month; sometimes as often as once a week; but as a distinct subject for talk, it has long ago been relieved of duty. There are sufficient reasons for this. Given a dinner company of six gentlemen to-day, it can easily happen that four of them—and possibly five—were not in the field at all. So the chances are four to two, or five to one, that the war will at no time during the evening become the topic of conversation; and the chances are still greater that if it becomes the topic it will remain so but a little while. If you add six ladies to the company, you have added six people who saw so little of the dread realities of the war that they ran out of talk concerning them years ago, and now would soon weary of the topic if you brought it up.

The case is very different in the South. There, every man you meet was in the war; and every lady you meet saw the war. The war is the great chief topic of conversation. The interest in it is vivid and constant; the interest in other topics is fleeting. Mention of the war will wake up a dull company and set their tongues going, when nearly any other topic would fail. In the South, the war is what A.D. is elsewhere: they date from it . . . . It shows how intimately every individual was visited, in his own person, by the tremendous episode. It gives the inexperienced stranger a better idea of what a vast and comprehensive calamity invasion is than he can ever get by reading books at the fireside.

## DEVELOPMENT THROUGH EXTENDED METAPHOR

An extended metaphor or **analogy** is a very effective way to develop an argument or illustrate a concept. It uses the known and familiar to explain the unfamiliar. The excerpt from *Life on the Mississippi* is also a vivid example of how a writer relates an experience through extended metaphor. Here is the introduction to an essay written by a student on the topic "All the World's a Stage."

All the world is indeed a stage. And we are the performers. Everything we do in life is a production, and we must constantly perform our best because, in life, there are no rehearsals. Each of us performs on a separate stage, some for a larger audience than others. But each performance, regardless of the size of the audience, is of equal importance, and each performer must meet the standard of life's most important critic—himself.

Here is a passage from Stephen Crane's novel *The Red Badge of Courage:*

The ground was cluttered with vines and bushes, and the trees grew close and spread out like bouquets. The creepers, catching against his legs, cried out harshly as their sprays were torn from the barks of trees. The swishing saplings tried to make known his presence to the world. He could not conciliate the forest. As he made his way, it was always calling out protestations. When he separated embraces of trees and vines the disturbed foliage waved their arms and turned their face leaves toward him.

Here is an illustrative passage from *The Education of Henry Adams*, published in 1918:

> For convenience as an image, the [dynamic theory of history] may liken man to a spider in its web, watching for chance prey. Forces of nature dance like flies before the net, and the spider pounces on them when it can; but it makes many fatal mistakes, though its theory of force is sound. The spider-mind acquires a faculty of memory, and, with it, a singular skill of analysis and synthesis, taking apart and putting together in different relations the meshes of its trap. Man had in the beginning no power of analysis or synthesis approaching that of the spider, or even of the honey-bee; he had acute sensibility to the higher forces. Fire taught him secrets that no other animal could learn; running water probably taught him even more, especially in his first lessons of mechanics; the animals helped to educate him, trusting themselves into his hands merely for the sake of their food, and carrying his burdens or supplying his clothing; the grasses and grains were academies of study. With little or no effort on his part, all these forces formed his thought, induced his action, and even shaped his figure.

## DEFINITION OR CLASSIFICATION

In this paragraph from a speech by Madeleine Kunin, she develops a key term by classifying its component parts:

> Political courage stems from a number of sources: anger, pain, love, hate. There is no lack of political motivation within women. We feel it all. Anger at a world which rushes toward saber-rattling displays of power. Pain at a world which ignores the suffering of its homeless, its elderly, its children. Hatred toward

the injustice which occurs daily as the strong over-
power the weak. And love for the dream of peace on
earth.

Here is a brief passage from *The Federalist #10* by James Madison:

>    . . . The two great points of difference between a
> democracy and a republic are: first, the delegation
> of the government, in the latter, to a small number
> of citizens elected by the rest; secondly, the greater
> number of citizens, and greater sphere of country,
> over which the latter may be extended.
>    The effect of the first difference is, on the one hand,
> to refine and enlarge the public views, by passing
> them through the medium of a chosen body of citi-
> zens, whose wisdom may best discern the true inter-
> est of their country, and whose patriotism and love of
> justice will be least likely to sacrifice it to temporary
> or partial considerations. Under such a regulation, it
> may well happen that the public voice, pronounced
> by the representatives of the people, will be more con-
> sonant to the public good than if pronounced by the
> people themselves, convened for the purpose.

## EXAMPLES IN ORDER OF IMPORTANCE

The most persuasive arguments are those in which the reasoning has a
cumulative effect. The skilled writer does not present the supporting details
of a thesis in random order; rather, the skilled writer presents details in
an order that stresses importance and significance. Here is how Abraham
Lincoln concluded his speech marking the celebration of Independence Day
in 1858:

>    . . . So I say in relation to the principle that all men
> are created equal, let it be as nearly reached as we
> can. If we cannot give freedom to every creature, let
> us do nothing that will impose slavery upon any other
> creature. Let us then turn this government back into
> the channel in which the framers of the Constitution
> originally placed it.

... Let us discard all this quibbling about this man and the other man—this race and that race and the other race being inferior, and therefore they must be placed in an inferior position—discarding our standard that we have left us. Let us discard all these things, and unite as one people throughout this land, until we shall once more stand up declaring that all men are created equal.

This excerpt is from one of the best-known speeches in Shakespeare's *Hamlet*. The character of Polonius is advising his son on how to conduct himself honorably as a university student in Paris:

... Give thy thoughts no tongue,
Nor any unproportioned thought his act.
Be thou familiar, but by no means vulgar.
Those friends thou hast, and their adoption tried,
Grapple them to thy soul with hoops of steel;
But do not dull thy palm with entertainment
Of each new-hatch'd, unfledged comrade. Beware
Of entrance to a quarrel, but being in,
Bear't that the opposed may beware of thee.
Give every man thy ear, but few thy voice;
Take each man's censure, but reserve thy
    judgment.
Costly thy habit as thy purse can buy,
But not express'd in fancy; rich, not gaudy;
For the apparel oft proclaims the man,
And they in France of the best rank and station
Are of a most select and generous chief in that.
Neither a borrower nor a lender be;
For loan oft loses both itself and friend,
And borrowing dulls the edge of husbandry.
This above all: to thine ownself be true,
And it must follow, as the night the day,
Thou canst not then be false to any man.
Farewell: my blessing season this in thee!

These models offer examples of only some of the ways in which writers develop ideas. As you read more widely, you will appreciate the extent to which every writer, especially the writer of essays, creates a form best suited to the subject and purpose. When you find a piece of writing you especially admire or find convincing, note how the author developed the ideas.

## Tone

When we speak of **tone** in writing we are referring to the attitude of the writer toward the subject and/or toward the reader. It is closely related to what we mean when we refer to someone's "tone of voice." Tone may range from *harsh* and *insistent* to *gentle* and *reflective*. There is as much variety of tone in writing as there is in human feeling. Some pieces—essays of opinion, for example—usually have a very distinct tone; other works, especially in fiction or personal expression, may have a more subtle and indirect tone.

Here is a list of adjectives to help you identify the tone or mood of a prose passage. Many have been gathered by students in their reading of Op-Ed page essays. These terms are part of the academic language you are expected to comprehend in reading and to use appropriately in discussing works of nonfiction. Each reflects a distinctive feeling; be sure to look up in a dictionary any that you are not sure about.

| | | | |
|---|---|---|---|
| admiring | cautious | informed | provocative |
| advisory | challenging | inquiring | questioning |
| affectionate | concerned | instructive | reasoned |
| alarmed | credible | intense | reflective |
| amused | critical | ironic | sad |
| anguished | curious | knowledgeable | sarcastic |
| appalled | cynical | melancholy | satirical |
| apprehensive | defensive | mocking | sentimental |
| argumentative | disappointed | mysterious | skeptical |
| arrogant | dismayed | nonchalant | surprised |
| assured | eerie | nostalgic | thoughtful |
| (with) awe | frank | objective | troubled |
| bewildered | grateful | offended | understanding |
| bitter | haughty | optimistic | whimsical |
| boastful | humorous | outraged | wondering |
| candid | indifferent | peaceful | |
| cautionary | indignant | probing | |

The Op-Ed pages of most newspapers offer daily examples of essays on current topics, representing widely varied methods of argument, style, and tone. *Ploughshares, McSweeneys, Zoetrope, Harper's Magazine, The*

*Atlantic Monthly*, and *The New Yorker* include excellent selections of essays and other examples of literary nonfiction. National magazines such as *Time* and *Sports Illustrated* also offer examples of feature writing and reporting on current issues. The list of Recommended Reading on page 215 also offers titles of books of nonfiction available in paperback.

# A GLOSSARY OF LITERARY TERMS AND TECHNIQUES

**abstract** In contrast to the *concrete*, abstract language expresses general ideas and concepts apart from specific examples or instances. Very formal writing is characterized by abstract expression. An *abstract* (n.) is a brief summary of the key ideas in a scientific, legal, or scholarly piece of writing.

**analogy** An expression of the similarities between things that are not wholly alike or related. (See, for example, the student essay on page 61.) See *metaphor* in A Glossary of Poetic Terms and Techniques, Chapter 5.

**anecdote** A very brief, usually vivid, story or episode. Often humorous, anecdotes offer examples of typical behavior or illustrate the personality of a character. Writers of biography and autobiography make extensive use of anecdote to reveal the lives of their subjects.

**antithesis** In formal argument, a statement that opposes or contrasts with a *thesis* statement. Informally, we use the term to refer to any expression or point of view completely opposed to another. In literature, even an experience or feeling may be expressed as the *antithesis* of another. See also *thesis*.

**argument** In persuasive writing or speaking, the development of reasons to support the writer's position; also the method of reasoning used to persuade. Informally, we may use the term to describe the development of a topic in any piece of exposition. Historically, it has also denoted a summary of a literary work's plot or main ideas.

**atmosphere** Closely related to *tone* or mood, it refers to a pervasive feeling in a work. Atmosphere often stems from setting and from distinctive characters or actions. For example, the atmosphere in many of Poe's stories is mysterious, troubling, even sinister, and Hawthorne's "Young Goodman Brown" reflects the threatening and ambiguous world of its Puritan setting.

**autobiography** A formally composed account of a person's life, written by that person. While we must trust, or be skeptical of, the reliability of the account, we often appreciate the firsthand narration of experience. Autobiography is also a rich source of information and insight into an historical period or into literary or artistic worlds. Autobiography, like the novel, has *narrative* and chronology. (See also *journal.)* We describe literary works that are closely based on the author's life as "autobiographical." Eugene O'Neill's *Long Day's Journey into Night* and Tennessee Williams's *The Glass Menagerie* are plays that reflect many details of their authors' lives.

**biography** A narrative, historical account of the life, character, and significance of its subject. Contemporary biography is usually researched in detail and may not always paint an admiring portrait of its subject. A critical biography of a literary figure includes discussion of the writer's works to show the writer's artistic development and career. Biographies of figures significant in history or public affairs also offer commentary on periods and events of historical importance.

**character** Characters are the imagined persons, created figures, who inhabit the worlds of fiction and drama. E. M. Forster distinguished between *flat* and *round* characters: Flat are those, like stereotypes, who represent a single and exaggerated human characteristic; round are those whose aspects are complex and convincing, and who change or develop in the course of a work. In good fiction, plot must develop out of character. The desires, values, and motives of characters account for the action and conflict in a plot.

**characterization** The method by which an author establishes character; the means by which personality, manner, and appearance are created. It is achieved directly through description and dialogue and indirectly through observations and reactions of other characters.

**concrete** Refers to the particular, the specific, in expression and imagery. That which is concrete can be perceived by the senses. Concrete also refers to that which is tangible, real, or actual, in contrast to the *abstract*, which is intangible and conceptual.

**conflict** In the most general sense, it identifies the forces that give rise to a plot. This term may identify an actual struggle between characters, anything from revenge to simple recognition or understanding. A plot may focus on conflict between characters and the forces of nature or society. These are essentially **external conflicts**. A work may also center on **internal conflicts**, characters' struggles to know or change themselves and their lives. Most works of fiction and drama contain more than one aspect of conflict. (See the discussion on page 47.)

**denouement** A French term meaning "untying a knot," it refers to the way the complications or conflict of a plot are finally resolved. It also refers to what is called the "falling action" in a drama, that part of the play that follows the dramatic climax and reveals the consequences of the main action for minor characters; it also accounts briefly for what happens in the world of the play after the principal drama is resolved. In Arthur Miller's *Death of a Salesman*, the "Requiem" may be considered a denouement; it accounts for the response to Willy's death by his wife, sons, and only friend. In Shakespeare's *Macbeth*, the climax is in the

scene following the death of Lady Macbeth in which Macbeth understands that he has destroyed all capacity for feeling and has rendered his
life meaningless; the denouement includes the battle in which Macbeth
understands that he cannot escape the witches' prophecy and is killed by
MacDuff, thus restoring the throne to the rightful heir, Malcolm.

**determinism** The philosophical view that human existence is determined
by forces over which humans have little or no control. The concept that
fate predestines the course of a character's life or a tragic figure's down-
fall is a form of determinism.

**episode** A series of actions or incidents that make up a self-contained part
of a larger narrative. Some novels are structured so that each chapter is
a significant episode. Fitzgerald's *The Great Gatsby* and Mark Twain's
*Huckleberry Finn* are good examples of this structure. A *scene* in a play
is often analogous to an episode in a narrative. Many television series are
presented in weekly episodes.

**essay** A general term (from French *essai*, meaning an attempt, a trying
out of something) to denote an extended composition, usually expository, devoted to a single topic. Essays may be composed to persuade,
to reflect on philosophical questions, to analyze a subject, to express
an opinion, or to entertain. As a literary form, the essay dates from the
sixteenth century and remains a popular and widely practiced form. The
essay by Francis Bacon on page 41 is a classic example. See *formal/
informal* essay.

**exposition** Writing whose purpose is to inform, illustrate, and explain. In
literature, exposition refers to those passages or speeches in which setting, offstage or prior action, or a character's background is revealed.
In *The Great Gatsby*, Nick Carraway pauses in the narrative to give the
reader additional information about Gatsby's background. The prologue
to Shakespeare's *Romeo and Juliet* is an example of exposition.

**flashback** A presentation of incidents or episodes that occurred prior
to the beginning of the narrative itself. When an author or filmmaker
uses flashback, the "present" or forward motion of the plot is suspend-
ed. Flashback may be introduced through the device of a character's
memory or through the narrative voice itself. William Faulkner's "Barn
Burning" and *Light in August* include vivid passages of memory and narrative flashback. Jack Burden's recounting of the Cass Mastern story in
Robert Penn Warren's *All the King's Men* is also a form of flashback.

**foreshadowing** A technique in which an author establishes details or
mood that will become more significant as the plot of a work progresses.
Thoughtful readers usually sense such details and accumulate them in
their memories. In one of the opening scenes of *Ethan Frome*, Ethan and
Mattie talk about the dangers of sledding down Starkfield's steepest hill;
and, in the second paragraph of "The Lottery," the boys are stuffing their
pockets with stones or making piles of them on the edge of the square.

**form** The organization, shape, and structure of a work. Concretely, form may refer to *genre* (see below), for example, the sonnet form, the tragic form. More abstractly, form also refers to the way we sense inherent structure and shape.

**formal/informal essay** The formal essay emphasizes organization, logic, and explanation of ideas, whereas the informal essay emphasizes the voice and perspective of the writer. In the latter, also called a *personal essay*, the reader is aware of the author's *persona* and is asked to share the author's interest in the subject.

**genre** A type or form of literature. Examples include *novel, short story, epic poem, essay, sonnet, tragedy.*

**image** Although the term suggests something that is visualized, an image is an evocation through language of *any* experience perceived directly through the senses. See also A Glossary of Poetic Terms and Techniques, Chapter 5.

**irony** In general, a tone or figure of speech in which there is a discrepancy (a striking difference or contradiction) between what is expressed and what is meant or expected. Irony achieves its powerful effect indirectly: in satire, for example, which often uses *understatement* or *hyperbole* to express serious criticism of human behavior and social institutions. We also speak of *dramatic irony* when the narrator or reader understands more than the characters do.

**journal** A diary or notebook of personal observations. Many writers use journals to compose personal reflection and to collect ideas for their works; the journals of many writers have been published. Students are often urged to keep journals as a way to reflect on their reading, compose personal pieces, and practice writing free of concern for evaluation.

**melodrama** A plot in which incidents are sensational and designed to provoke immediate emotional responses. In such a plot, the "good" characters are pure and innocent and victims of the "bad" ones, who are thoroughly evil. The term refers to a particular kind of drama popular in the late nineteenth century and, later, in silent films and early Westerns. A work becomes melodramatic when it relies on improbable incidents and unconvincing characters for strong emotional effect.

**memoir** A form of autobiographical writing that reflects on the significant events the writer has observed and on the interesting and important personalities the writer has known.

**monologue** In a play, an extended expression or speech by a single speaker that is uninterrupted by response from other characters. A monologue is addressed to a particular person or persons, who may or may not actually hear it. Ring Lardner's short story "Haircut" is an example of monologue as a method of narration. In it, a barber tells the story to a customer (the reader) who is present but does not respond. See also *dramatic monologue* in A Glossary of Poetic Terms and Techniques, Chapter 5.

**motivation** The desires, values, needs, or impulses that move characters to act as they do. In good fiction the reader understands, appreciates, and is convinced that a character's motivation accounts for the significant incidents and the outcome of a plot.

**narrative point of view** The standpoint, perspective, and degree of understanding from which a work of narrative fiction is told. See *omniscient point of view, objective point of view.*

**narrator** The character or author's *persona* that tells a story. It is through the perspective and understanding of the narrator that the reader experiences the work. In some works, the narrator may inhabit the world of the story or be a character in it. In other works, the narrator is a detached but knowledgeable observer.

**naturalism** Closely related to *determinism,* naturalism depicts characters who are driven not by personal will or moral principles but by natural forces that they do not fully understand or control. In contrast to other views of human experience, the naturalistic view makes no moral judgments on the lives of the characters. Their lives, often bleak or defeating, simply *are* as they are, determined by social, environmental, instinctive, and hereditary forces. Naturalism was in part a reaction by writers against the nineteenth century Romantic view of humans as the masters of their own fate. It is important to note, however, that none of the Naturalistic writers in America (Crane, Dreiser, London, Anderson, and Norris chief among them) presented a genuinely deterministic vision. Several of these authors began their careers in journalism and were drawn to the Naturalistic view of life as a result of their own experience and observation of life in the United States. See also *realism.*

**objective point of view** In fiction or nonfiction, this voice presents a story or information, respectively, without expressed judgment or qualification. A fundamental principle of journalism is that news *reports* should be objective. Ernest Hemingway's short story "The Killers" is an example of fiction rendered in a completely detached, objective point of view.

**omniscient point of view** Spoken in third person (*she, he, it, they*), this is the broadest narrative perspective. The omniscient narrator speaks from outside the story and sees and knows everything about the characters and incidents. Omniscient narration is not limited by time or place. In **limited omniscient** point of view, the author may choose to reveal the story through full understanding of only one character and limit the action to those incidents in which this character is present.

**persona** A term from the Greek meaning "mask," it refers in literature to a narrative voice created by an author and through which the author speaks. A narrative persona usually has a perceptible, even distinctive, personality that contributes to our understanding of the story. In Nathaniel Hawthorne's *The Scarlet Letter,* the omniscient narrator has a distinctive persona whose attitudes toward Puritan society and the characters' lives are revealed throughout the novel.

**plot** The incidents and experiences of characters selected and arranged by the author to create a meaningful narrative. A good plot is convincing in terms of what happens and why.

**poetic justice** The concept that life's rewards and punishments should be perfectly appropriate and distributed in just proportions. In Ring Lardner's short story "Haircut," Jim Kendall's ironic fate is an example of poetic justice: He is a victim of one of his own crude and insensitive practical jokes.

**point of view** In nonfiction, this denotes the attitudes or opinions of the writer. In narrative fiction, it refers to how and by whom a story is told: the perspective of the narrator and the narrator's relationship to the story. Point of view may be *omniscient*, where the narrator knows everything about the characters and their lives; or it may be *limited* to the understanding of a particular character or speaker. Point of view may also be described as *objective* or *subjective*. *Third-person* narrative refers to characters as "he, she, it, they." *First-person* narrative is from the "I" point of view. J. D. Salinger's *The Catcher in the Rye* and Twain's *Huckleberry Finn* are told in the first person. *Second-person* narrative, the "you" form, is rare but is found in sermons addressed to a congregation or in essays of opinion addressed directly to a leader or public figure: "You, Mr. Mayor (Madame President), should do the following . . ." Thomas Friedman and Gail Collins occasionally write pieces in the second-person voice for the Op-Ed page of *The New York Times*.

**prologue** An introductory statement of the dramatic situation of a play or story. Shakespeare's *Romeo and Juliet* begins with a brief prologue. The first two pages of Fitzgerald's *The Great Gatsby* are a prologue to the story Nick Carraway will tell.

**prose** Most of what we write is prose, the expression in sentences and phrases that reflect the natural rhythms of speech. Prose is organized by paragraphs and is characterized by variety in sentence length and rhythm.

**protagonist** A term from Ancient Greek drama, it refers to the central character, the hero or heroine, in a literary work.

**realism** The literary period in the United States following the Civil War is usually called the Age of Realism. Realism depicts the directly observable in everyday life. Realistic writers seek to *present* characters and situations as they would appear to a careful observer, not as they are imagined or created by the author. After 1865, American writers became increasingly interested in the sources of power and force, and in the means to survival and success, in an increasingly materialistic society. For writers of this period, realism was a literary mode to express a *naturalistic* philosophy. See also *naturalism, verisimilitude*.

**rhetoric** From Ancient Greece, the art of persuasion in speech or writing achieved through logical thought and skillful use of language.

**rhetorical question** A question posed in the course of an *argument* to provoke thought or to introduce a line of reasoning.

**romance** A novel or tale that includes elements of the supernatural, heroic adventure, or romantic passion. Hawthorne's *The Scarlet Letter* is a romance, not because it is a love story but because it goes beyond *verisimilitude* in dramatizing elements of demonic and mystical forces in the characters and their lives.

**satire** A form or style that uses elements of irony, ridicule, exaggeration, understatement, sarcasm, humor, or absurdity to criticize human behavior or a society. All satire is **ironic** (see above) in that meaning or theme is conveyed in the discrepancy between what is said and what is meant, between what is and what should be, between what appears and what truly is. While satire is often entertaining, its purpose is serious and meant to provoke thought or judgment. The verses of Alexander Pope are often extended satire, and many poems by e. e. cummings are satiric. In prose, much of the writing of Mark Twain is satire; *Huckleberry Finn* is the most striking example. Other American writers of satire include Sinclair Lewis, Dorothy Parker, Edith Wharton, Joseph Heller, and Tom Wolfe. On television, *Saturday Night Live*, and *The Simpsons* are good examples of contemporary satire, as was *The Colbert Report*.

**short story** This form is distinguished from most novels not simply by length but by its focus on few characters and on a central, revealing incident. In short stories, however, there is as much variety in narrative point of view, subject, and technique as there is in novels. Edgar Allan Poe characterized the short story as "a short prose narrative, requiring from a half-hour to one or two hours in its perusal."

**soliloquy** A form of *monologue* in which a character expresses thoughts and feelings aloud but does not address them to anyone else or intend other characters in the work to hear them. In essence, the audience for a play is secretly listening in on a character's innermost thoughts. Macbeth's reflection on "Tomorrow, and tomorrow, and tomorrow . . . " is the best-known soliloquy in the play.

**speaker** The narrative voice in a literary work (see *persona*). Also, the character who speaks in a *dramatic monologue*.

**symbol** Most generally, anything that stands for or suggests something else. Language itself is symbolic; sounds and abstract written forms may be arranged to stand for virtually any human thought or experience. In literature, symbols are not codes to crack—they are not "hidden meanings." Symbols are real objects and *concrete* images that lead us to *think about* what is suggested. They organize a wide variety of ideas into single acts of understanding. They embody not single "meanings" but suggest whole areas of meaning.

**theme** Roughly analogous to thesis in an essay, this is an observation about human experience or an idea central to a work of literature. The *subject* of a work is in the specific setting, characters, and plot. Theme in a work of fiction is what is meaningful and significant to human experience generally; themes are the ideas and truths that transcend the specific characters and plot. Shakespeare's *Macbeth* is about an ambitious nobleman who, encouraged by his equally ambitious wife, murders the king of Scotland in order to become king himself. The themes in *Macbeth* include the power of ambition to corrupt even those who are worthy and the mortal consequences of denying what is fundamental to one's nature.

**thesis** The central point, a statement of position in a formal or logical argument. Also used to refer to the topic, or controlling, idea of an essay. Use of the term *thesis* implies elaboration by reasons and examples. See *antithesis*.

**tone** The attitude of the writer toward the subject and the reader. See also A Glossary of Poetic Terms and Techniques, Chapter 5.

**transition** A transition is a link between ideas or sections in a work. In prose arguments, single words such as *first, second . . . moreover,* and *therefore* or phrases such as *in addition, on the other hand,* and *in conclusion* serve as transitions. In fiction, a brief passage or chapter may serve as a transition. In *The Great Gatsby,* the narrator pauses from time to time to "fill in" the reader and to account for the passage of time between the dramatic episodes that make up the novel's main plot.

**turning point** In drama and fiction, the moment or episode in a plot when the action is moved toward its inevitable conclusion.

**verisimilitude** A quality in fiction and drama of being "true to life," of representing that which is real or actual. Verisimilitude in fiction is often achieved through specific, vivid description and dialogue; first-person narration also creates the effect of verisimilitude. In drama it may be enhanced through means of set, costumes, and lighting that are realistic in all their details.

(See also, in Chapter 5—A Glossary of Poetic Terms and Techniques.)

# Chapter 5

# READING POETRY

## INTRODUCTION

### How to Read a Poem

How should you read a poem? Aloud. Several times. And never quickly. Here is a short poem about baseball. As you read, pay attention first to what the poem by Robert Francis says.

### Pitcher

His art is eccentricity, his aim
How not to hit the mark he seems to aim at,
His passion how to avoid the obvious,
His technique how to vary the avoidance.
The others throw to be comprehended. He
Throws to be a moment misunderstood.
Yet not too much. Not errant, arrant, wild,
But every seeming aberration willed.
Not to, yet still, still to communicate
Making the batter understand too late.

Now, read the poem again, with particular attention to the varied length of the statements; read from comma to comma or period to period as you would in prose. When you reach the end of the first and fifth lines, for example, pause very slightly—but do not stop. After several readings, you will not only appreciate what Robert Francis undertands about the art of pitching but also feel the way in which the rhythm of the poem is also the rhythm of pitching.

In poetry we are meant to sense a structure and to feel the rhythm. (See **meter*** and **rhythm**.) The structure and rhythm of poetry may be formal, informal, even "free." Poetry is also characterized by its directness of effect and by its concentration—ideas and feelings are expressed in relatively few words. Karl Shapiro says, "Poems are what ideas *feel like*." Robert Francis's poem is about what good pitching *feels like*.

---

*Terms in bold type are defined in A Glossary of Poetic Terms and Techniques at the end of the chapter.

This poem, by Emily Dickinson (1830–1886), recalls the feeling of mourning:

> After great pain, a formal feeling comes—
> The nerves sit ceremonious, like Tombs—
> The stiff Heart questions was it He, that bore,
> and Yesterday, or Centuries before?
>
> The Feet, mechanical, go round—
> Of Ground, or Air or Ought—
> A Wooden way
> Regardless grown,
> A Quartz contentment, like a stone—
>
> This is the Hour of Lead—
> Remembered, if outlived,
> As Freezing persons, recollect the Snow—
> First—Chill—then Stupor—then the letting go—

In this poem, Dickinson recreates what it feels like suddenly to encounter a snake in the grass:

> A narrow Fellow in the Grass
> Occasionally rides—
> You may have met Him—did you not
> His notice sudden is—
> The Grass divides as with a Comb—
> A spotted shaft is seen—
> And then it closes at your feet
> And opens further on—
>
> He likes a Boggy Acre
> A Floor too cool for corn—
> Yet when a boy, and Barefoot—
> I more than once at Noon
> Have passed, I thought, a Whip lash
> Unbraiding in the Sun
> When stooping to secure it
> It wrinkled, and was gone—

Several of Nature's People
I know, and they know me—
I feel for them a transport
Of cordiality—

But never met this Fellow
Attended, or alone
Without a tighter breathing
And Zero at the Bone—

Where the writer of prose may seek immediate clarity of meaning above all, the poet often seeks **ambiguity**, not to create "confusion," but to offer multiplicity of meaning, in single words, in images, in the meaning of the poem itself. Look again at "Pitcher." Might this poem also be a reflection on the art of poetry itself? It is because of such richness in meaning that poems often require several readings.

The experience of poetry is conveyed in vivid **imagery**, which appeals to the mind and to the senses. It is often expressed in **figurative language**, that is, words and comparions that are not literal but that imaginatively create original, vivid, and often unexpected images and associations. (See **metaphor** and **simile**.) Finally, in poetry there is particular significance in the way words and lines sound. The story or experience is enhanced through musical effects. A poem should be heard or felt!

In this poem by Laurence Binyon, a boy kept home from school with a fever, is dazzled by the light of the sun as it comes out after rain, and he no longer regrets being "…a captive/Apart from his schoolfellows."

### The rain was ending, and light

THE rain was ending, and light
Lifting the leaden skies.
It shone upon ceiling and floor
And dazzled a child's eyes.

Pale after fever, a captive
Apart from his schoolfellows,
He stood at the high room's window
With face to the pane pressed close,

And beheld an immense glory
Flooding with fire the drops
Spilled on miraculous leaves
Of the fresh green lime-tree tops.

Washed gravel glittered red
To a wall, and beyond it nine
Tall limes in the old inn yard
Rose over the tall inn sign.

And voices arose from beneath
Of boys from school set free,
Racing and chasing each other
With laughter and games and glee.

To the boy at the high room-window,
Gazing alone and apart,
There came a wish without reason,
A thought that shone through his heart.

I'll choose this moment and keep it,
He said to himself, for a vow,
To remember for ever and ever
As if it were always now.

A note on reading this poem: do not read to emphasize regular meter and rhyming pattern; remember, read from comma to comma, period to period. For example, the second and third stanzas should be read with only slight pauses at the commas and through the third stanza, where there is no end punctuation, in as few breaths as possible. The fourth stanza completes the vivid image of the "immense glory" the boy sees as he looks out the window.

# STRUCTURE AND LANGUAGE IN POETRY

All the traditional poetic forms stem from an oral tradition, in which poetry was sung or recited. The **epic** and the **ballad** are the oldest forms of **narrative poetry**, but modern poets also tell stories in narrative verse. (Robert Frost's "Out, Out—" is a well-known example.) Most of the poetry we read today, however, is **lyric** poetry.

Think of the lyric poem as a song; in the Ancient Greek tradition, the lyric poem was meant to be sung to the accompaniment of a lyre, a small harplike instrument. Indeed, we speak of the words for a song as its lyrics. The ancient form is evident in the songs for Shakespeare's plays, in the tradition of the nineteenth-century art song, and in the twentieth-century ballads and songs. The ancient form is evident in the songs for Shakespeare's plays, in the tradition of the nineteenth-century art song, and in the twenti-eth-century ballads and songs we associate, for example, with Rodgers and Hart, Cole Porter, and Stephen Sondheim and sung by Frank Sinatra, Barbra Streisand, among many others, including Tony Bennett in his duets with Lady Gaga.

Lyric poems are relatively brief and are expressed in the voice (that is, from the point of view) of a single speaker. They express a powerful emo-tion, usually captured in a significant experience or dramatic situation. A lyric poem, like a song, often tells a story, but it does so in nonnarra-tive form. The **speaker** (or "poet") may recall an experience, or render it directly, in order to understand its meaning and then reveal it to the reader. Thus, many lyric poems are *meditations, reflections,* or *recollections* of experience that lead to a *discovery*, to an emotionally powerful *recognition* of the meaning of the experiences. The effect of the poem is to convey that meaning directly, to engage readers in such a way that they share the expe-rience, feel the emotion, with the speaker. The poems by Robert Francis, Emily Dickinson, and Laurence Binyon on the previous pages are examples of lyrics.

This poem by Robert Penn Warren appeared on a past Regents ELA exam.

### Old Photograph of the Future

That center of attention—an infantile face
That long years ago showed, no doubt, pink and white—
Now faded, and in the photograph only a trace
Of grays, not much expression in sight.

(5)  That center of attention, swathed in a sort of white dress,
Is precious to the woman who, pretty and young,
Leans with a look of surprised blessedness
At the mysterious miracle forth-sprung.

In the background somewhat, the masculine figure
(10)  Looms, face agleam with achievement and pride.
In black coat, derby at breast, he is quick to assure
You the world's in good hands—lay your worries aside.

The picture is badly faded. Why not?
Most things show wear around seventy-five,
(15)  And that's the age this picture has got.
The man and woman no longer, of course, live.

> They lie side by side in whatever love survives
> Under green turf, or snow, and that child, years later,
> stands there
> While old landscapes blur and he in guilt grieves
> (20) Over nameless promises unkept, in undefinable despair.

In this poem, the speaker expresses the profound feelings of guilt and despair he feels in looking at an old photograph of himself and his parents when he was an infant. The **tone** of the poem is reflective, that of an elegy. The mood at the end is one of regret and loss as the speaker recalls his dead parents, confronts his own age, "the age this picture has got," and grieves at the "nameless promises unkept." Although the narrator speaks of "that child, years later" who "stands there . . . and . . . in guilt grieves," the intensity and privacy of feeling at the end indicate that the speaker is that child. The narrative voice and the lack of specific identification of the characters serve to emphasize the passage of time and underscore the fact that looking at the photograph leads the "child," now old, to reflect on his entire life.

The structure is simple and easy to observe: five **quatrains** with alternating **rhyme**; each quatrain is self-contained—ends with a period—and tells a part of the story. The first fifteen lines of the poem describe the picture and the "characters" in it. Note that the final section of the poem begins with the last line of the fourth quatrain, the description having concluded in line 15. Line 16 both ends the narrator's rendering of the photograph and also begins the "conclusion," which is the significance of the experience of looking at the photograph.

The rhythm within lines is varied and often broken by dashes or other pauses; this rhythm allows us to share the speaker's questions and reflections. The rhythm of the fourth stanza slows as each line completes a thought. In contrast, the final stanza flows into a single, long gesture of recognition and regret.

The experience of looking at the picture—in which he is the "center of attention"—leads the speaker to reflect on whether he has satisfied the "promises" that the "mysterious miracle" of his birth meant to his awed and proud parents. The photograph also leads the speaker to reflect on the unfulfilled promises of his own life.

There is little in the way of figurative language in this poem. The imagery, however, reveals more than a description of a photograph, and the paradox in the title reveals one of the poem's central **themes**, the cycle of birth, life, and death. On rereading Warren's poem, with our appreciation of the poet's experience in mind, we perceive how the third and fourth lines are more than a description of the photograph—they also suggest the speaker's age. He sees himself (in the photo and metaphorically) as "faded . . . only a trace of grays, not much expression in sight." The repetition of the fact that he was the "center of attention" (in the photograph and in his parents' lives) makes more poignant the grief over "promises unkept" at the end.

The poet offers only a few details of the photograph, but they are the details many of us will recognize from our own photographs of grandparents and great-grandparents: the father "In the background somewhat" and in formal pose—"in black coat, derby at breast"—the child (girl or boy) in "a sort of white dress." It is, of course, such widely shared experience that is both the poem's form and its theme.

In this poem by Theodore Roethke, the speaker recalls a significant experience from childhood:

### Child on Top of a Greenhouse

The wind billowing out of the seat of my britches,
My feet crackling splinters of glass and dried putty,
The half-grown chrysanthemums staring up like accusers,
Up through the streaked glass, flashing with sunlight,
A few white clouds all rushing eastward,
A line of elms plunging and tossing like horses,
And everyone, everyone pointing up and shouting!

Try repeating just the verbs of this poem, feeling their dramatic energy. The repetition of "-ing" forms also creates what is called **internal rhyme**, while the words "like," "sunlight," "white," "line" form the pattern of sound called **assonance**.

In this poem by Donald Hall the speaker also recalls an important childhood experience:

### The Sleeping Giant
(A Hill, So Named, in Hamden, Connecticut)

The whole day long, under the walking sun
That poised an eye on me from its high floor,
Holding my toy beside the clapboard house
I looked for him, the summer I was four.

I was afraid the waking arm would break
From the loose earth and rub against his eyes
A fist of trees, and the whole country tremble
In the exultant labor of his rise;

Then he with giant steps in the small streets
Would stagger, cutting off the sky, to seize
The roofs from house and home because we had
Covered his shape with dirt and planted trees;

And then kneel down and rip with fingernails
A trench to pour the enemy Atlantic
Into our basin, and the water rush,
With the streets full and the voices frantic.

That was the summer I expected him.
Later the high and watchful sun instead
Walked low behind the house, and school began,
And winter pulled a sheet over his head.

In this poem, a child's fearful and vivid imagination is sparked by **personification** of the hill near his house. This poem is particularly effective because it recalls for us the fact that small children are literal and that they tend to give names and human character to inanimate things. This child actually sees—and fears—the sleeping giant. Note too how the images of the sun in the first and last stanzas both unify the poem and denote the passage of time. Finally, there is a gentle **irony** in the final line that suggests that the child, no longer fearful, can now "play" with the metaphor of the sleeping giant, as "winter pulled a sheet over his head."

Shakespeare's Sonnet 30 illustrates several of the formal aspects of verse:

### When to the sessions of sweet silent thought

When to the sessions of sweet silent thought
I summon up remembrance of things past
I sigh the lack of many a thing I sought
And with old woes new wail my dear time's waste:

(5) Then can I drown an eye, unused to flow,
For precious friends hid in death's dateless night,
And weep afresh love's long-since-canceled woe,
And moan th'expense of many a vanished sight;

Then can I grieve at grievances forgone,
*(10)* And heavily from woe to woe tell o'er
The sad account of fore-bemoaned moan,
Which I new pay as if not paid before.
But if the while I think on thee, dear friend,
All losses are restored and sorrows end.

The structure of the Shakespearean **sonnet** is three **quatrains** and a closing **couplet**. The **rhyme scheme** is *abab/cdcd/efef/gg*. This pattern allows us to feel the structure of the poem, to track the development of the ideas. The couplet, with its similar end rhyme and self-contained thought, contrasts the feelings expressed in the previous 12 lines and concludes the poem.

We find in this Shakespearean sonnet, as well, examples of **alliteration** and assonance: The first quatrain features alliteration in the many words that begin with "s." Lines 7 through 12 offer assonance in the repetition of "oh" sounds, which are also examples of **onomatopoeia**—that is, the sounds reflect the meanings of the words. Lines 4 and 10 also illustrate what is called internal rhyme.

## THEME IN POETRY

Some lyric poems may assert a belief. Others may be a comment on the nature of human experience—love, death, loss or triumph, mystery and confusion, conflict and peace, on the humorous and the ironic, on the imagined and the unexpected in all its forms. Some poems reflect on the nature of time, of existence. Many lyrics are about poetry itself. These aspects of human experience are what we refer to as the themes of poetry.

In this well-known sonnet, Number 55, Shakespeare asserts that poetry confers immortality, that it can prevail over the most powerful forces of time. Note how the central idea is developed in the three quatrains and how the couplet—in its thought and its rhyme—concludes the development of that idea.

#### Not marble, nor the gilded monuments

Not marble, nor the gilded monuments
Of princes, shall outlive this pow'rful rhyme;
But you shall shine more bright in these contents
Than unswept stone besmeared with sluttish time.

When wasteful war shall statues overturn,
And broils root out the work of masonry,
Nor Mars his sword nor war's quick fire shall burn
The living record of your memory.

'Gainst death and all-oblivious enmity
Shall you pace forth; your praise shall still find room
Even in the eyes of all posterity
That wear this world out to the ending doom.
So, till the judgment that yourself arise,
You live in this, and dwell in lovers' eyes.

In this lyric by Carl Sandburg, the poet suggests that poetry is "about" the meaning in life itself.

## Last Answers

I WROTE a poem on the mist
And a woman asked me what I meant by it.
I had thought till then only of the beauty of the mist,
     how pearl and gray of it mix and reel,
And change the drab shanties with lighted lamps
     at evening into points of mystery quivering with
     color.
  I answered:
The whole world was mist once long ago and some
     day it will all go back to mist,
Our skulls and lungs are more water than bone and
     tissue
And all poets love dust and mist because all the last
     answers
Go running back to dust and mist.

The best-known lyrics, however, are probably love poems—Sonnet 116 of Shakespeare, for example:

## Let me not to the marriage of true minds

Let me not to the marriage of true minds
Admit impediments. Love is not love
which alters when it alteration finds,
Or bends with the remover to remove.

O, no, it is an ever-fixed mark
That looks on tempests and is never shaken;
It is the star to every wand'ring bark,
Whose worth's unknown, although his height be taken.

Love's not Time's fool, though rosy lips and cheeks
Within his bending sickle's compass come;
Love alters not with his brief hours and weeks,
But bears it out even to the edge of doom.
    If this be error and upon me proved,
    I never writ, nor no man ever loved.

In this lyric by Claude McKay, the poet is overcome with longing for his homeland on the island of Jamaica.

## The Tropics in New York

Bananas ripe and green, and ginger-root,
    Cocoa in pods and alligator pears,
And tangerines and mangoes and grape fruit,
    Fit for the highest prize at parish fairs,

Set in the window, bringing memories
    Of fruit-trees laden by low-singing rills,
And dewy dawns, and mystical blue skies
    In benediction over nun-like hills.

My eyes grew dim, and I could no more gaze;
    A wave of longing through my body swept,
And, hungry for the old, familiar ways,
    I turned aside and bowed my head and wept.

# TONE

**Tone** in poetry, as in prose and all forms of human communication, expresses the *attitude* of the speaker toward the reader or listener and toward the subject. Tone in literature is as varied as the range of human experience and feeling it reflects. When we speak of the *mood* of a piece of writing, we are also speaking of tone, of an overall feeling generated by the work.

Here are some terms to help you recognize and articulate tone or mood:

| | | |
|---|---|---|
| ambiguous* | insistent | reconciled |
| amused | ironic* | reflective |
| angry | melancholy | regretful |
| bitter | mournful | reminiscent |
| celebratory | mysterious | satiric* |
| elegiac (from elegy*) | nostalgic | sorrowful |
| grateful | optimistic | thoughtful |
| harsh | paradoxical* | understated* |
| humorous | questioning | |

# WRITING ABOUT POETRY/EXPLICATION

When you are asked to *explicate* a poem, you are being asked to look closely at it and "unfold" its meaning, line by line, idea by idea. Explication combines paraphrase with close reading of form. You are explaining both the content *and* the form: the ideas and meaning as well as the structure and poetic elements.

To begin an explication, read the poem several times to discover what it says. Who is the speaker? What is the subject? the dramatic situation? What theme or experience is central to the poem? What is the tone or mood? Try to summarize or paraphrase the poem as a whole. Then note the formal details: What is the pattern of organization? What is the movement of ideas and feeling? of images and metaphors? How do stanzas or arrangement of lines reveal that? How do rhyme, meter, and rhythm contribute to the experience, to the meaning of the poem? (The commentary that follows Robert Penn Warren's "Old Photograph of the Future" on page 79 is an example of explication.)

---

*These terms are defined in A Glossary of Poetic Terms and Techniques at the end of the chapter.

# POETRY ON EXAMINATIONS

On examinations, such as the Regents ELA exam and the AP Literature and Composition exam, the multiple-choice questions are designed to measure your skill at close reading and *explication*. You are expected to recognize and identify the elements of poetry. (See A Glossary of Poetic Terms and Techniques.) In addition, you are usually required to compose an essay/ explication of a poem on the AP Literature and Composition exam, and such essays are commonly assigned in high school and college literature courses. *Analysis*, which requires detailed examination of particular elements of a poem or passage, is usually reserved for course assignments. The thoughtful student will, of course, develop skill in both explication and analysis.

# A HANDFUL OF POEMS FOR FURTHER READING

In this excerpt from an extended essay in verse, Alexander Pope reflects on how poets express meaning through sound and rhythm.

### An Essay on Criticism

True ease in writing comes from art, not chance,
As those move easiest who have learned to dance.
'Tis not enough no harshness gives offense,
The sound must seem an echo to the sense:
Soft is the strain when Zephyr gently blows,
And the smooth stream in smoother numbers flows;
But when loud surges lash the sounding shore,
The hoarse, rough verse should like the torrent roar.

The horror and loss of war are often expressed through irony. Here is Stephen Crane's reflection on war:

## Do Not Weep, Maiden, for War Is Kind

Do not weep, maiden, for war is kind.
Because your lover threw wild hands against the sky
And the affrighted steed ran on alone,
Do not weep.
War is kind.

      Hoarse, booming drums of the regiment
      Little souls who thirst for fight
      These men were born to drill and die.
      The unexplained glory flies above them,
      Great is the battle-god, great, and his kingdom—
      A field where a thousand corpses lie.

Do not weep, babe, for war is kind.
Because your father tumbled in the yellow trenches,
Raged at his breast, gulped and died,
Do not weep.
War is kind.

      Swift blazing flag of the regiment,
      Eagle with crest of red and gold,
      These men were born to drill and die.
      Point for them the virtue of slaughter,
      Make plain to them the excellence of killing
      And a field where a thousand corpses lie.

Mother whose heart hung humble as a button
On the bright splendid shroud of your son,
Do not weep.
War is kind.

In this poem, by Walt Whitman (1819–1892), the speaker moves from the observation of a spider to a reflection on the soul's search to understand all existence.

## A Noiseless Patient Spider

A noiseless patient spider,
I mark'd where on a little promontory it stood isolated,
Mark'd how to explore the vacant vast surrounding,
It launch'd forth filament, filament, filament, out of itself,
Ever unreeling them, ever tirelessly speeding them.

And you O my soul where you stand,
Surrounded, detached, in measureless oceans of space,
Ceaselessly musing, venturing, throwing, seeking the
    spheres to connect them,
Till the bridge you will need be form'd, till the ductile
    anchor hold,
Till the gossamer thread you fling catch somewhere,
    O my soul.

In this brief poem by Alfred, Lord Tennyson (1809–1892) the language and imagery convey the experience of both the observer and of the eagle itself.

## The Eagle

He clasps the crag with crooked hands;
Close to the sun in lonely lands,
Ringed with the azure world, he stands.

The wrinkled sea beneath him crawls;
He watches from his mountain walls,
And like a thunderbolt he falls.

Here, in free verse, is Whitman's vision of eagles:

## The Dalliance of Eagles

Skirting the river road, (my forenoon walk, my rest,)
Skyward in air a sudden muffled sound, the dalliance
    of the eagles,
The rushing amorous contact high in space together,
The clinching interlocking claws, a living, fierce,
    gyrating wheel,
Four beating wings, two beaks, a swirling mass tight
    grappling,
In tumbling turning clustering loops, straight downward
    falling.
Till o'er the river pois'd, the twain yet one, a moment's
    lull,
A motionless still balance in the air, then parting, talons
    loosing,
Upward again on slow-firm pinions slanting, their
    separate diverse flight,
She hers, he his, pursuing.

And here is a poet, Katharine Lee Bates, who takes delight in playing with the names and characters of various fish; the result is a collection of puns, wordplay, and forms of internal and external rhyme.

## Don't You See?

THE day was hotter than words can tell,
So hot the jelly-fish wouldn't jell.
The halibut went all to butter,
And the catfish had only force to utter
A faint sea-mew—aye, though some have doubted,
The carp he capered and the horn-pout pouted.
The sardonic sardine had his sly heart's wish
When the angelfish fought with the paradise fish.
'T was a sight gave the bluefish the blues to see,
But the seal concealed a wicked glee—
The day it went from bad to worse,
Till the pickerel picked the purse-crab's purse.

And the crab felt crabbedder yet no doubt,
Because the oyster wouldn't shell out.
The sculpin would sculp, but hadn't a model,
And the coddlefish begged for something to coddle.
But to both the dolphin refused its doll,
Till the whale was obliged to whale them all.

In the first of these two poems by Robert Browning (1812–1889) the rich
and varied imagery recreates the journey of a lover to his beloved and, in
the second, his return to the "world of men."

### Meeting at Night

The grey sea and the long black land;
And the yellow half-moon large and low;
And the startled little waves that leap
In fiery ringlets from their sleep,
As I gain the cove with pushing prow,
And quench its speed i' the slushy sand.

Then a mile of warm sea-scented beach;
Three fields to cross till a farm appears;
A tap at the pane, the quick sharp scratch
And spurt of a lighted match,
And a voice less loud, through its joys and fears,
Than the two hearts beating each to each.

### Parting at Morning

Round the cape of a sudden came the sea,
And the sun looked over the mountain's rim:
And straight was a path of gold for him,
And the need of a world of men for me.

In this sonnet, George Meredith (1828–1909) imagines the desire of this fallen angel, now Satan, to return to the heavens he once inhabited.

## Lucifer in Starlight

On a starred night Prince Lucifer uprose.
Tired of his dark dominion swung the fiend
Above the rolling ball in cloud part screened,
Where sinners hugged their spectre of repose.
Poor prey to his hot fit of pride were those.
And now upon his western wing he leaned,
Now his huge bulk o'er Afric's sands careened,
Now the black planet shadowed Arctic snows.
Soaring through wider zones that pricked his scars
With memory of the old revolt from Awe,
He reached a middle height, and at the stars,
Which are the brain of heaven, he looked, and sank.
Around the ancient track marched, rank on rank,
The army of unalterable law.

In this well-known sonnet by Percy Bysshe Shelley (1792–1822) we experience the ironic fate of a once proud and arrogant king.

## Ozymandias

I met a traveler from an antique land
Who said: Two vast and trunkless legs of stone
Stand in the desert. Near them, on the sand,
Half sunk a shattered visage lies, whose frown,
And wrinkled lip, and sneer of cold command,
Tell that its sculptor well those passions read
Which yet survive, stamped on these lifeless things,
The hand that mocked them and the heart that fed;
And on the pedestal these words appear:
"My name is Ozymandias, king of kings:
Look on my works, ye Mighty, and despair!"
Nothing beside remains. Round the decay
Of that colossal wreck, boundless and bare,
The lone and level sands stretch far away.

Romantic poets and painters were fond of celebrating sunsets. Here is an excerpt from "Enough Has Been Said of Sunset," by Iris Barry.

> LIGHT—imperceptible as
> One thin veil drawn across blackness:
> Is it dawn? . . .
> Comes the twitter-whistle of sleepy birds
> Crescendo . . .
> Now bright grayness creeping
> Drowns the dark; and waves of sea-wind
> Rock the thin leaves . . .
> A door bangs; sharp barks from dogs released,
>       scampering.
> After some silence, footsteps.
> And the rising bustle of people
> Roused by the day-break.

Here is what dawn "feels like" to William Carlos Williams:

### Metric Figure

> THERE is a bird in the poplars—
> It is the sun!
> The leaves are little yellow fish
> Swimming in the river;
> The bird skims above them—
> Day is on his wings.
> Phoenix!
> It is he that is making
> The great gleam among the poplars.
> It is his singing
> Outshines the noise
> Of leaves clashing in the wind.

These poems represent only a few examples of the great variety of expression in verse. Your own textbooks and anthologies offer many more examples; and the list of Recommended Reading at the end of the book includes titles of collections readily available in paperback. You will also find the addresses of some excellent websites devoted to poetry. You should read as widely as possible, and always read aloud!

# A GLOSSARY OF POETIC TERMS AND TECHNIQUES

**allegory**  A narrative, in prose or verse, in which abstract ideas, principles, human values or states of mind, are *personified*. The purpose of the allegory is to illustrate the signficance of the ideas by dramatizing them. *Parable* and *fable* are particular kinds of allegory, in which a moral is illustrated in the form of a story.

**alliteration**  The repetition of initial consonant sounds in words and syllables. This is one of the first patterns of sound a child creates (for instance "ma-ma," "pa-pa"). The children's stories of Dr. Seuss use alliteration and assonance. Poets use alliteration for its rich musical effect: "Fish, flesh, and fowl commend all summer long/Whatever is begotten, born, and dies" (Yeats); for humor: "Where at, with blade, with bloody, blameful blade/He bravely broached his boiling bloody breast" (Shakespeare); and to echo the sense of the lines: "The iron tongue of midnight hath told twelve" (Shakespeare).

**allusion**  A reference to a historical event, to Biblical, mythological, or literary characters and incidents with which the reader is assumed to be familiar. Allusion may, with few words, enrich or extend the meaning of a phrase, idea, or image. Allusion may also be used for ironic effect. In his poem "Out, out . . ." Robert Frost expects the reader to recall from Macbeth's final soliloquy the line, "Out, out brief candle!" Such expressions as "a Pandora's box" or "Achilles heel" are also forms of allusion.

**ambiguity**  Denotes uncertainty of meaning. In literature, however, especially in poetry, we speak of *intentional* ambiguity, the use of language and images to suggest more than one meaning at the same time.

**assonance**  The repetition of vowel sounds among words that begin or end with different consonants. Sonnet 30 of Shakespeare (page 82) and "Child on Top of a Greenhouse" by Theodore Roethke (page 81), for example, are rich in assonance. Some poets may vary end rhymes with assonance; for example, Emily Dickinson (page 76) does it here: "The Feet, mechanical, go round—Of Ground, or Air, or Ought—,"

**ballad**  Narrative poem, sometimes sung, that tells a dramatic story.

**blank verse**  Unrhymed *iambic pentameter*, usually in "paragraphs" of verse instead of stanzas. Shakespeare's plays are composed primarily in blank verse. For example, from *Macbeth* (Act I, Scene 5):

> Your face, my Thane, is as a book where men
> May read strange matters. To beguile the time,
> Look like the time; bear welcome in your eye,
> Your hand, your tongue; look like the innocent flower,
> But be the serpent under't . . .

**connotation** The feelings, attitudes, images, and associations of a word or expression. Connotations are usually said to be "positive" or "negative." See also discussion on page 148 in Chapter 8—Vocabulary.

**couplet** Two lines of verse with similar meter and end rhyme. Couplets generally have self-contained ideas as well, so they may function as stanzas within a poem. In the English (Shakespearean) *sonnet*, the couplet concludes the poem. (See the sonnets on pages 82–84.) Also many scenes in Shakespeare's plays end with rhymed couplets: "Away, and mock the time with fairest show/False face must hide what the false heart doth know" (*Macbeth* Act I, Scene 7).

**denotation** That which a word actually names, identifies, or "points to." Denotation is sometimes referred to as "the dictionary definition" of a word.

**dramatic monologue** A poem in which a fictional character, at a critical or dramatic point in life, addresses a particular "audience," which is identifiable but silent. In the course of the monologue, we learn a great deal, often ironically, about the character, who is speaking and the circumstances that have led to the speech. Robert Browning is the best-known nineteenth-century poet to compose dramatic monologues; "My Last Duchess" is a famous example. In the twentieth century, such poets as Kenneth Fearing, E. A. Robinson, T. S. Eliot ("The Love Song of J. Alfred Prufrock"), Robert Frost, and Amy Lowell have composed well-known dramatic monologues.

**elegy** A meditative poem mourning the death of an individual.

**epic** A long narrative poem often centering on a heroic figure who represents the fate of a great nation or people. *The Iliad* and *The Odyssey* of Homer, *The Aeneid* of Vergil, and the Anglo-Saxon *Beowulf* are well-known epics. Milton's *Paradise Lost* and Dante's *The Divine Comedy* are examples of epic narratives in which subjects of great human significance are dramatized. *Omeros,* by Derek Walcott, is a contemporary example of an epic poem.

**figurative language** The intentional and imaginative use of words and comparisons that are not literal but that create original, vivid, and often unexpected images and associations. Figurative language is also called *metaphorical language*. See *metaphor* and *simile*.

**free verse** A poem written in free verse develops images and ideas in patterns of lines without specific metrical arrangements or formal rhyme. Free verse is distinguished from prose, however, because it retains such poetic elements as assonance, alliteration, and figurative language. The poetry of Walt Whitman offers striking examples.

**hyperbole** An exaggerated expression (also called overstatement) for a particular effect, which may be humorous, satirical, or intensely emotional. Hyperbole is the expression of folk tales and legends and, of course, of lovers: Romeo says to Juliet, "there lies more peril in thine eye/Than twenty of their swords." Hyperbole is often the expression of any overwhelming feeling. After he murders King Duncan, Macbeth looks with horror at his bloody hands: "Will all great Neptune's ocean wash this blood/Clean from my hand . . . ?" In her sleepwalking scene, Lady Macbeth despairs that "All the perfumes of Arabia will not sweeten this little hand." And every one of us has felt, "I have mountains of work to do!"

**Iambic pentameter** The basic meter of English speech: "I think I know exactly what you need/and yet at times I know that I do not." Formally, it identifies verse of ten syllables to the line, with the second, fourth, sixth, eight, and tenth syllables accented. There is, however, variation in the stresses within lines to reflect natural speech—and to avoid a "sing-song" or nursery rhyme effect. Most of the dialogue in Shakespeare's plays is composed in this meter. See *blank verse*.

**Image** Images and imagery are the heart of poetry. Although the term suggests only something that is visualized, an image is the recreation through language of *any* experience perceived directly through the senses. For example, Tennyson's "The Eagle" (page 89) is composed of striking visual images. The feelings of fear and of mourning in Emily Dickinson's poems are also images. In "Pitcher" (page 75) we feel the motion of pitching.

**Internal rhyme** A pattern in which a word or words within a line rhyme with the word that ends it. Poets may also employ internal rhyme at irregular intervals over many lines. The verbs in Theodore Roethke's poem "Child on Top of a Greenhouse" (page 81) create the effect of internal rhyme.

**irony** In general, a tone or figure of speech in which there is a discrepancy—(a striking difference or contradiction)—between what is expressed and what is meant or expected. Irony may be used to achieve a powerful effect indirectly. In satire, for example, it may be used to ridicule or criticize. Stephen Crane's poem "Do Not Weep, Maiden, for War Is Kind" (page 88) is intensely ironic, both in the stanzas apparently seeking to comfort those whose lovers, fathers, and sons have died and in the contrasting stanzas of apparent celebration of the glories of war. We also speak of *dramatic irony* in fiction in which the reader understands more than the characters do. Ring Lardner's short story "Haircut" is an excellent example.

**lyric** A general term used to describe poems that are relatively brief and expressed in the voice of a single *speaker* (narrative voice). Lyric poems express a powerful emotion revealed in a significant experience or observation. (See discussion on page 78.)

**metaphor** A form of analogy. Through metaphor, a poet discovers and expresses a similarity between dissimilar things. The poet use metaphors to imaginatively find common qualities between things we would not normally or literally compare. As a figure of speech, metaphor is said to be implicit or indirect. This contrasts to *simile* (see page 98), where the comparison is expressed directly. In his final soliloquy, Macbeth uses a series of metaphors to express the meaninglessness of his own life: "Life's but a walking shadow, a poor player . . . it is a tale told by an idiot . . . ."

**meter** and **rhythm** Rhythm refers to the pattern of movement in a poem. As music has rhythm, so does poetry. Meter refers to specific patterns of stressed and unstressed syllables. See *iambic pentameter.*

**ode** A meditation or celebration of a specific subject. Traditional odes addressed "elevated" ideas and were composed in elaborate stanza forms. Keats's "Ode to a Nightingale" and "Ode to Autumn" are particularly fine examples. Modern odes may address subjects either serious or personal. One well-known contemporary ode is Pablo Neruda's "Ode to My Socks."

**onomatopoeia** The use of words whose sound reflects their sense. "Buzz," "hiss," and "moan" are common examples. Shakespeare's Sonnet 30 shows how the sounds and rhythm of whole lines may be onomatopoetic.

**oxymoron** Closely related to *paradox*, oxymoron is a figure of speech in which two contradictory or sharply contrasting terms are paired for emphasis or ironic effect. Among students' favorite examples are "jumbo shrimp" and "army intelligence." Poets have written of the "wise fool," a "joyful sadness," or an "eloquent silence."

**paradox** An expression, concept, or situation whose literal statement is contradictory, yet which makes a truthful and meaningful observation. Consider the widely used expression "less is more," for example. Shakespeare's play *Macbeth* opens with a series of paradoxes to establish the moral atmosphere in which "foul is fair." John Donne's famous poem "Death Be Not Proud" ends with the paradox "Death thou shalt die," and the title of Robert Penn Warren's poem "Old Photograph of the Future" is a paradox.

**personification** A form of metaphor or simile in which nonhuman things—objects, plants and animals, forces of nature, abstract ideas—are given human qualities; for example, "The half-grown chrysanthemums staring up like accusers" (Roethke, page 81), "the walking sun/that poised an eye on me from its high floor" (Hall, page 81), "Time . . . the thief of youth" (Milton), and "Blow winds, and crack your cheeks! Rage! Blow!" (Shakespeare).

**prose poem** This form appears on the page in the sentences and paragraphs of prose yet its effect is achieved through rhythm, images, and patterns of sound associated with poetry.

**quatrain** Stanza of four lines. The quatrain is the most commonly used stanza form in English poetry. Quatrains may be rhymed, *abab, aabb, abba,* for example, or they may be unrhymed. The sonnets of Shakespeare (pages 82–83), the poem by Laurence Binyon (page 77), "Old Photograph of the Future" (page 79), and "The Sleeping Giant" (page 81) are also composed in quatrains.

**rhyme** In general, any repetition of identical or similar sounds among words that are close enough together to form an audible pattern. Rhyme is most evident when it occurs at the ends of lines of metrical verse. The *quatrains* of Shakespeare's Sonnet 55 (pages 83–84) have alternating rhyme as do those of Robert Penn Warren's poem "Old Photograph of the Future" (page 79).

**rhyme scheme** A regular pattern of end rhyme in a poem. The rhyme scheme in Shakespeare's sonnets, for example, is *abab/cdcd/efef/gg*.

**satire** A form or style that uses elements of irony, ridicule, exaggeration, understatement, sarcasm, humor, or absurdity to criticize human behavior or a society. All satire is *ironic* (see page 96) in that meaning or theme is conveyed in the discrepancy between what is said and what is meant, between what is and what should be, between what appears and what truly is. While satire is often entertaining, its purpose is serious and meant to provoke thought or judgment. The verse of Alexander Pope is often extended satire, and many poems by e. e. cummings are satiric.

**simile** An expression that is a direct comparison of two things. It uses such words as *like, as, as if, seems, appears*. For instance: "A line of elms plunging and tossing like horses" (Theodore Roethke); "Mind in its purest play is like some bat" (Richard Wilbur); "I wandered lonely as a cloud" (William Wordsworth).

**soliloquy** A form of monologue found most often in drama. It differs from a dramatic monologue in that the speaker is alone, revealing thoughts and feelings to or for oneself that are intentionally unheard by other characters. In Shakespeare's plays, for example, the principal characters' reflections on how to act or questions of conscience are revealed in their soliloquies. Hamlet's "To be, or not to be . . ." is probably the most famous dramatic soliloquy in English.

**sonnet** A poem of fourteen lines in *iambic pentameter* that may be composed of different patterns of stanzas and rhyme schemes. The most common forms are the English, or Shakespearean, sonnet, which consists of three quatrains and a closing couplet, and the Italian sonnet, which consists of an *octave* of eight lines and a *sestet* of six lines.

**speaker** The narrative voice in a poem. Also, the character who speaks in a *dramatic monologue*. The poems "The Sleeping Giant" and "Old Photograph of the Future" have distinctive speakers who are also the central characters in the dramatic experience of the poem.

**stanza** The grouping of lines within a poem. A stanza provides the basic organization and development of ideas, much as a paragraph does in an essay. Many stanza patterns have a fixed number of lines and a regular pattern of rhyme; the poems of Robert Penn Warren (page 79) and Donald Hall (page 81) are good examples. Poets, however, often create stanzas of varying length and form within a single poem. A stanza that ends with a period, completing an idea or image, is considered "closed," while a stanza that ends with a comma or with no punctuation, is called "open," indicating that there should be very little pause in the movement from one stanza to another. Roethke's poem "Child on Top of a Greenhouse" (page 81) is an example of a poem composed in a single stanza.

**symbol** Most generally, anything that stands for or suggests something else. Language itself is symbolic; sounds and abstract written forms may stand for almost any human thought or experience. Symbols are real objects and *concrete* images that lead us to think about what is suggested. Symbols organize a wide variety of ideas into single acts of understanding. They embody not single "meanings" but suggest whole areas of meaning.

**tone** The attitude or feeling of the speaker toward the subject. Tone may also refer to the dominant mood of a poem. (See discussion of *tone* on page 86.)

**understatement** Expression in which something is presented as less important or significant than it really is. The first and third stanzas of Stephen Crane's "Do Not Weep, Maiden" (page 88) ironically understate the horror of death in battle and the loss for those who mourn. Understatement is often used for humorous, *satiric,* or *ironic* effect. Much of the satire in *Huckleberry Finn* stems from Huck's naive and understated observations. One particular form of understatement, actually a double negative, includes such expressions as "I was not uninterested," which really means "I was interested," or "He was not without imagination," which really means "He had some imagination."

# Chapter 6

# WRITING ABOUT LITERATURE: A GENERAL REVIEW

For most students, writing papers and responding to essay questions on exams are the most challenging aspects of their course work. Writing requires that you articulate and focus your understanding of what you read. Like all good writing, writing about literature not only demonstrates to others what you understand and think but also obliges you to clarify *for yourself* what you truly know. That process is sometimes hard, but it is worthwhile. Writing is essential to developing your critical reading and thinking skills.

## TOPICS FOR LITERARY ESSAYS

Much of your writing about literature is done in response to assignments and exam questions. Students are also urged to maintain notes and journals. For essays, instructors may assign very specific topics, or they may offer general subjects that require you to develop your own topic and controlling idea.

In your literature courses and exams you will find that the majority of the questions focus on **character**. Because essay topics may apply to many works of nonfiction you read—personal essay, memoir, and autobiography in particular—the term *character* should be understood to refer to any persons, not exclusively to those of fiction and drama.

As you think about characters in the literature you read, keep the following questions in mind: What are a character's values and motives? beliefs and principles? moral qualities? strengths and weaknesses? illusions or delusions? For what is a character searching? striving? devoting his or her life? What significant decisions and actions does a character take? What are the consequences of those decisions and actions? To what extent does a character "succeed" or "fail"? understand or fail to understand?

Literature also seeks to account for the forces outside individuals, that is, the external forces that influence the direction and outcome of their lives. These "forces" range from those of nature and history to the demands of family, community, and society. The response of individuals to inner and outer forces is what literature considers and dramatizes. (See Chapters 4 and 5 for discussions of reading literature and for glossaries of important terms and techniques.)

# TOPIC AND FOCUS

As any essay must, your paper must have a clear purpose, a controlling idea; moreover, the development of the purpose must be convincing to the reader. *Focus* means in writing, as it does in a photograph, that the subject is clear! We can see it, even recognize it. And, if the photographer/writer has "framed" the material properly, we can perceive the relationship of the background details to the principal subject. When you take a picture of your best friend at camp, or of the place you most want to remember from a vacation trip, you keep the lens of your camera directed at what is most important—not at the tree next to your friend, not at the bus that took you to Niagara Falls.

# SELECTION OF SIGNIFICANT DETAILS

One of the most widely observed characteristics of short stories is that they are very selective in detail. The author of a short story includes only those elements of setting, character, and plot that reveal the significance of the central incident. In "The Lottery," for example, we do not know when the story takes place, we do not even know the name of the town or where it is located, and we know little about the lives of individual characters. Those details are not *significant*—they do not matter—to the story Shirley Jackson tells; comparable details *are* significant in "Haircut," and, therefore, Ring Lardner includes them.

To achieve focus in your essays about works of literature, you must exercise the same rigorous process of selection. However interesting you may find a particular incident or aspect of a character, do not include those details if they do not directly explain or clarify your topic.

# DEVELOPING THE TOPIC

Many of the common methods of developing arguments are discussed in Chapter 4—Reading Prose. Here are some of those methods as they might be used to develop essays on works of literature:

## Comparison/Contrast

Although *compare* means to identify similarities, and *contrast* means to identify differences, the term *comparison* is often used for a discussion that examines both similarities and differences among the items being compared. This is one of the most useful approaches, and one of the most commonly used, because the process of comparing helps sharpen thought. To compose a meaningful comparison, the writer must understand the objects of comparison in detail.

Any literary aspect found in two or more works may serve as a basis for comparison. For example, one could compare the effective use of first-person narration in *The Great Gatsby* and *Ethan Frome,* or in *The Catcher in the Rye* and *Huckleberry Finn.* Although the circumstances of their lives are vastly different, the fact that both Ethan Frome and Jay Gatsby fail to achieve what they most desire—a life with the women they love—offers a rich possibility for comparison and contrast. "Haircut" and "The Lottery" share common elements of setting and irony. *Othello* and *Romeo and Juliet* have a common theme—the tragic destruction of great love.

Comparison may, of course, focus on much narrower topics and be confined to a single work. The best way to develop notes for a comparison is first to list the aspects common to the items under comparison, then to list for each all the specific details that differentiate them. Finally, as you do in preparation for any essay, you select those that are most significant.

## Analysis

Analysis requires detailed examination of a particular aspect of a literary work. The purpose of an analytic paper is to show the significance of that aspect to the meaning of the work as a whole. Examples of analytic topics include the use of time in Miller's *Death of a Salesman,* the imagery of light and dark in *Othello,* and the extended metaphor in Emily Dickinson's poem "I Taste a Liquor Never Brewed."

## Classification

Classification organizes objects, people, and other living things into categories; it is a process of identifying and relating. In discussions of literature, classification may be an important part of an essay, or it may constitute a topic in its own right. An essay in which the writer shows how a particular work exemplifies a **genre** is considered classification: *The Scarlet Letter* as a **romance**; Shakespeare's *Macbeth* as Elizabethan **tragedy**; Dreiser's *Sister Carrie* as **naturalism**.

## Cause and Effect

Many of the topics for writing and discussion of literature may be developed by showing how circumstances or actions have direct and observable consequences. Demonstrating actual cause and effect, however, requires careful thinking and attention to detail. Cause and effect are more easily demonstrated in logic and chemistry than in human experience.

Literary topics that focus on **plot** often lend themselves to cause and effect development because essentially any plot is built on cause and effect: specific circumstances, actions, or decisions lead to others and have consequences in the lives of the characters. Plot summary alone does *not* establish cause and effect; it simply relates "what happened." Cause-and-effect argument requires the writer to show how and why incidents are related.

## Exemplification

Whenever you cite specific details to support a thesis, and when you choose the works you will use to answer the literature question in Part B of Session Two, you are using exemplification. *To exemplify* means to illustrate the meaning of a general concept through use of specific examples. This method is fundamental to the development of nearly any essay or literary topic.

# LOOKING AT KEY TERMS IN LITERATURE QUESTIONS

**Identify**   To name and also to characterize and to place in context; sometimes you may be required to state the significance of what you are identifying. Often identification includes linking characters to the theme or experience that serves as the topic.

**describe**   To give the essential characteristics of a person, object, or experience. If you are asked to describe, your choice of details or characteristics must reveal your understanding of a larger question. Why are these details relevant to the topic? Description alone will not be the focus of a literature topic.

**explain/show/discuss**   These terms indicate the most important parts of a question, which will be developed in the body of an essay. Once you have identified and described your subject, you must interpret and demonstrate the significance of your examples and details; you must offer evidence, using specific references, to support your argument.

# USING FLUENT AND PRECISE LANGUAGE

Effective writing is characterized by interesting and vivid language, and "use of precise and engaging language" is among the criteria for evaluation of Regents essays. From the list of what writers *do*, here are some terms to help you articulate your observations about creation of plot:

> *convey, create, delineate, depict, describe, dramatize, foreshadow, illustrate, invent, portray, present, recreate, reveal, select, shock, show, symbolize*

The following terms offer precision and variety in discussing details of a plot:

> *affair, circumstance, climax, development, episode, event, experience, incident, instance, juncture, moment, occasion, occurrence, opportunity, scene, situation*

Terms useful in referring to *character* include:

> *disposition, identity, individuality, makeup, mettle, nature, persona, personality, self, spirit, temperament*

Finally, here is a list of adjectives collected by students to describe some of the many relationships and attitudes among characters in literature (and in our own lives!):

> *admiring, affectionate, bitter, cautious, compassionate, curious, deceitful, disapproving, disdainful, dishonest, distant, envious, false, fearful, generous, hostile, indifferent, loving, optimistic, reluctant, resentful, reserved, respectful, scornful, sincere, skeptical, stern, suspicious, sympathetic, treacherous, watchful*

(See also Using Synonymies to Enhance Your Writing in Chapter 7.)

# CHOOSING YOUR OWN TOPIC: REPRESENTATIVE LITERARY SUBJECTS AND THEMES

In many high school and college literature courses, students must select their own topics for writing. The subjects of literature are as varied as human experience itself, and below are some of the many themes authors dramatize. You will encounter these as topics in class discussion and as topics for essays and examination questions. These topics may, of course, serve for discussion of more than one work in an essay.

# Topics That Focus on Character

- In many works of literature, an important theme is an **individual's achievement of self-knowledge as a result of undergoing an ordeal**. This self-knowledge may be a recognition of the individual's own strengths, weaknesses, values, prejudices, aspirations, or fears. Identify the individual and the self-knowledge he or she achieves. Using specific references from the work, explain how the ordeal led the individual to the self-knowledge.
- **Nature** can have different effects on different people. It can defeat someone with its power; it can inspire someone with its beauty. Identify the character; using specific references, show how he or she was either defeated or inspired by nature.
- It has been said that to live with **fear** and not be overcome by it is the final **test of maturity**. Explain what fear a character lives with; show how the character "passes" or "fails" the test of maturity on the basis of his or her response to that fear.
- A commonly held belief is that **suffering strengthens an individual's character**. The suffering can be physical, mental, or emotional. Identify the individual; describe the nature of the suffering; explain how the suffering did or did not strengthen the individual's character.
- Sometimes a person **struggles to achieve a goal** only to discover that, once the goal is achieved, the results are not what was expected.
- In many works of literature there are characters who are **troubled by injustice** in society, such as poverty, discrimination, or lawlessness, and **who try to correct** the injustice. Identify the character and the injustice, explain what actions the character takes; discuss whether or not the efforts are successful.
- In many works, characters who love one another or share a special friendship often face **obstacles to their relationship**. Sometimes characters overcome the obstacle; sometimes they are defeated by it. Identify the characters and the obstacle; explain how the characters overcome or are defeated by the obstacle; discuss the effect this outcome (the success or failure, not the obstacle) has on the relationship.
- In many works of literature, **a character sacrifices something of value** in order to achieve something of greater value.
- Sometimes a character faces a **conflict between his or her conscience** and the standards of behavior expected by others. Identify the character; explain the specific nature of the conflict; discuss how the character was affected by this conflict.
- In many works of literature, a character reaches a **major turning point** in his or her life. From that point onward, the character undergoes a significant change.
- Characters in works of literature frequently **learn about life or themselves** by taking risks.

- The phrase **"rite of passage"** describes a situation in which a young person is faced with an experience that results in his or her becoming mature. Explain the experience; discuss how the young person matures as a result of the way in which he or she deals with the experience.
- In many works of literature, characters are **challenged by unfamiliar environments**. Show how the character was or was not successful in meeting the challenge.
- Some individuals in literature **try to do what they believe is right**, even though they face opposition.
- In some works of literature, an important character **makes a mistake that advances the reader's understanding of that individual**.
- Confusion, danger, or tragedy sometimes results when **one character misunderstands the words or actions of another character**.
- In many works of literature, a character **struggles against circumstances that seem to be beyond his or her control**. Sometimes the character is victorious, sometimes not.

## Topics That Focus on Literary Elements and Techniques

While topics that focus on character may be the most common in literature courses or on exams, various literary elements also provide topics for essays. The AP literature exam, for example, often features a question based on a literary element or technique.

- Some authors are especially successful at creating **a memorable visual image** that contributes to the reader's understanding of a work. Identify the image and its importance; show how the image contributes to the meaning of the work.
- In many works of literature, the **setting** contributes to the reader's understanding of the central conflict in the plot. Describe the setting; show how it contributes to the reader's understanding of the conflict on which the plot hinges.
- Authors often create a **predominant mood** in a work of literature. Using specific references, discuss incidents that convey that mood and explain the importance of mood to the work.
- Authors sometimes use **foreshadowing** to help develop the plot of a work. Foreshadowing usually takes the form of incidents that seem to be unimportant at first, but take on added significance later. Discuss examples of foreshadowing and show how they contribute to the overall effect and meaning of the work.
- A work of literature may be defined as **a classic** because it promotes deep insight into human behavior, presents a universal theme, or uses

language in an exceptional way. Show how a particular work meets the above definition of the term *classic*.
- Through their work, some **authors reveal their acceptance or rejection of values** held by society. Identify the value; state whether the author accepts or rejects it; using specific references, show how the author reveals his or her attitude toward that value.
- In literature, **symbols** are used to reinforce the central idea or to represent characters. Using specific references, explain how the symbol in a particular work enriches the reader's understanding of either the central idea or a character.
- The **narrative point of view** is significant to the effect and meaning of a literary work. Illustrate the truth of this statement by specific references to a work of literature.

# AUDIENCE AND LITERATURE ESSAYS

Most teachers mention audience in the assignments they give; if it is not clear for whom you are writing, it is a good idea to ask before you complete an assignment. For most outside examinations, including the Regents, assume that you are writing for a reader who is familiar with the works of literature but who has not considered the topic; background discussion and *detailed* explanation of plot are not needed.

# A NOTE ON CONCLUSIONS

No essay, however brief, should simply stop. Even if you run out of time or things to say, try not to telegraph that information to the reader. A conclusion must come back to the topic, must complete the discussion, in a way that leaves the reader feeling convinced by what you have written. On examinations, most students close with a brief, summative conclusion that highlights the relationship of the literary work or works to the topic or restates the thesis of the essay. Even if the reader of a short essay does not really *need* the conclusion to appreciate your argument, the obligation to compose a conclusion keeps you focused on the topic.

Student writers are urged to avoid the following in their conclusions: the expression "what this paper has shown . . ." or "As you can see . . ."; a reminder that Shakespeare was a great playwright or that Mark Twain was an important figure in American literature; a confession that the reader *really* liked or did not like a particular work. Above all, the conclusion is not the place to introduce a new topic or tack on an idea that properly belongs in the body of the essay.

# Chapter 7

# WRITING ON DEMAND

Writing has always been an important part of a student's education as well as an essential skill for a successful professional life. The National Commission on Writing is only one of the more recent initiatives in American education to emphasize the importance of good writing among our students. American colleges and universities also seek independent assessment of students' writing skills as part of the admissions process. In this chapter you will find some guidelines for effective writing on demand.

## WRITING TO INFORM OR PERSUADE

### A General Review

Much of the work you do in high school or college requires writing to demonstrate your ability to understand, analyze, and organize information and ideas. On exams and essays for science and social studies courses, as well as in English and writing courses, you are expected to do many of the following:

- Tell your audience (readers) what they need to know
- Use specific, accurate, and relevant information
- Use a tone and level of language appropriate for the task and audience
- Organize your ideas in a logical and coherent manner
- Follow the conventions of standard written English

These guidelines are also reminders of what your teachers mean when they direct you to compose a "well-written essay" on a given topic.

### Personal Narrative

Here is an example of an informal essay written in response to a specific task. It is a good example of what is meant by **tone and level of language** appropriate for the audience. The essay is also organized in a logical and coherent manner.

109

---

**Task:** A representative of a middle school in your district has invited you to speak at the middle school graduation ceremonies on the topic "Getting Off to a Good Start in High School." Write a brief speech that you would give to the students, stating your recommendations for a successful start in high school. Use specific reasons, examples, or details to support your recommendations.

---

### Sample Student Response

*Not so long ago, I too was sitting where you are now, thinking and worrying about what my life in high school would be like. Will I stand out? Will I make friends? How should I approach people? Will my classes be too difficult? Will I be able to cope with the stress? These questions kept badgering me throughout the summer before ninth grade. I was especially nervous about starting school because I had just moved to a new neighborhood and did not know a single person.*

*By the end of the summer, the thought that especially frustrated me was that I would have no one to eat lunch with on the first day of school. This does not seem like such a big deal but it bothered me a lot. I knew that at the high school people went out to eat with a group of friends. I had no one to go out with. I told myself that I still had a week before school started and did not need to worry.*

*The first day of school finally arrived. As I neared the high school, I felt helpless and lonely. I wanted to plead with my mom to turn the car around and go back home. But I reluctantly got out of the car and slowly approached the front entrance of the school.*

*Luckily, I found my first class and quickly took a seat in the front. I felt as if all eyes were on me. The new kid. The freak. While everyone was talking and laughing about their summer, I sat in my seat trying to look as though I was busy fiddling with my notebook. I couldn't wait to get out of the classroom. I wanted to run home and hide, for this was one of the most difficult experiences of my life.*

*Things started to look better around fifth period. I got up the courage and started talking to people. I even went out to lunch with a few girls and had a comfortable time. I was not totally relaxed but knew that I would adapt and soon make more friends.*

*I have just finished my junior year in high school. I have many friends and am very happy in my school. I will be a senior this coming September and expect to experience new ideas and challenges. I am now starting to think about what I want to do with my life and what colleges I might want to attend. Soon I will be leaving high school and will again feel the nervousness and anxiety that all of you are going through in preparing for high school. I guess what we are experiencing is not trepidation but life, and what to expect in the future. You may be scared now, but be confident that you will overcome those fears and the experiences will only make you stronger.*

### Analysis

Although this speech is more a personal narrative than a list of recommendations, the writer/speaker clearly understands the purpose of the task and understands her audience:

"Not so long ago, I too was sitting where you are now. . . ." The diction is informal, the tone is conversational, and first-person narrative is highly appropriate for the occasion.

The theme is established in the opening sentence, but the speaker's main point is not stated until the very end: "You may be scared now, but . . . you will overcome those fears . . . and [be] stronger." She leads her audience to this conclusion by narrating her own feelings and experiences, starting with a series of "fears" she knows her listeners have. The narrative covers a period of many weeks, but it is made coherent by specific references to time: "throughout the summer . . . by the end of summer . . . on the first day of school . . . my first class . . . around fifth period . . . lunch." She also uses a reference to time to come back to the present and bring the speech to a close: "I have just finished my junior year. . . ."

The ideas are well expressed; and the paragraph in which the writer describes what it was like to sit in her first class—"The new kid." "The freak."—pretending to be busy with her notebook is especially vivid and convincing. We also trust the speaker when she tells us that she had "a comfortable time" at lunch but that she "was not totally relaxed" either. If she had claimed that after lunch all her fears had disappeared, we would not believe her. This is also a good example of what is meant by honesty in writing: it rings true in our ears. This piece would be even better if the writer had included more specific examples of how she overcame her fears.

## Persuasive Writing

Here are two examples of what is called persuasive writing, pieces that develop and support an opinion on a particular topic. In contrast to the essay of argument in Part 2 of the Regents ELA exam, which must be based on evidence from given sources, these essays are developed with the writer's own reasoning and examples. Note what makes each a successful argument.

---

**Task:** The students in your science class have been invited to submit essays on topics of current interest or controversy for possible publication on the Op-Ed page of the school newspaper.

---

### Sample Student Response

*Using Animals for Scientific Research*

*The question of whether or not to use animals as subjects for scientific research is a difficult one. Those in opposition claim that using animals in research is inhumane, while those holding a diametrically opposing view maintain that it is a necessary evil whose long-term benefits far outweigh the sacrifice of a handful of animals. I am an ardent supporter of the latter view. I feel that the use of animals is justified by the benefits that are reaped by all of mankind, and that halting the use of animals as subjects would greatly impede advancements in the field of medicine.*

*One example of the tremendous benefits that animal research can bring about is the case of the discovery of insulin by Dr. William Banting and his assistant, Charles Best. Before this amazing discovery, diabetes mellitus was a devastating and inevitably fatal disease. The extent of treatment that doctors could offer afflicted patients was a starvation diet, which prolonged life only for a short time and caused the obviously detrimental and painful effects of virtual starvation.*

*When Dr. Banting came up with a unique idea that linked the cause of the disease to a hormonal secretion of the pancreas, a potential way to control this deadly disease arose. But the idea had to be tested and proven successful before it could be offered to human patients. Dr. Banting proceeded with his experiments, using fifteen dogs as his subjects. Although several of the dogs did die as a result of the experiment, the benefits that society gained because of the tests are infinitely greater. If those opposed to utilizing animals in testing had their way, the concept would have died prematurely because there would have been no way to test the idea. Fortunately for the field of science and for the millions of diabetics that have lived in the past few decades, Dr. Banting was able to find this treatment.*

*As a diabetic, I am greatly indebted to the work of Dr. Banting and the studies he conducted using animals as subjects. Today, I am not only alive, but healthy and active. I cannot help but be a supporter of animal testing because I owe my life to it. I understand how one may object to senseless cruelty to animals and the wasting of their lives worthlessly. But using animals strictly for scientific use is not "senseless cruelty" and it is clearly justified.*

---

### Analysis

This is a good example of a short essay of opinion because the student has chosen a subject that he could develop with expertise and compelling personal experience; it also demonstrates his skill in organizing and presenting an argument.

One of the most effective ways to approach a controversial topic is to "acknowledge the opposition." Indicate that you recognize, and even respect, the opposing view. This writer agrees that the question "is a difficult one," but goes on to say he is "an ardent supporter" of animal testing. Note that he skillfully saves his personal reasons for the end, first developing a factual but dramatic example of the benefits of testing for millions of people. Introducing his personal reasons earlier would have made the argument less persuasive because he would have appeared less objective. The conclusion is emotionally effective when he says, "I cannot help but be a supporter of animal testing because I owe my life to it." More importantly, the writer demonstrates skillful argument when he says, "I understand how one may object. . ." and closes with a distinction between scientific experiment and "senseless cruelty." This essay would be a good contribution to an Op-Ed page.

---

**Task:** The editor of your local newspaper has proposed that businesses that hire high school graduates pay them salaries in proportion to their grades from the last two years of high school; that is, the higher a graduate's grades for the last two years of high school, the higher the salary. Write a letter to the editor in which you state your opinion of the proposal. Use specific reasons, examples, or details.

## Sample Student Response

*I vehemently oppose the proposal that graduates be paid salaries in proportion to their grades for the last two years of high school.*

*First, grades should not affect the equal opportunity of all workers to receive the same paycheck for the same work. It must be taken into account that there are many factors that influence a student's grades in high school. For example, one student may have a harder course load than another student with higher grades. It is unfair to compare grades from different level classes. Perhaps a student does not do well on tests, but is an excellent student in class. Participation and the ability to speak one's mind are very beneficial in a career, yet that is not reflected by grades. Furthermore, if a student has an inborn proficiency in a subject (and gets good grades), it is unfair to assume that that student works hard to achieve his or her scores. An average student works harder and may still not get the same scores. Hard work and dedication are important factors in choosing an employee, but these factors cannot always be relayed by a report card.*

*There are other factors besides grades that play a role in whether a student is right for a job. The applicant may have experience in the field of interest, but the proposed system would not take this into account. Perhaps a student has been a volunteer or has been active in clubs and organizations outside of school. By looking at his or her track record with reference to involvement in organizations, the student's ability to follow through would be noted. This is an important factor to take into account when hiring a worker.*

*Also, grades do not indicate strength of personal character, an important determinant in the selection of an employee. One must not make the generalization that a student with good grades is also a good person, and that a student with poor grades is not a good person. Only a personal interview can give the employer some sense of personal character of the worker. Positive interactions with other workers are vital to the success of a business.*

*Finally, by locking in different salaries and pay rates based on high school grades, the employer is creating unnecessary competition and tension in the workplace. A worker with a lower salary may not work as hard, as a result. The worker with the lower salary might be treated differently, or unfairly, by the employer by not being encouraged to work up to potential.*

*Thank you for your attention to this matter. Perhaps now an employee will be viewed as a person, and not as a report card. Everyone deserves a fair chance.*

---

**Analysis**

This essay would receive a relatively good evaluation because it expresses a clear and thoughtful opinion, it is well organized, and it is excellent in its development; on the other hand, the essay is not always focused on the specific topic. The letter begins well, with a clear statement of position, and the first section makes several important points about the limited significance of grades. Note, however, that the argument shifts from a discussion of how workers should be paid to how they should be hired in the first place. The second section makes several good points, but it too refers to *hiring* workers. The writer comes back to the topic of differentiated pay only in the third full paragraph.

If the writer had followed her statement of opinion with a *because* statement and a summary of her main points, she could have established the focus needed. This writer clearly took time to gather good examples and reasons, but she did not always show how they related to the topic. The task directed the student to write a letter to an editor and to write *the body of the letter only*, but such letters are really essays of argument and must have focus and coherence to be effective. Composing "letters" of this kind is a very good way to practice writing persuasive essays.

---

# WRITING FROM A PROMPT

On many examinations and in high school or college courses, you will encounter the term *prompt*. This term is used to refer in general to any set of directions for a writing task. In the theater, the prompter is the one who gives an actor or singer in danger of forgetting his or her lines the phrase that he or she needs to remember to continue the performance. In writing, a prompt serves to recall ideas or stimulate discussion. A prompt is also meant to inspire, or even provoke. A prompt may be in the form of a task and directions, as in the examples above, or it may be in the form of a quote or even a photograph—anything that offers the writer a subject and a reason to produce a piece of writing.

Here are two examples of persuasive writing where the prompt was in the form of a quote only; the writers had to establish controlling ideas and develop the examples on their own.

## "All the World's a Stage"

*William Shakespeare once wrote, "all the world's a stage and all the people players . . ." This well-known phrase has stuck in people's minds through time because theater is a prominent medium in society; whether it's an amphitheater in ancient Rome or Broadway in New York City, crowds of people are drawn to the theater every day.*

*The theater appeals to people for many different reasons. Some attend the theater to escape from the harsh realities of life for a little while. While sitting in a dark auditorium and watching trials and disputes played by live actors in front of you, it is very easy to forget your own problems. Other people find the theater simply entertaining. Plays and musicals involve audiences because they stimulate the senses and the mind. And some people go to the theater as a social event.*

*But theater is not only something to be watched. For many people, theater is their life. Every day, more and more people are becoming actors and actresses in hopes of becoming rich and famous. And for some people, that dream actually comes true. Many actors join the world of theater for their love of expressing themselves through their bodies, the tools of the trade. Nothing can compare to that adrenaline rush an actor gets just before he or she steps on stage in front of hundreds of people who all have their eyes focused on him or her, and the applause of an audience is all the gratitude some actors need to feel appreciated.*

*Many people don't realize that theater goes beyond the actors though, and that is where they are deceived. Sometimes the technical aspect of a production is more interesting than the acting is. A Broadway production can have a set with more complicated plans than a skyscraper building. Shows like "Phantom of the Opera" can have over twenty major trap doors and more than ninety minor ones. There are dozens of people in charge of sound, lighting, props, and costumes that no one ever sees or thinks about when sitting in the audience. There is just that wonderful feeling that these things just magically happen; no one seems to be responsible.*

*The theater is an art that will live on for a long time to come, as long as people take the time to support it. The magic of a show that enthralls most viewers, though, is a culmination of the hard work, time, and dedication of many people who never get credit for their actions. But Shakespeare was right because, for many people in the theater, all the world is a stage.*

### "All the World's a Stage"

*All the world is indeed a stage. And we are the performers. Everything we do in life is a production, and we must constantly perform our best because, in life, there are no rehearsals. Each of us performs on a separate stage, some for a larger audience than others. But each performance, regardless of the size of the audience, is of equal importance, and each performer must meet the standard of life's most important critic—himself.*

*As a high school student, I often find that there exists much pressure to perform: pressure to perform academically, pressure to perform in sports, pressure to perform in social situations, and countless others. Furthermore, there are many individuals for whom I constantly must perform. At this juncture in life, parents, teachers, friends, and others comprise what I often perceive as an overwhelmingly large audience, which is sometimes overly critical.*

*As I grow older, I am learning to accept new responsibilities, and I find that my role in life is changing. Often in life, we cannot constantly adhere to a routine performance; sometimes we must improvise. The improvisation, or adjustment to new responsibility, is often difficult though of critical importance to a successful production. In life, I have come to expect the unexpected and have done my best to deal with new situations. As performers, we must not allow tragedy, depression, and self-doubt to unnerve us. Instead, we must cope, adjust, and continue to perform.*

*Throughout my performance I have received evaluation from many critics, some of which I have taken better than others. No matter how many critics we have, we should remind ourselves that we are our most important critics, for of life's performance we will make the ultimate evaluation. Even though all the world's a stage, each of us need be concerned with only one performance.*

---

**Analysis**

The first essay stumbles at the beginning: The introduction has a central idea, but it is not well expressed and there is no coherence in the reference to ancient Rome. This essay reads like a first draft, and perhaps the writer was pressed for time. It would be improved not only in revision of the opening paragraph but also in the transitions. This writer begins too many sentences with *and* or *but*, and the language is not always fluent or precise. The writer, however, does establish organization and some unity in the opening of the second paragraph: "The theater appeals to people for many different reasons."

The writer also shows skill in development by moving from the role of theater for audiences to its importance for participants. The concluding sentence also works well because it relates the major part of the essay to a fresh meaning of the quote. In this case, a good conclusion rescues an essay with a weak introduction.

The second essay is effective because of the exceptional way in which the writer developed the topic as an extended metaphor. The essay is brief, but it is absolutely focused; every detail supports the central idea, the comparison of one's life to a dramatic performance. The writer has maintained a consistent point of view and has developed the topic in a creative way.

---

# EVALUATING COMPOSITION

Every student has seen on a paper or an essay test the comment "develop this point more." The Regents rubric on page 229 is a reminder that one of the most important criteria in evaluating essays for class or for an exam is the extent to which the topic has been developed to achieve the writer's purpose. Simply to announce a subject and say that you have thoughts on that subject is not enough.

For any topic, the student must show skill in establishing a central idea and in creating an effective way to develop it. All compositions must be unified and expressed in fluent and precise language, and they must follow the conventions of standard written English. (See Guide to Standard Written English beginning on page 161.)

# PREPARING FOR ESSAY EXAMS

Nearly all the writing you have done, both personal and for school, serves as preparation. Just as an athlete or musician practices regularly in order to have the skills to draw on in a performance, high school students are developing their skills whenever they compose written responses. Reflect on what you know your strengths and weaknesses are. To review, go over the essays and exams you have written in high school; note what is consistently strong and what needs revision; review carefully your teachers' comments.

Good writers are also readers. Read good writing, observe what makes it effective, emulate it, and imitate for practice what you admire. In serious magazines and in the editorial pages, letters to the editor, and Op-Ed sections of newspapers you can often find good essays of argument on current topics. (See also Recommended Reading on page 215 for suggested works and authors of nonfiction.)

To succeed in any assigned task, you need to know what is expected and how you will be evaluated. Review the Regents exam scoring guides, which describe the criteria for scoring the written responses.

# WRITING ON TIMED EXAMINATIONS

If you are writing an essay for an examination, you do not have time for extensive preparation, but you can learn to condense the kind of thinking and notetaking you do for course assignments into a process for planning an examination response. How to begin?

## Gather Your Ideas

*First*, be sure you understand the task or the meaning of the topic. One way to do that is to rephrase the question into a topic assertion. This may not be original, but if a restatement of the question serves as a topic sentence for your introduction and gets you started—use it! You may not use such statements in your final essay, but the fact that you can express them for yourself means you understand what the question expects or that you have something to say about the topic

If you are creating your own topic, be sure you know what you want to say about it. This may seem obvious, but only when you sketch or outline can you be sure you have sufficient material for an essay. Use the brainstorming techniques you have learned in class or workshops. For example, if you have practiced "freewriting" in the past or have written journal entries as a way of developing ideas, take a few minutes to address the topic in that way, without regard to organization or "getting it absolutely right." Similarly, you can just note down in words or phrases everything the prompt brings to mind. It is better to note more ideas than you can use than to discover after twenty-five minutes that you have too few.

## Organize

*Second*, take a few minutes to make a plan or outline. All essay writing requires this step. Do not leave it out, even on the SAT, in which you have only 25 minutes for the essay. The outline may consist of only phrases or a brief list to remind you of the points you want to make. Consider possible lines of argument. That is, answer for yourself the questions "How can I prove that? What information in the text (if given) can I quote or paraphrase as evidence? How can I show or persuade someone who is interested in what I have to say? What do I know or believe that will make my discussion convincing?" Finally, decide on the order that is best: chronological? sequence of cause and effect? order of importance or intensity? (Common methods of developing ideas in essays are reviewed, with examples, in Reading Nonfiction, Chapter 4.)

## Compose

The essays you write for the Regents exam and for the SAT are, of course, "tests." You are not being asked to demonstrate acquired knowledge so much as you are to demonstrate how well you can communicate in standard written English what you understand about the given subjects and texts or what you think about a particular issue. What is being assessed is your ability to articulate a controlling idea and support it with reasons and appropriate examples. On the Regents exam, you must also be able to work from given texts and write for clearly defined purposes and audiences.

Concentrate on good development—not a finished product. An essay that reveals critical thinking and coherence and effectively develops several appropriate examples or reasons with command of sentence variety and language will receive a high score even if it remains somewhat unfinished or lacks a formal conclusion. Remember, on the SAT optional essay you are writing what will be evaluated as a first draft. Regents essays are viewed as somewhat more "finished," but those too are understood to have been written in only one sitting.

## Edit as You Go

The time you take in planning is also well spent because on-demand writing requires you to edit and revise as you compose your response. If you still make spelling errors in commonly used words, make a deliberate effort to look for those errors and correct them on the exams. A few neatly corrected spelling or usage errors are not only acceptable, they reveal the writer's ability to edit his or her own work. (See Chapter 9 on Grammar and Usage and Chapter 10 on Punctuation.)

# USING SYNONYMIES TO ENHANCE YOUR WRITING

Included in the expectations for any well-written essay is use of language that is vivid and appropriate; the rubrics for scoring Regents essays include "use of original, fluent, and precise language." The term *synonymy* refers to words that can be grouped according to general meaning; that is, they all denote or describe a specific instance of a general concept. Reviewing and creating synonymies will help you develop the vivid and precise language characteristic of good writing. Below are some examples of synonymies for commonly used but often vague or overused expressions.

**to cause**

| | | | |
|---|---|---|---|
| bring about | generate | originate | raise |
| create | give rise to | persuade | spawn |
| effect | incite | produce | |
| engender | invent | promote | |
| excite | lead to | provoke | |

**to change**

| | | | |
|---|---|---|---|
| adapt | develop | grow | revise |
| adjust | deviate | mature | rework |
| alter | differ | metamorphose | transform |
| amend | digress | modify | turn (into) |
| become | diverge | modulate | vary |
| convert | diversify | mutate | |
| correct | edit | progress | |
| depart | evolve | remake | |

**to look upon someone/something**

| | | | |
|---|---|---|---|
| analyze | discern | judge | scrutinize |
| appraise | dismiss | observe | stereotype |
| censure | distinguish | perceive | summarize |
| classify | esteem | ponder | typecast |
| conclude | evaluate | reckon | value |
| condemn | honor | regard | view |
| consider | hypothesize | review | watch |
| deem | infer | ruminate | |

## to look down upon someone/something

| | | | |
|---|---|---|---|
| belittle | diminish | frown upon | ridicule |
| censure | discredit | have disdain for | scorn |
| condescend | disfavor | hold inferior | shame |
| condemn | disgrace | humiliate | shun |
| degrade | disparage | ignore | taunt |
| demote | disregard | jeer | vilify |
| depreciate | show disrespect | mock | |
| deride | embarrass | rebuke | |
| devalue | find fault with | reject | |

## bad

| | | | |
|---|---|---|---|
| abhorrent | detrimental | inequitable | scandalous |
| atrocious | devilish | infamous | scurrilous |
| awful | dirty | inferior | shameless |
| base | disquieting | loathsome | sinful |
| belittling | evil | malevolent | sinister |
| blemished | false | malign | slanderous |
| calumnious | fiendish | marred | sour |
| catastrophic | foul | mean | spiteful |
| contemptible | fraudulent | merciless | spoiled |
| corrupt | grotesque | monstrous | squalid |
| counterfeit | hateful | nefarious | tasteless |
| criminal | heinous | negative | terrible |
| cruel | hellish | notorious | unethical |
| damaged | hideous | odious | unscrupulous |
| deceptive | horrible | ominous | vile |
| defective | horrid | perverse | villainous |
| defiled | horrific | putrid | wicked |
| delinquent | immoral | rotten | |
| depraved | imperfect | ruthless | |
| despicable | impish | scabrous | |

## effective

| | | | |
|---|---|---|---|
| capable | dazzling | forceful | persuasive |
| cogent | dramatic | impressive | potent |
| commanding | effectual | influential | powerful |
| compelling | efficacious | lively | strong |
| convincing | emotional | moving | telling |

## caring

| | | | |
|---|---|---|---|
| affectionate | devoted | giving | selfless |
| benevolent | doting | goodhearted | sympathetic |
| bountiful | empathetic | humane | tender |
| compassionate | empathic | kind | thoughtful |
| concerned | fond | loving | warm |
| courteous | generous | philanthropic | warmhearted |

## due to

| | | | |
|---|---|---|---|
| as a consequence of | because of | from | on account of |
| as a result of | by reason of | in light of | resulting from |
| because | caused by | in view of | |
| | following from | induced by | |

## hard/difficult

| | | | |
|---|---|---|---|
| arduous | fatiguing | intricate | strong |
| bitter | galling | labyrinthine | tiresome |
| challenging | grievous | mighty | toilsome |
| complex | grim | oppressive | tough |
| daunting | harsh | relentless | unattainable |
| demanding | Herculean | resistant | unbending |
| enigmatic | impenetrable | rigorous | uncompromising |
| esoteric | impossible | serious | unyielding |
| exacting | impregnable | severe | wearisome |
| exhausting | inflexible | sharp | |
| exigent | insurmountable | strenuous | |

## sad/depressing (depressed)

| | | | |
|---|---|---|---|
| abject | dejected | forsaken | somber |
| aching | desolate | gloomy | sorrowful |
| aggrieved | despairing | joyless | tormenting |
| bereaved | disconsolate | lugubrious | tragic |
| bereft | discontent | melancholy | unhappy |
| bleak | distraught | miserable | upset |
| blue | distressing | morose | wretched |
| cheerless | down | painful | |
| dark | forlorn | saddening | |

123

**same**

| | | | |
|---|---|---|---|
| akin | compatible | generic | parallel |
| alike | conformable | homogeneous | photocopy |
| allied | conforming | identical | related |
| analogous | congruent | imitation | replica |
| associated | consonant | indiscernible | same |
| clone | copy | inseparable | shared |
| cognate | correspondent | interchangeable | similar |
| collective | corresponding | joint | synonymous |
| common | duplicate | like | tantamount |
| comparable | equal | matching | twin |
| comparative | equivalent | mutual | |

# A GLOSSARY OF TERMS FOR WRITING*

**anecdote**  A brief story or account of a single experience, often biographical, which illustrates something typical or striking about a person. Anecdotes, like parables, are effective as vivid, specific examples of a general observation or quality.

**argument**  The development of reasons, examples to support a thesis; narrowly, to outline a position on an issue or problem with the intent to clarify or persuade. Argument is also used in a broad sense to refer to the way a writer develops any topic.

**audience**  For the writer this term refers to the intended reader. Awareness of an audience determines, for example, what the writer may assume a reader already knows, level of diction, and tone.

**coherence**  A piece of writing has coherence when the logical relationship of ideas is evident and convincing. In a coherent discussion, statements and sections follow one another in a natural, even inevitable way. A coherent discussion hangs together; an incoherent one is scattered and disorganized.

**cohesion**  This refers to the grammatical and usage aspects of writing. Cohesive writing means that the connection of ideas within each sentence and at the paragraph level is clear and that the writing follows the conventions of standard written English.

**controlling idea**  This refers to the writer's thesis or main idea. It asserts what the writer has to say <u>about</u> the topic or question.

**conventions**  These are the "rules" or common guidelines for punctuation, spelling, and usage.

**description**  The expression in words of what is experienced by the senses. Good description recreates what is felt, seen, heard—sensed in

---

*Many of the terms in this glossary are also discussed in Chapter 4, Reading Prose.

any way. We also use the term describe to mean *identify, classify, characterize,* even for abstract ideas. Description permits readers to recreate the subject in their own imaginations.

**development** This refers to the choice and elaboration of examples, reasons, or other details that support an argument or illustrate a controlling idea. (See also the rubric for scoring Regents essays in Appendix D.)

**diction** This refers to word choice. Diction may be formal or informal, complex or simple, elegant or modest, depending on the occasion and the audience. The language we use in casual conversation is different from the language we use in formal writing. The good writer uses language that is varied, precise, and vivid; the good writer has resources of language to suit a wide range of purposes.

**exposition** The development of a topic through examples, reasons, details, which explain, clarify, show, instruct—the primary purpose of exposition is to convey information. Much of the writing assigned to students is referred to as expository writing: Through exposition you can demonstrate what you have learned, discovered, understood, appreciated.

**focus** This refers to the way a writer contains and directs all the information, examples, ideas, reasons in an essay on the specific topic.

**narrative** Because it tells a story, narrative has chronological order. Narrative method is commonly used in exposition when examples are offered in a chronological development.

**position paper** A form of persuasive writing, a position paper is meant to generate support for an issue or cause; the essay is based on specific evidence that can be cited to support the writer's argument. A position paper may also evaluate solutions or suggest courses of action.

**prompt** This refers to a set of directions for a writing task; may also be a quote or passage meant to stimulate a piece of writing.

**tone** In writing, tone refers to the attitude of the writer toward the subject and/or toward the reader. Tone may range from *harsh and insistent* to *gentle and reflective.* There is as much variety of tone in writing as there is in human feeling. Some pieces, essays of opinion, for example, usually have a very distinct tone; other works, especially in fiction or personal expression, may have a more subtle and indirect tone. (See discussion of Tone on page 65 in Reading Prose and on page 86 in Reading Poetry.)

**transition** Words or phrases used to link ideas and sections in a piece of writing. Common transitions include *first, second . . . in addition . . . finally; on the other hand, moreover, consequently, therefore.* Transitions make the development of an argument clear.

**unity** In the narrowest sense, unity refers to focus: The ideas and examples are clearly related to the topic and to one another. In the largest sense, unity refers to a feature of our best writing: All elements—ideas, form, language, and tone—work together to achieve the effect of a complete and well-made piece.

# Chapter 8

# VOCABULARY

Formal vocabulary study may begin as early as kindergarten; associating meaning with different sounds begins virtually at birth. As all students have discovered, however, there always seem to be new words to learn. Every novel, essay, or newspaper article we read is likely to include some new expressions or unfamiliar words. Deliberately studying new words and preparing for tests on them is certainly one way to expand our vocabularies, and every serious student has developed a method for such study. But if you do not continue to use those new words—that is, read, speak, and write with them—they may be forgotten soon after the test.

The thousands of words you *know* were acquired through repeated use over time and through association with their contexts, that is, through reading and listening. As you study vocabulary words associated with a course in English, social studies, or science, you are learning them in a context, and you are also expanding your reading and writing vocabularies. Every word you study should create some kind of image for you: try to associate it with a phrase, an experience or feeling, an object or person, an action or incident. If you have no image, you do not truly know the word yet.

The vocabulary you are expected to know and use, and that will be assessed on the Regents ELA, the SAT, and the ACT exams, is the language of literary authors, essayists, historians, and scientists. On the Regents ELA exam, this means that your mastery of relevant vocabulary will be assessed through questions about the meanings of words within the extended reading comprehension passages. You will also be expected to understand how particular words or expressons establish tone and clarify an author's meaning in the texts for analysis. This shift in how vocabulary is assessed represents a shared goal of the Common Core aligned state exams (Regents, PARCC, SBAC) and the SAT and ACT. For high school students, this means less need to study exotic and unfamiliar vocabulary in isolation; rather, students will need to be able to understand—and use—what is called academic language.

In the next section, you will find examples of what is meant by academic language. At the end of the chapter, you will find three collections of words to review as well. The first represents words that have been tested on Regents exams over several years. The second is a list compiled by high school students from their reading of the Op-Ed pages of *The New York Times* and other sources. The third, from published book reviews, was also compiled by students. Each list offers the thoughtful reader and writer a rich source of vocabulary in current use.

# ACADEMIC LANGUAGE

Academic language is the language you use to express understanding of texts in class discussion, lecture, and writing. It is the language of interpretation, analysis, evaluation, and explanation. This term also refers to the language of a particular subject or discipline: literature, history, biology, economics, art, and so on. Reviewing the glossaries of literary and poetic terms and the terms for writing is another way of strengthening your command of academic language.

Here is a list of **verbs**, followed by their noun and adjective forms, commonly used to express how nonfiction texts are written and how arguments are developed. You will recognize many of these terms from the list of What Writers Do at the beginning of Chapter 4.

| | | |
|---|---|---|
| allege | allegation | alleged, allegedly |
| analyze | analysis | analytic, analytically |
| apply | application | |
| argue | argument | argumentative |
| arrange | arrangement | |
| articulate | | |
| assemble | | |
| assert | assertion | assertive |
| assess | assessment | |
| associate | association | |
| assume | assumption | |
| categorize | category | categorical |
| cite | citation | |
| characterize | characterization | |
| claim | (a/the) claim | |
| clarify | clarification | |
| classify | classification | |
| compare | comparison | |
| compile | compilation | |
| complement | (a/the) complement | complementary |
| compose | composition | |
| comprehend | comprehension | comprehensive |
| conclude | conclusion | conclusive |
| construct | construct, construction | |
| contend | contention | contentious |
| contradict | contradiction | contradictory |
| contrast | contrast | contrasting |
| correlate | correlation | correlative |
| criticize | criticism | critical, critically |
| critique | (a/the) critique | |

128

| | | |
|---|---|---|
| debate | (a/the) debate | debatable |
| deduce | deduction | deductive, deductively |
| defend | defense | defensive |
| define | definition | definitive |
| demonstrate | demonstration | demonstrative |
| derive | derivation | derivative |
| design | (a/the) design | |
| develop | development | |
| differentiate | differentiation | |
| discern | discernment | discerning |
| discover | discovery | |
| discuss | discussion | |
| distinguish | distinction | distinguished |
| elaborate | elaboration | elaborate, elaborately |
| emphasize | emphasis | |
| estimate | estimation | |
| evaluate | evaluation | |
| exaggerate | exaggeration | |
| examine | examination | |
| exclude | exclusion | |
| explain | explanation | |
| explore | exploration | exploratory |
| focus | (a/the) focus | |
| form | (a/the) form | formal, formally |
| formulate | formulation | |
| frame | | |
| generalize | generalization | |
| highlight | highlight | |
| hypothesize | hypothesis | hyhpothetical |
| identify | identification | |
| illustrate | illustration | |
| imply | implication | |
| include | inclusion | inclusive |
| infer | inference | inferential, inferentially |
| influence | influence | influential |
| inquire | inquiry | |
| integrate | integration | |
| interpret | interpretation | interpretive |
| introduce | introduction | |
| investigate | investigation | |
| judge | judgment | judgmental, judgmentally |
| mean | meaning | meaningful |
| modify | modification | |
| observe | observation | |
| oppose | opposition | |

| | | |
|---|---|---|
| organize | organization | |
| originate | origin | original |
| outline | (a/the) outline | |
| paraphrase | paraphrase | |
| persuade | persuasion | persuasive |
| predict | prediction | predictive |
| presume | presumption | presumptive |
| project | projection | |
| propose | proposition | |
| recall | recollection | |
| refer | reference | referential |
| report | report | |
| represent | representation | |
| respond | response | responsive |
| review | review | |
| select | (a/the) selection | selective, selectively |
| sequence | (a/the) sequence | sequential, sequentially |
| specify | specification | |
| speculate | speculation | speculative |
| state | statement | |
| structure | (a/the) structure | structural, structurally |
| suggest | suggestion | suggestive |
| summarize | summary | summarily |
| support | support | supportive |
| suppose | supposition | supposed, supposedly |
| symbolize | symbol | symbolic |
| synthesize | synthesis | |
| translate | translation | |
| utilize | utilization | |
| vary | variation | |
| verify | verification | |

Note: The *-ed* (past participle) forms of all these verbs are also used as modifiers: *assembled, classified, identified*, and so on. The adjective/adverb forms listed previously are widely used as separate forms and some have differences in meaning from the verb and noun forms.

Here is a list of **nouns and adjectives** used to identify and describe rhetorical methods as well as a writer's tone and purpose:

| | |
|---|---|
| abstraction | abstract |
| analogy | analogous |
| approach | |
| | appropriate |
| | approximate |

| | |
|---|---|
| argument | argumentative |
| aspect | |
| audience | |
| authenticity | authentic |
| background | |
| chronology | chronological |
| coherence | coherent |
| concision | concise |
| | concrete |
| consequence | consequentially |
| consistency | consistent, consistently |
| constancy | constant |
| context | contextually |
| credibility | credible |
| criterion/criteria | |
| detail | |
| diction | |
| dimension | |
| direction | direct |
| effect | effective |
| element | elemental |
| equivalence | equivalent |
| | essential |
| evidence | evident |
| example | |
| excerpt | |
| exercise | |
| expository | exposition |
| extract | extraction |
| fact | factual |
| factor | |
| feature | |
| | figurative, figuratively |
| fragment | |
| frequence | frequent |
| general | generally |
| graph | graphic |
| highlight | |
| image | |
| inclination | |
| indirection | indirect |
| intention | intentional |
| irony | ironic |
| irrelevance | irrelevant |

| | |
|---|---|
| literalness | literal, literally |
| logic | logical, logically |
| metaphor | metaphorical |
| method | *methodical |
| motivation | motivating |
| narration | narrative |
| narrator | |
| objectivity | objective |
| opinion | opinionated |
| order | ordered |
| origin | original |
| pattern | |
| perspective | |
| plagiarism | plagiarized |
| plan | |
| plausibility | plausible |
| point of view | |
| possibility | possible |
| primary | |
| priority | *prior |
| probability | probable |
| process | |
| profile | |
| prompt | |
| proposition | |
| purpose | purposeful |
| relevance | relevant |
| revision | revised |
| sequence | sequential |
| series | |
| signal | |
| significance | significant |
| source | |
| speaker | |
| specificity | specific |
| strategy | strategic |
| structure | |
| style | stylistic |
| subject | *subjective |
| subsequence | subsequent |
| substitution | substitute |
| succinctness | succinct |
| summary | |
| survey | |

| | |
|---|---|
| technique | technical |
| theme | |
| thesis | |
| tone | |
| topic | *topical |
| transition | |
| uniqueness | unique |
| validity | valid |
| variation, variety | varied |
| viewpoint | |
| voice | |

*Note: As in the list of verbs, some nouns and adjectives with a common derivation may have differences in meaning.

Throughout *Let's Review*, you will find sources of what is meant by academic language, along with glossaries of terms for fiction, nonfiction, poetry, and writing. Your ability to recognize examples of various literary and rhetorical elements strengthens your comprehension; you will also be expected to use them appropriately when you write essays of argument and text analysis.

# UNFAMILIAR AND ARCHAIC LANGUAGE

Here is some of the vocabulary you will encounter as you read and discuss what are considered authentic or historically significant texts. Some of the words are familiar in their current use; but, the meanings offered here are from texts as early as the 16th century, including works of Shakespeare, and are also found in 18th, 19th , and early 20th century writings in English.

## Verbs

| | |
|---|---|
| **address** | to consider, think about, speak to |
| **apprise** | to give verbal or written notice |
| **behold** | to observe with care, witness |
| **breach** | to break through |
| **discover** | to learn, to disclose |
| **dispose** | to be inclined |
| **divine** | to guess, figure out, foresee |
| **endeavor** | to try, attempt a task or challenge |
| **fashion** | to form or make something |

| | |
|---|---|
| forbear | to pause, delay, avoid voluntarily or decline to do something |
| have | to prefer, think, believe, consider, think about |
| peruse | to read or examine with care |
| relish | to enjoy, take delight in |
| smart | to cause pain |
| suffer | to put up with, tolerate |
| thirst | to have an intense desire for something |
| thwart | to oppose, frustrate or defeat |
| want | to fail, be deficient or lacking |
| witness | to see by personal presence, observe directly |
| wreak | to revenge, throw or dash with violence |

## Nouns

| | |
|---|---|
| appendages | arms and legs |
| appetite | desire, interest |
| ardor | passion |
| aught, naught | anything, nothing |
| conveyance | vehicle |
| countenance | look, appearance |
| dominion | area of authority, knowledge or power |
| eloquence | artful, expressive speech |
| faculties | senses, aptitudes, abilities |
| fashion | a distinctive or habitual manner |
| forebearance | patience, tolerance |
| grievance | suffering, distress; grudge, resentment |
| humor | temperament |
| idleness | unimportance, uselessness, emptiness |
| infirmity | weakness, disorder; personal failing |
| justice | accuracy, wisdom |
| labors | efforts |
| nature | disposition, inherent quality |
| perusal | reading, consideration |
| petulance | irritability, contrariness |
| rapture | extreme joy or pleasure; passionate intensity |
| sensibility | acuteness of perception; capacity to feel or perceive |
| temper | disposition of mind |
| vanity | emptiness, untruth, unfruitful labor |
| virtue | strength of character, bravery, valor; moral excellence |

## Adjectives

| | |
|---|---|
| base | corrupt, vile |
| bumptious | arrogant, brash |
| clever | intelligent, skilled |
| familiar | agreeable in conversation, not formal or distant |
| idle | unimportant, trivial |
| imbued | tinged, affected with |
| infirm | weak of mind, body, or will |
| petulant | pert, wanton, sour in temper |
| prevailing | having effect; persuading, succeeding |
| puerile | childish, trifling, weak |
| rough | coarse in manners, uncivil; terrible, dreadful |
| sensible | having perception by the mind or the senses |
| sober | serious, calm, subdued |
| stout | bold, intrepid, brave |
| sublime | high in excellence, lofty, grand |
| wholesome | contributing to health of mind, conducive to good |

# STUDYING NEW WORDS

## Learning in Context

Even the most diligent student cannot reasonably expect simply to memorize—out of context—the hundreds, even thousands, of words on Regents and SAT lists. Recent studies also confirm that vocabulary study confined to lists of words without a context or pattern of association—as with a particular work of literature, for example—does not result in long-term retention. Moreover, the practice of recording dictionary definitions alone gives only general and sometimes misleading information about the meaning and correct use of words. Learning words means learning their precise meanings, connotations, and appropriate context.

Unless you are working with an unabridged dictionary, which often includes illustrative examples in sentences or phrases, you are likely to find in a desk dictionary only brief definitions, general in nature, and possibly a list of synonyms. This limited information is valuable as a *reference*, especially if you are reading a passage and need to know a word's meaning in order to understand the passage. Learning the full meaning of unfamiliar words, however, requires more active study. In the sections below you will find recommendations for ways to prepare and organize your vocabulary study.

# ROOTS AND PREFIXES FROM LATIN AND GREEK

Although English is certainly not derived from Greek and Latin only, familiarity with the Greek or Latin forms in English words is often useful to students taking vocabulary tests. Recognition of root meanings in particular may help you determine the correct answer for a word you may not be sure of. Even more important, however, is the value of knowing the Latin and Greek origins of English when you are first studying new words. When you are aware of the meanings of the individual parts of a word you often can form an image for it. Think of the Latin root *spect*, for example. This root means *look into, observe, behold* and, with variations in spelling *spec* and *spic*, is the base of many English words: *inspect, introspect, expect, respect, speculate, spectacle, spectacular, conspicuous*—and many others. Even the word *spy* is related to this Latin root.

When you are looking up words in the dictionary, do not skip over the etymology—the section that shows you in abbreviated form the origin and history of a word. Grouping words by related origin can be a very useful way to organize when you are studying large groups of new words; by using their common origin, you will learn to associate a new word with others you already know. It is the process of forming associations in meaning, forming images, and knowing contexts that permits you to learn efficiently—and to remember—the words you study. (Familiarity with roots and prefixes is also very helpful in understanding spelling patterns, as you will see in Chapter 11.)

Listed below, with examples, are many of the Latin and Greek roots found in English. (As you review the meanings of these roots, provide additional examples from your own knowledge; you should also guess about possible examples—then look them up in a dictionary to confirm your guess.) This process is a demonstration of what is meant by *active* vocabulary study. It means you are thinking about a word and associating it with others you know.

As you examine the list of Greek and Latin roots common in English, you should be struck by how familiar many of these forms are. You should also note that all these roots denote specific actions or ideas. Knowing the meanings of these elements as you study new words, or review familiar ones, will give you specific images or experiences to associate with them. This in turn will make the meaning of many words more vivid and easier to remember than will an abstract definition or list of synonyms alone.

# LATIN ROOTS

| Forms | Meaning | Examples |
| --- | --- | --- |
| *alter* | other | altercation, alternative |
| *ami (amicus)* | friend | amiable, amicable, amity |
| *amor* | love | amorous, enamored |
| *anima* | breath, mind, spirit | animation, unanimous, inanimate, animosity |
| *bell (bellum)* | war | bellicose, belligerent, antebellum |
| *cad (cadere), cid* | to fall | decay, decadence, deciduous |
| *cap, cip* | contain | captivate, capacity, capable |
| *capit (caput)* | head | capital, capitol, recapitulate |
| *cede, ceed, cess (cedere)* | to move, yield | proceed, accede, exceed, precede, excess, success, procession |
| *cept (capere)* | to take, seize, hold | intercept, reception, accept |
| *cid, cis (caedere)* | to cut, kill | precise, incisive, homicide |
| *clam, claim (clamare)* | to cry, call out | exclaim, proclaim, clamor |
| *clud, clus (claudere)* | to shut, close | include, exclusion, recluse |
| *cred (credere)* | to believe, loan, trust | creditable, incredible, credulous |
| *culp (culpa)* | fault, guilt | culpable, exculpate |
| *cur, curs (currere)* | to run | course, cursor, current, incur, precursor, recur |
| *dict (dicere)* | to say, tell | dictator, diction, edict, predict |
| *doc (docere)* | to teach | doctor, docile, indoctrinate |
| *duc, duct (ducere)* | to lead | deduce, induction, conduct |
| *err (errare)* | to go, lead astray | error, erroneous, erratum |
| *err (errer)* | to travel, wander | errand, arrant, erratic |
| *fac, fact, fect, fic (facere)* | to make, do | affect, defect, effect, facsimile, factor, artificial, deficit |
| *fer (ferre)* | to bear, carry | inference, offer, reference |
| *fid (fidelitas)* | faith, loyalty | infidel, perfidious, diffident |
| *flect, flex (flectere)* | to bend | reflex, reflection, flexibility |
| *flu, fluct, flux (fluere)* | to flow | affluent, fluctuation, fluent, influence, influx |
| *fund (fundare) (fundus)* | to base, bottom | (to) found, fundamental, profundity |
| *fus (fundere)* | pour | effusive, foundry, fusion |
| *gen (genus) (genare)* | kind, sort, birth, to beget | genre, heterogenous, genetic, generate, progenitor, genocide |
| *grad, gress (gradus)* | to walk, go, stage or step | digress, graduate, progress, grade, gradient, retrograde |
| *greg (gregis)* | flock, herd, group | egregious, gregarious, integrate |
| *her, hes (haerere)* | to cling, stick | adhesive, coherence, inherently |
| *ject, jet (jacere)* | to throw | inject, projection, jettison |
| *jud, jur, jus (jus)* | to judge; to swear just, right; law | abjure, adjudicate, prejudge, jury, justification, perjury |
| *lat (latus)* | borne, carried | correlative, related, superlative |
| *leg (legis, lex)* | law | legality, legislative |
| *locus* | place | location, locale, locomotive |

| | | |
|---|---|---|
| *locu, loqu (loqui)* | to speak | eloquent, loquacious, soliloquy, |
| *locutor* | speaker | interlocutor, locution, obloquy |
| *lude (ludere)* | to play | interlude, ludicrous, prelude |
| *mit, mitt, mis, miss (mittere)* | to dispatch, send, to let go | emit, permit, remit, submissive, commission, missile, permission |
| *mob, mot (movere)* | to move | demote, motivate, promote, commotion, mobility |
| *mor, mort (mortis)* | death | immortal, mortality, mortified |
| *ped (pedis)* | foot | expeditious, impede, pedestrian |
| *pel, puls (pellere)* | to drive, push | compel, dispel, impulse, repel, compulsive, repellent |
| *pend, pens (pendere)* | to hang, weigh, pay | append, compensate, dependent, impending, pension, pensive |
| *ple, plet (plere)* | to fill | complete, complement, deplete |
| *plen (plenus)* | full | plentiful, replete |
| *pon, pos, posit (ponere)* | to place, put | component, depose, propose, juxtapostion, impose, opponent |
| *port (portare)* | to carry | comport, deportment, purport, portable, portfolio |
| *pot, poten, poss (posse)* | to be able | impossibility, omnipotent, potential |
| *rad (radius)* | root, spoke (wheel) | eradicate, radical, radiation |
| *rect, reg (regula) (regire)* | right, straight to guide, rule | direction, rectified, regal regimen, regime |
| *rupt (rumpere)* | to break, burst | disrupt, corrupt, interruption |
| *sat (satis)* | enough | dissatisfy, insatiable, saturated |
| *sci (scire)* | to know | conscience, omniscient, prescience, scientific |
| *scrib, script (scribere)* | to write | describe, inscription, scripture |
| *sect (sectare)* | to cut | dissect, intersection |
| *secu, sequ (sequi)* | to follow | consequence, obsequious, sectarian, sequel |
| *sed, sid, sess (sedere)* | to sit | dissidence, possess, residual, sedation, sedentary |
| *sent, sens (sentire)* | to feel | consensus, insensitive, sentient |
| *son (sonus)* | sound | consonant, dissonance, sonic, sonogram, sonority, unison |
| *spec, spect, spic (spectare)* | to look at, observe | auspicious, conspicuous, expect, inspect, respect, spectacular |
| *spir, spirit* | to breathe | inspiration, respiratory, spirit |
| *sta, state, stit (stare)* | to stand | constitute, instability, obstacle, stability, status |
| *strict, string (stringere)* | to draw tight | constrict, restriction, stringent |
| *sume, sump (sumere)* | to take | assume, consume, presumption |
| *tact, tang, ting, tig (tangere)* | to touch | contact, contiguous, intangible, tactile, tangential |

| | | |
|---|---|---|
| ten, tain (tenere) | to hold, keep | abstain, pertain, restrain, tenacious, untenable |
| tend, tens (tendere) | to reach, stretch | contend, intensity, portent, pretentious, tendency |
| tort (torque) | to twist | contortion, extort, tortuous |
| tract (trahere) | to draw, pull | distract, intractible, protracted, retraction |
| ver (veritas) | truth | aver, veracity, verification |
| vers, vert (vertere) | to turn | adverse, aversion, diversity, inadvertent, reversion, subvert, version, versification |
| vid, vis (videre) (video) | to see | evident, improvident, supervise, revision, visage, visionary |
| vit, viv (vivere) (viva) | to live; life | revival, survive, vivacious, unviable |
| vinc, vict (vincere) | to conquer | conviction, eviction, invincible |
| voc, voke (vocare) | to call | advocate, equivocal, invocation, provocative, revoke, vocation |
| volv, volu (volvere) | to roll, turn | convoluted, evolution, revolving |

## GREEK ROOTS

| Forms | Meaning | Examples |
|---|---|---|
| anthrop | man, humankind | anthropocentric, misanthropist, philanthropy |
| arch | rule, ruler | anarchy, patriarchal |
| astr, astron | star | astronomical, disastrous |
| bio | life, living things | biography, microbiology |
| chron | time | anachronistic, chronic |
| cosm (kosmos) | order, universe | cosmic, microcosm |
| demo | among the people | democratic, demography |
| gen | birth, race | genesis, progeny |
| gno, gnosis | know | agnostic, diagnosis, gnomic |
| gram, graph | write, writing | epigrammatic, biography |
| log, logue | word, reason | analogy, illogical, prologue |
| lect, lex | language, speak | dialect, lexical |
| lysis | dissolution, destruction | catalyst, paralysis |
| metr | measure | diametric, metrical |
| morph | form, shape | amorphous, metamorphose |
| mne, mnes | memory, remember | amnesty, mnemonic |
| onym | a name | eponymous, synonym |
| opti, optic | eye, sight | optical, synopsis |
| path (pathos) | feeling, suffering | apathy, empathetic, pathetic |
| ped | child | pediatrician, pedagogy, pedantic |
| phon | sound | euphony, phonetic, symphonic |

Prefixes are units of one or two syllables that are not words in themselves but that have distinct meanings. The addition of a prefix to the beginning of an existing word (what is called a *stem* or *root)* creates a word with an additional meaning. The spelling variations for many of the prefixes listed below are reminders that in English the spelling of a prefix will be altered to match the root to which it is attached. For example, *ad*, which means *to* or *toward*, is attached to many words in English; the *d* often changes to the first letter of the word to which it is added, making the resulting new forms easier to pronounce. (See the examples below as well as those in Chapter 11—Spelling.)

## LATIN PREFIXES

| Forms | Meaning | Examples* |
|-------|---------|-----------|
| a, ab, abs | away, from | abdicate, absence, abstraction |
| a, ad (ac, af, al, etc.) | to, toward | absent, acclimate, adherent, alliteration, assign, attribution |
| ambi | both, around | ambiance, ambiguous, ambidextrous, ambivalent |
| ante | before | antebellum, antecedent |
| bene, ben | good, well | beneficial, beneficent, benign |
| circum | around | circumnavigate, circumstances, circumlocution |
| co (col, com, cor) | together | coincidence, collaboration, commiserate, correspondence |
| contra, contro, counter | against, opposite | contradiction, controversy, counterfeit, counteract |
| de | away, down, from | deduction, deterrence, deviate |
| dis (di, dif) | apart, away; not; separate | disavow, disdain, disappear, disregard, disperse, discern |
| en (var. of in) | make, put into | enable, enhance, encourage |
| equ, equi | equal, even | equable, equanimity, equivalence, equivocate |
| ex (e, ef) | away from, out | efface, effective, ejection, exodus, expiration |
| in (il, im, ir) | in, within | immersion, impending, innate |
| in (il, im, ir) | not, without | illegible, imprudent, incognito |
| inter | among, between | intercede, intermediary, interim |
| magn | great | magnificence, magnanimous |
| mal | bad, evil | malevolent, malice, malefactor, malign, malignant |
| ob (oc, of, op) | to, toward; against; over; totally | objection; obdurate, obnoxious; obfuscate; obsolete, obliterate |
| omni | all | omnipotent, omniscient |
| per | completely; through | perceive, perdurable, pervasive |
| post | after | posterity, posthumous |

| | | |
|---|---|---|
| *pre* | before, in advance | pre-empt, preclude, premonition |
| *pro* | before, forward | proclivity, prodigy, profane |
| *re* | again | reiterate, reverberate, retort, revise, remember |
| *retro* | backward | retrogression, retroactive |
| *se* | apart, aside | secession, sedition, select |
| *sub (suf, sup, sus)* | from below, under | subsidize, substandard, suffuse, suppress, sustenance |
| *super* | above, over | supercilious, superfluous, supervise, supersede |
| *tra, trans* | across, beyond | transgression, transcend |

## GREEK PREFIXES

| Forms | Meaning | Examples |
|---|---|---|
| *a, an* | not, without | agnostic, anarchy, apathetic |
| *ana* | back, backward according to; through | anagram, anachronistic, anapest analogy, analysis |
| *ant, anti* | against, opposite | antipathy, antithesis, antipodes |
| *auto* | self | autonomous, autocracy |
| *cata* | down | cataclysm, catalyst, catastrophe |
| *dia* | through, between | dialect, dialogue, diameter |
| *dys* | bad, ill, difficult | dysfunctional, dyspeptic |
| *epi* | upon | epicenter, epigram, epilogue |
| *eu* | good, well | euphemism, euphoria, eugenics |
| *hetero* | different | heterodox, heterogeneous |
| *homo* | alike, same | homogeneous, homonym |
| *macro* | large, long duration | macrocosm, macroscopic |
| *meta, met* | after, beyond; changed | metaphor, metaphysical, metamorphosis |
| *micro* | small | microscope, microbe |
| *mon, mono* | one, single | monotheism, monolith |
| *pan* | all, complete | panacea, pandemonium |
| *pro* | before; favorable | prophecy; propitiate |
| *proto* | first, primary | protagonist, prototype |
| *sym, syn* | together, with | symmetry, synergy, synopsis |

* When you review the lists for study at the end of the chapter you will notice how many words in English are formed with these prefixes. Use those lists to add to the examples offered here.

Here is the first group of vocabulary words from the Regents exams list on page 149. Note how many are formed from the Greek or Latin prefixes reviewed on the previous pages.

| | | | |
|---|---|---|---|
| **ab**dicate | **ad**monish | amorphous | aspire |
| **ab**errant | **ad**versity | **ana**chronistic | assay |
| **ab**horrent | **af**flict | **an**ecdotes | astute |
| abridgment | agrarian | animation | asylum |
| absolve | **al**lot | **ap**pease | atrocious |
| acclaim | **al**lure | **ap**prehend | audacity |
| accost | **al**ly | arbitrator | **auto**nomous |
| accredit | **alter**cation | archaic | avarice |
| acme | amass | ardent | averse |
| acquiesce | **ambi**ance | armistice | aversion |
| acquittal | **ambi**dextrous | **ar**ray | avidly |
| adage | **ambi**guous | **ar**rogantly | azure |
| adhere | **ambi**valent | ascendancy | |
| **ad**junct | amnesty | ashen | |

In many of these examples, the meaning of the original prefix has been absorbed into the meaning of the entire word, in **adage** and **allot**, for example. The highlighted prefixes illustrate, however, how extensively Greek and Latin forms are found in English.

# A NOTE ON SYNONYMS AND USING A THESAURUS

As thoughtful students and careful writers know, synonyms are rarely equivalents. Synonyms are words closely related in meaning to a given word, but they should not be considered equally interchangeable with it.

Here is a list of synonyms for **acquiesce** that you might gather from a thesaurus:

| | | | |
|---|---|---|---|
| accede | capitulate | concur | permit |
| accept | come to terms | conform | submit |
| agree to | with | consent | surrender |
| allow | comply with | give in | yield |
| assent | concede | grant | |

This list is very helpful in enriching your understanding of the word, especially because it includes several terms that emphasize that there is a sense of giving in, of reluctance, in **acquiesce**. The closest synonyms in this list are *accede, come to terms with, conform, give in, yield. Capitulate, submit,* and *surrender* accurately reflect the connotation of the word, but they denote a more forceful sense of defeat than does *acquiesce*. The others, *accept, agree to, concur, consent, permit*, are less precise because they reflect only the general meaning and do not denote the sense of reluctance and the lack of enthusiam inherent in **acquiesce**.

Learning to distinguish among variations in meaning and context is an important part of developing your vocabulary. It is also essential to the craft of good writing. In Chapter 6, Writing About Literature, and Chapter 7, Writing on Demand, you will find several *synonymies*, which are words grouped by general meaning or connotation. The purpose of the *synonymies* is to help you develop precision and variety in your own writing. You should review those as part of your vocabulary study as well.

# ORGANIZING VOCABULARY STUDY

Another way to work with lists such as the ones at the end of this chapter is to *sort* them, much as you would sort playing cards. Depending on the card game you are playing, you might sort a hand by suit, by numerical sequence, or by kind. You can sort a group of words in various ways as well: by part of speech, by connotation, by human or abstract qualities, and so on. Many students create their own flash cards for the words they study, which makes sorting in various ways easy.

Here are some suggestions for how you might sort the first group of words from the Regents list (page 149). First, sort by part of speech. In the list below, the *verbs* are printed in bold type:

## VERBS

| | | | |
|---|---|---|---|
| **abdicate** | adversity | anecdote | asylum |
| aberrant | **afflict** | animation | atrocious |
| abhorrent | agrarian | **appease** | audacity |
| abridgment | **allot** | **apprehend** | autonomous |
| **absolve** | allure | arbitrator | avarice |
| **acclaim** | **ally** | archaic | averse |
| **accost** | altercation | ardent | aversion |
| **accredit** | **amass** | armistice | avidly |
| acme | ambiance | **array** | azure |
| **acquiesce** | ambidextrous | arrogantly | |
| acquittal | ambiguous | ascendancy | |
| adage | ambivalent | ashen | |
| **adhere** | amnesty | **aspire** | |
| adjunct | amorphous | **assay** | |
| **admonish** | anachronistic | astute | |

143

Then classify the group of verbs further as either *transitive* or *intransitive;* that is, according to the nature of the action they denote and the nature of the objects, if any, they take. When you look up these words in a dictionary, they will be identified as *v.i.* or *v.t.* Transitive verbs (*v.t.*) take a direct object; the action is directed from the subject to an object. For example, "She *admonished* (scolded, warned) the unruly child" and "King Midas *amassed* (accumulated) a fortune in gold." *Direct objects*, of course, may be persons and living creatures, or they may be things, even abstractions: "She quickly *apprehended* the danger she was in."

*Intransitive verbs* (*v.i.*) denote actions that are contained within the subject or that signify what we call states of being: "He *adhered* strictly to his ethical principles." *Adhere* connotes a state of mind, an attitude.

The distinction between transitive and intransitive action is not always easily made, but one way to demonstrate the difference is to make an active statement passive. For example, we can reverse the statement "She admonished the child" and turn it into "The child was admonished by her." The statement above about King Midas can be expressed in the passive as "A fortune in gold was amassed by King Midas." Although transitive actions may be reversed in this way, intransitive actions do not reverse. For example, the sentence "The principles were adhered by him" has no meaning. Some verbs may function both as transitive and intransitive. A simple example is the verb *to sink*: "The small sailboat sank during the heavy storm" (*v.i.*), but "The submarine fired a torpedo that sank the enemy battleship." (*v.t.*).

Most verbs in this first group are transitive, so it would be useful to sort them by the kinds of objects they take; that is, whether they denote actions directed at persons or at things and abstractions. You would, of course, note this information as you look up each unfamiliar word in a dictionary. Here is the list of verbs further sorted:

## ACTIONS DIRECTED AT PERSONS

to **absolve** (free from, relieve) someone of guilt or responsibility

to **acclaim** (praise, honor) a person's performance, action, or work

to **accost** (approach, confront) someone

to **admonish** (caution, scold) someone for misbehavior or inaction

to **afflict** (burden, attack) someone with suffering or illness

to **appease** (conciliate) a person, a nation, or a government

to **apprehend** (catch, capture) a suspect or a criminal

## ACTIONS DIRECTED AT THINGS OR ABSTRACTIONS

to **abdicate** (relinquish, abandon) a throne, a responsibility

to **accredit** (certify, recognize) a school or university, the value of an idea

to **allot** (distribute, assign) funds, resources

to **amass** (gather, accumulate) a fortune, an army

to **append** (add, match) a section, passage, body of information

to **apprehend** (understand, comprehend, capture) an idea, a concept

to **articulate** (verbalize, clarify, explain) ideas, feelings, understanding

to **array** (arrange) a display, a number of objects

to **assay** (measure, evaluate) a task, a situation

to **assert** (declare, claim, affirm, profess) ideas, an opinion, a judgment

## INTRANSITIVE ACTIONS

to **acquiesce** (give in to, agree reluctantly) in demands of others

to **adhere** (hold, cling to, comply) to demands or to principles

to **ally** (join, support) with another person, group, or nation

to **aspire** (strive, seek) to a goal, an achievement

For purposes of study, these verbs could be shuffled, and then resorted, by *connotation*. Which are generally positive in feeling and association, and which are negative? There are many words for which this is not a useful distinction, but appreciation of connotation is often essential to fully understanding the meaning of a word.

## POSITIVE

| | | |
|---|---|---|
| absolve | accredit | ally |
| acclaim | adhere | aspire |

## NEGATIVE

| | | |
|---|---|---|
| abdicate | acquiesce | afflict |
| accost | admonish | appease |

As you make your notes or compose your flash cards, be sure to include connotation if it is relevant. A dictionary usually does not define a word by its connotation; you must infer it from the meanings and examples offered.

## NOUNS

The *nouns* are in bold type:

| | | | |
|---|---|---|---|
| abdicate | **adversary** | anachronistic | aspire |
| aberrant | **adversity** | **anecdote** | **assay** |
| abhorrent | afflict | **animation** | assert |
| **abridgment** | affluent | appease | astute |
| absolve | agrarian | append | **asylum** |
| **acclaim** | allot | apprehend | atrocious |
| accost | **allure** | apprehensive | **audacity** |
| accredit | **ally** | **arbitrator** | autonomous |
| **acme** | **altercation** | archaic | **avarice** |
| acquiesce | amass | ardent | averse |
| **acquittal** | **ambiance** | **armistice** | **aversion** |
| **adage** | ambidextrous | **array** | avidly |
| adamant | ambiguous | arrogant | azure |
| adhere | ambivalent | articulate | |
| adjunct | **amnesty** | **ascendancy** | |
| admonish | amorphous | ashen | |

As you look at a collection of nouns, try to group them in various ways based on the kinds of things or persons they name. Note that in this group only two, **adversary** and **arbitrator,** name persons. This list, however, includes several political or legal terms that would form a useful group for study:

| | |
|---|---|
| **acquittal** | **arbitrator** (arbitration) |
| **adversary** (adversarial) | **armistice** |
| **ally** | **ascendancy** |
| **amnesty** | **asylum** |

A small group of terms is related to literature:

| | | |
|---|---|---|
| **abridgment** | **adage** | **anecdote** |

Other terms name attitudes or feelings. (Note the contrast in connotation here.)

## POSITIVE

acclaim                animation

## NEGATIVE

audacity          aversion          avarice

Finally, there are nouns that name forces, situations, conditions, and other concepts.

acme              ambiance        allure              array

## ADJECTIVES

The *adjectives* are in bold type:

| | | | |
|---|---|---|---|
| abdicate | adversary | **anachronistic** | aspire |
| **aberrant** | adversity | anecdote | assay |
| **abhorrent** | afflict | animation | assert |
| abridgment | **affluent** | appease | **astute** |
| absolve | **agrarian** | append | asylum |
| acclaim | allot | apprehend | **atrocious** |
| accost | allure | **apprehensive** | audacity |
| accredit | ally | arbitrator | autonomous |
| acme | altercation | **archaic** | avarice |
| acquiesce | amass | **ardent** | **averse** |
| acquittal | ambiance | armistice | aversion |
| adage | **ambidextrous** | array | avidly |
| **adamant** | **ambiguous** | **arrogant** | **azure** |
| adhere | **ambivalent** | articulate | |
| **adjunct** | amnesty | ascendancy | |
| admonish | **amorphous** | **ashen** | |

Because adjectives modify—that is, qualify, limit, or describe—nouns, a useful way to group them is by the nature of what they describe. For example, some of the adjectives in the list above describe human behavior or *actions*:

**aberrant**          **abhorrent**          **atrocious**

(all strongly negative in connotation)

Several adjectives describe human *attitudes, feelings, aspects of character*:

## NEGATIVE

adamant          ambivalent          arrogant

## POSITIVE

ardent          astute          avid

Still others characterize *the way people appear or express themselves:*

ambiguous          ambivalent          apprehensive          averse

*Language* may be:

ambiguous          anachronistic          archaic

Two adjectives relate to color:

ashen          azure

One term, **ambidextrous,** describes a physical characteristic.

This particular group contains no adverb forms, but for many of the adjectives in the list, the adverb is formed by adding *-ly.* For example:

| | | |
|---|---|---|
| aberrantly | apprehensively | avidly |
| adamantly | astutely | |
| ambiguously | atrociously | |

**Reminder:** If you prepare your own note cards for study, be sure to include all forms of the word. For example, your notes for **ambivalent** (adj.) would also include **ambivalence** (n.). This is how the lists of academic vocabulary on page 128 are organized.

These groups overlap and should be combined in different ways as you work through larger numbers of words. The process of sorting, or reshuffling, as new categories and associations occur to you is a very effective way to learn new words. Each time you sort, you are actively thinking about a word in a particular context and are associating it with other words; this process is essential to making a word a permanent part of your reading and writing vocabulary.

# VOCABULARY FOR STUDY

Below are lists of words that have been collected from past Regents exams, Op-Ed pages, and book reviews. You will recognize many of them from the section on academic language.

## Vocabulary from Regents Exams

| | | | |
|---|---|---|---|
| abdicate | admonish | amorphous | aspire |
| aberrant | adversity | anachronistic | assay |
| abhorrent | afflict | anecdotes | astute |
| abridgment | agrarian | animation | asylum |
| absolve | allot | appease | atrocious |
| acclaim | allure | apprehend | audacity |
| accost | ally | arbitrator | autonomous |
| accredit | altercation | archaic | avarice |
| acme | amass | ardent | averse |
| acquiesce | ambiance | armistice | aversion |
| acquittal | ambidextrous | array | avid |
| adage | ambiguous | arrogantly | azure |
| adhere | ambivalent | ascendancy | |
| adjunct | amnesty | ashen | |
| | | | |
| badger | belied | blatant | breach |
| barrage | bemused | bleary | brevity |
| bask | benevolent | boisterous | |
| beguile | berate | brazen | |
| | | | |
| cache | charisma | commencement | converse |
| carnage | chasm | commiserate | convivial |
| celebrated | clandestine | conception | craven |
| chafe | clique | congeal | credence |
| chagrin | coalition | consecrate | crestfallen |
| charade | collate | constrict | cringe |
| | | | |
| dauntless | deified | desist | discreet |
| de facto | deluge | desolate | dissidence |
| debonair | delve | deter | dissuade |
| decrepit | demeaning | detest | divulge |
| deduce | denizen | diffuse | domain |
| deferred | depict | dilemma | dredge |
| deflect | deride | diminutive | dynamic |
| defunct | derogatory | discord | |

| | | | |
|---|---|---|---|
| eccentric | encore | envoy | euphoric |
| edify | endorse | equanimity | eviction |
| eject | endow | equilibrium | exemplary |
| elicit | enfeeble | equitable | exodus |
| elude | enhance | equivocal | exonerate |
| elusive | ensnare | eradicate | expedite |
| embroil | entail | erratic | exploitation |
| eminence | entreaty | escapade | exulted |
| | | | |
| facet | feasible | flail | fortitude |
| fallible | fiasco | fleeting | fortuitous |
| fanatic | fidelity | forage | fracas |
| fanfare | finesse | foreboding | frugal |
| farcical | finite | formidable | futility |
| | | | |
| garish | genuine | grate | guise |
| garrulous | geriatric | gratuity | guttural |
| gaudy | gesticulate | grievously | |
| genial | grapple | grisly | |
| | | | |
| hallowed | harrowing | heretical | homage |
| harangue | heinous | hinder | humid |
| | | | |
| idiosyncrasies | impertinent | indisputably | insomnia |
| ignoble | imprudent | induce | insubordinate |
| illuminate | inadvertent | infernal | insurgent |
| immutable | inaugural | infringe | inundated |
| impartial | incensed | ingenuity | invoked |
| impending | incessant | inherent | irate |
| imperative | incognito | inimitable | irksome |
| imperceptible | incompetent | innocuous | irrational |
| imperiled | incorrigible | insatiable | itinerant |
| imperious | indignant | insolent | |
| | | | |
| jeer | jovial | jut | |
| jocular | juncture | | |
| | | | |
| lacerated | latent | lesion | lucrative |
| lackluster | lateral | lineage | lugubrious |
| lament | lavish | liquidate | lull |
| languorously | laxity | loquacious | |

madcap
maim
malefactor
malice
malleable

marauding
martial
meager
mediate
melancholy

meticulous
militant
misconstrue
misgivings
mitigate

mollify
morose
mortify
mundane
muzzle

nefarious
negligible
nepotism

niche
nimble
nonentity

nostalgia
notorious
nullification

nuptial
nurture

obliquely
obliterate
obstinate
oligarchy

omnipotent
omniscient
onslaught
opportune

optimum
oscillate
oust
ouster

override

pacifism
palatable
pandemonium
parable
paraphrase
penchant
perjury
perpetual

perplexity
philanthropic
piety
pinnacle
placid
plague
plausible
plight

poise
precariously
precipice
precludes
prestige
prevail
procrastinate
prodigious

profoundly
proponent
protrude
prowess
proxy
putrid

qualms

quandary

ramification
rampant
ramshackle
rancid
rant
rapport
ravenous

recalcitrant
reciprocal
recoil
recrimination
rectify
refute
reminiscent

reparation
repercussion
repress
resolute
retort
revamped
reverberate

revulsion
roster
rouse
rue
ruinous
russet

sacrosanct
salve
sanction
sanctity
saunter
scandalous
scathing
scrupulous
scrutiny
seedy

sheen
shortcomings
shrewd
singularly
skeptical
skulk
sleek
slipshod
smolder
sporadic

squalor
stalwart
stark
stealthily
strew
strut
subliminal
submissive
subside
subsidize

substantiate
subtlety
sullen
sumptuous
superfluous
suppress
surcease
surreptitious
swagger
synopsis

tainted     throng     transient     trudge
tally     token     trauma     tumult
tawny     topple     traverse
tenacity     transcend     trifling

unassuming     unnerve     unpalatable     utilitarian
uncanny     unobtrusive     unscrupulous

vanquish     verbatim     viable
variance     verbose     vigilance
vehement     veritable     virtually

waive     whack     wrangle
warily     wield     wrath
weather (vb.)     wily     writhe

yield

zenith

# Vocabulary from Op-Ed Pages

a priori     ad hoc     amiss     arcane
abdicate     adamant     amorphous     archetype
aberration     addled     androgyny     archive
abrogation     aegis     annals     ardent
abysmal     affidavit     annotate     artifice
abyss     affront     anoint     ascribe
accede     aggrieved     antidote     assessment
acclimate     agnostics     antipathy     assimilate
accolade     albeit     apathy     assuage
accrue     alleviate     append     asylum
acrimonious     allude (to)     arbiter     au courant
actuary     amalgamation     arbitrage     audit
acumen     ambivalence     arbitrary     autonomous

barrage     berth     blighted     bureaucrats
beguile     besmirch     blunder     burgeoning
beleaguered     bias     brass (slang def.)
benighted     bipartisan     brute (vb.)
bereft     blatant     budgetary

| | | | |
|---|---|---|---|
| cacophony | civics | concubine | convocation |
| cajole | clandestine | condone | covet |
| callous | clerical | confrere | crafty |
| canard | coda | conspiratorial | craven |
| candor | coffer | constituent | credibility |
| canonical/canon | collusion | contemporaries | cul-de-sac |
| capitulate | compliant | contend | cupidity |
| cataclysmic | complicit | contender | curtail |
| caveat | compound (vb.) | contingent | cushy |
| censure | compulsion | conundrum | cynical |
| chasm | concede | convene | cynicism |
| chimera | conciliate | conversant | |
| circumspect | conciliatory | conversely | |

| | | | |
|---|---|---|---|
| daunting | demur | despot | dispirit |
| debase | demystify | deter | disposition |
| decadence | denounce | detract | disquieting |
| decibel | denuded | didactic | dissemble |
| decree | denunciation | disavow | disseminate |
| decry | deplorable | discernible | dissident |
| deferment | depredation | discourse | dissipate |
| defrocked | deprivation | discretion | diversity |
| defunct | derail | discretionary | don (vb.) |
| deluded | derangement | disenchantment | doting |
| demagogue | deregulation | disingenuous | Draconian |
| demise | deride | disjointed | |
| demonize | derisive | dispel | |

| | | | |
|---|---|---|---|
| earmark | enclave | equivocate | exorbitant |
| egregious | enfranchise | eradicate | expenditure |
| electorate | enmesh | erode | expostulate |
| elixir | ennobling | ethos | expunge |
| eminence | ennui | eugenics | exude |
| empathetic | envoy | eviscerate | |
| empathy | epitomize | exhort | |
| encapsulate | equanimity | exonerate | |

| | | | |
|---|---|---|---|
| fallacious | firebrand | forlorn | frothing |
| farcical | fiscal | formidable | furor |
| fedora | flounder (vb.) | formulate | fusillade (fig.) |
| feint | flummoxed | fray (n.) | futility |
| fiasco | fodder (fig.)* | frenetic | |
| finagle | folly | fritter (vb.) | |

---

*In this case, consider the figurative meaning of the words.

| | | | |
|---|---|---|---|
| gaffe | gaudy | gouging | gubernatorial |
| gag rule | gauge | grapple | guffaw |
| galvanize | gerrymander | grim | |
| garner | glut | grotesque | |

| | | | |
|---|---|---|---|
| habeus corpus | hapless | hectoring | hubris |
| hackneyed | harbor (vb.) | heresy | hyperbole |
| hamlet | heckle | hoosegow (slang) | |

| | | | |
|---|---|---|---|
| iconography | importune | indignity | insular |
| ideological | impunity | ineptitude | integrity |
| idiosyncratic | incendiary | infiltrate | interlocking |
| idyllic | incessant | infirmity | intransigence |
| ignominious | incipient | inflationary | inure |
| ilk | incite | infuse | invaluable |
| impede | incontrovertible | inherent | inviolate |
| imperil | incumbent | innuendo | irk |
| implement (vb.) | indefatigable | inquisitorial | irredentism |
| implicit | indigenous | insignia | |

| | | | |
|---|---|---|---|
| lacerate | largess | leery | lout |
| laconic | latent | leitmotif | lucid |
| lambaste | laureate | levitate | |
| languish | lebensraum | litany | |

| | | | |
|---|---|---|---|
| malady | maudlin | molder | mortar |
| malaise | megalomaniac | monolith | murky |
| malign | meritorious | morass | myopic |
| manifestation | meticulous | moratorium | |
| mantra | milieu | moribund | |
| martyr | mimesis | morose | |

| | | |
|---|---|---|
| nadir | nexus | nuance |
| nascent | nomadic | |

| | | | |
|---|---|---|---|
| obfuscate | odious | oppression | overweening |
| obsolescence | ominous | outlay | |
| obstreperous | omnipresent | overhaul | |
| oddity | oncology | overt | |

| | | | |
|---|---|---|---|
| palliative | perennial | plunder | prohibitive |
| panacea | peripheral | pogrom | proliferate |
| pandering | pernicious | polarization | proliferation |
| paradox | peroration | polemic | propensity |
| paramount | perpetuate | polyglot | protocol |
| parochial | perquisite | portend | provocation |
| parsimonious | perversion | pragmatism | prurience |
| partisan (adj.) | pillage | prattle | psyche |
| passel | pinnacle | preeminent | pugnacity |
| pathology | pious | preempt | pundit |
| patrician | pique | preclude | purport |
| pedantic | placable/placate | presage | purvey/purveyor |
| peevish | plaudits | probity | pusillanimous |
| pejorative | plight | profound | pyrotechnics |
| penchant | plummet | progeny | |

| | | |
|---|---|---|
| quagmire | quaver | quintessential |
| qualm | quibble | |

| | | | |
|---|---|---|---|
| rabid (fig.) | recidivism | resolute | rhetoric |
| rakish | reconcile | resonance | rifle (vb.) |
| rancor | rectitude | restorative | rogue |
| rapacious | rejoinder | retributive | rudimentary |
| rapprochement | relegate | reverberate | ruse |
| raucous | reparations | reverence | |
| *realpolitik* | replete | revile | |

| | | | |
|---|---|---|---|
| salve (vb.) | siphon | staid | sullen |
| sartorial | snare | stark | summarily |
| sashay | snide | staunch | sumptuary |
| scion | sobriquet | steely eyed | sunder |
| scoff | sophomoric | stint | supersede |
| scourge | sordid | stipend | supplant |
| seamy | sorghum | strident | surfeit |
| self-effacing | sovereignty | stringent | swindle |
| sham | spate | stymie | sword of |
| shaman | speculative | subsidize | Damocles |
| shore up | staggering | substantive | sycophant |
| shudder | stagnation | subterfuge | synergy |

| | | | |
|---|---|---|---|
| temporal | throng | tout | troupe |
| temporize | thwart | transgression | tsunami |
| tenacity | torpor | transitory | turbulent |
| tendentious | totter | treacherous | |

undergird
undermine
undiluted

unduly
unencumbered
unfettered

unilateral
universality
unprecedented

unrelenting
unscrupulous
usurp

vagaries
venality
veracity
verdant

vestige
vexing
viable
victimize

vigilante
vilify
visceral
vituperation

volatile
voyeurs

waffling
wallow
wastrels

welter
wheedling
winnow

writ
writhe
wrongheaded

xenophobia

zeal

zeitgeist

# Vocabulary from Book Reviews

accolade
accretion
accrue
acerbic
acolyte
acrimonious
acumen
adage
adduce
adherent

adumbrate
adversity
aesthetic
albeit
alluring
amatory
amiable
amok
anapest
ancillary

animus
annotate
antipodes
aphrodisiac
aplomb
apotheosis
arbiter
arbitrary
archaic
ardor

arduous
arsenal
ascetic
asinine
aspire
attenuate
austere
authorial

banal
barren
bathetic
bedraggled

bemused
bestiality
bevy
bifurcation

blight
blithe
bohemian
boorish

boulevardier
bowdlerize
Byzantine

cache
cadence
canny
catharsis
caveat
chafe
charisma
chastening
chastise

chic
clandestine
cleric
cloying
coffer
cohere
coherence
colloquial
compendious

compendium
complicity
congenial
consign
contend
contrivance
copious
counterpoise
covert

credo
cribbed
crotchety
cupidity
curmudgeon
cursory

| | | | |
|---|---|---|---|
| dash | demigod | dichotomy | divagation |
| daunting | denouement | didactic | divergence |
| debunk | deploy | discursive | droll |
| deft | despotic | dispense | duplicity |
| delineate | detritus | dispossess | dysfunctional |
| delude | devolve | dither | dystopia |
| | | | |
| eccentric | ensconce | esoteric | exigency |
| eclectic | entreaty | espouse | existential |
| edify | envisage | esthetic | expansive |
| egregious | epigraph | ethereal | expatriate |
| elegy | epitomize | ethos | expurgate |
| elocution | equanimity | evangelical | exultant |
| elucidate | eradicate | evocative | |
| enclave | Eros | exacerbate | |
| encomium | eschew | exhort | |
| | | | |
| fabulist | farce | foray | fruition |
| facsimile | fervid | forbearance | furtive |
| faction | florid | formulaic | |
| | | | |
| galvanize | gorgon | guile | |
| gamut | grapple | gustatory | |
| | | | |
| hackneyed | harrowing | hewn (details) | |
| hagiography | hedonism | | |
| | | | |
| iconoclast | implacable | ineffable | intercede |
| iconography | impresario | ineffectual | intractable |
| idiosyncratic | incoherent | inept | inured |
| idyll/idyllic | incongruous | inextricably | invidious |
| ignite (fig.) | incur | insidious | irreverent |
| imminent | indelible | insinuation | itinerant |
| imperative | indeterminate | insouciance | |
| impetus | indigenous | intelligentsia | |
| | | | |
| jarring | jettison | jostle | Joycean |
| | | | |
| kamikaze | | | |
| | | | |
| lacuna | largess | loquacious | lyricism |
| lament | libertine | Lothario | |
| languish | lilting | lucid | |
| lapidary | litigious | lucrative | |

157

| | | | |
|---|---|---|---|
| macabre | mawkish | minutiae | mosaic |
| malaise | melodrama | misogyny | muddle |
| malevolent | mendacious | mogul | murky |
| malign | mercurial | moldering | musing |
| manifold (adj.) | mien | mordant | muster |
| matrix | milieu | moribund | myopia |

| | | | |
|---|---|---|---|
| naiveté | natter | nonpareil | nuance |
| narcissistic | nihilism | non sequitur | |
| nascent | nimble | noxious | |

| | | | |
|---|---|---|---|
| obfuscation | opprobrium | ostensible | ostracize |

| | | | |
|---|---|---|---|
| palatable | penumbra | portent | prevaricate |
| pantheon | perdurable | portentous | prodigious |
| paradigm | peregrination | practitioner | prosaic |
| pathos | perennial | pragmatic | protean |
| paucity | petulance | prattle | punitive |
| pedagogical | piety | precocious | purport |
| pelt (vb.) | placebo | premonition | |
| penchant | plodding | prescient | |

| | | |
|---|---|---|
| querulous | quintessential | quotidian |
| query | quixotic | |

| | | | |
|---|---|---|---|
| rancor | recalcitrant | reverence | riveting |
| rapacious | recapitulate | revile | rudimentary |
| rapture | relegate | rhetorical | ruminate |
| rancor | repatriation | ricochet | |
| raucous | replete | riff | |
| reap | repository | risible | |

| | | | |
|---|---|---|---|
| sagacity | sedentary | stanch | sunder |
| salacious | self-effacement | standoffish | supercilious |
| sally forth | sepulchral | staunch | surreptitious |
| sap (vb.) | shaman | stilted | surrogate |
| savor | shenanigans | stultifying | symbiosis |
| scatological | snippet | sublimate | symmetry |
| scourge | solicitous | sublime | synoptic |
| scuttlebutt | spurn | subterfuge | |
| searing | squander | succumb | |

158

| | | | |
|---|---|---|---|
| taut | titillating | transient | trenchant |
| teeter | torpid | transitory | trilogy |
| temporal | tortuous | transmogrify | truism |
| thrall | traffic (vb.) | travail | tweak |
| throng | transcendent | treatise | |

| | | | |
|---|---|---|---|
| unabashed | uncanny | unfathomable | unflinching |

| | | | |
|---|---|---|---|
| vacillate | venality | vignette | vitriol |
| valediction | verisimilitude | vindictiveness | voluminous |
| vapid | vernacular | virtuosity | vortex |
| venal | vicissitude | vis à vis | votary |

| | | |
|---|---|---|
| waft | wend | withal |
| welter | whimsy | |

# Chapter 9

# GRAMMAR AND USAGE FOR THE CAREFUL WRITER: A GUIDE TO STANDARD WRITTEN ENGLISH

The grammar of a language is its logic. We observe the conventions of standard usage in order to write and speak clearly, in order to communicate precisely what we mean. This section reviews those aspects of grammar and usage you are expected to know and to apply.

On the Regents ELA exam, your command of the conventions—standard written English—is evaluated by how well you write the essay of argument and the text analysis. On the SAT, your command of the grammar and usage is assessed in the writing and language section and on the optional essay; the ACT exam includes a specific section on grammar and usage, sentence structure, and mechanics (see Chapter 10 for Punctuation Guidelines and Reminders).

None of these exams requires you to identify errors in usage by name, but a review of the essential terms and structures will help you to recognize errors and to understand how to correct them. What are the essentials?

## REVIEWING THE FUNDAMENTALS

### The Parts of Speech

Below are the parts of speech that you should review. These include the noun, pronoun, adjective, verb, and adverb, as well as conjunction, preposition, and interjection.

# NOUN

Names or identifies persons, creatures, objects, ideas. The articles *the, a, an* usually precede and signal a noun. For example:

| | | |
|---|---|---|
| book | education | history |
| child | English | politics |
| climate | happiness | woman |

# PRONOUN

Replaces or "stands in for" nouns or other pronouns already stated; the noun or pronoun referred to (replaced) is the **antecedent**.

*Subject Forms:*      I, you, he/she/it, we, you, they

*Object Forms:*      me, you, him/her/it, us, you, them

*Possessive Forms:*      mine, yours, his/hers/its, ours, yours, theirs

*Relatives:*      that, which, who, whom, whose, whoever, whomever

# ADJECTIVE

Modifies nouns, that is, it describes, limits, specifies, what a noun names. For instance:

| | | |
|---|---|---|
| *tall* woman | *young* child | *illustrated* book |
| *temperate* climate | *American* history | *public* education |

# VERB

Denotes any *action*: run, talk, think, intend, suggest, play, strike, have, do; or *state of being*: appear, seem, be, feel. The principal parts of a verb are as follows:

*Infinitive:*      to run, to talk, to think, to intend, to appear, to seem

*Simple past:*      ran, talked, thought, intended, appeared, seemed

*Present participle:*      running, talking, thinking, intending, appearing, seeming

*Past participle:*      (has) run, (has) talked, (has) thought, intended, appeared, seemed

## ADVERB

Modifies verbs; it indicates the manner, quality, or degree of an *action*.

run *swiftly*       talk *loudly*       think *clearly*

play *well*       strike *suddenly*

Adverbs also function as *intensifiers*; that is, they indicate the degree or intensity of modifiers, both adjectives and adverbs.

*rather* tall woman       *very* young child

talk *too* loudly       *nearly* complete project

## CONJUNCTION

A word that connects two or more words or groups of words.

*Coordinating conjunctions:*       and, but, yet, so, for

*Subordinating conjunctions:*       because, although, since, while, if, until, when, unless, before, after

There are a tall woman *and* a young child.

We will stay home *if* it rains.

*Because* he trains regularly, he plays well.

## PREPOSITION

Expresses relationships of time, space, or position.

| | | | |
|---|---|---|---|
| above | behind | in | under |
| across | beside | into | within |
| after | between | on | without |
| at | except | over | |
| before | for | to | |

## INTERJECTION

An expression that begins or interrupts a sentence to express a particular feeling.

*Ouch!*, that hurts.       *Oh*, how interesting!       *Bravo!*

# Phrases, Clauses, and Sentences

While we may express feelings and give commands with single words, our most useful expression is in words grouped in phrases, clauses, and sentences.

## PHRASE

A meaningful group of words. There are many kinds of phrases in English. Here are some common examples:

*A noun and its modifiers:*

the large brick building          the tall young woman

*A verb and its auxiliaries* (to show different tenses):

has run                          will arrive
should have been done

*A preposition and its object:*

across the room                  in the final chapter
down the hill                    on the roof

*A participle and its object or modifiers:*

opening the door carefully       sensing danger
returning after many years*      walking slowly

## CLAUSE

A meaningful group of words that contains a verb and its subject.
Clauses are *dependent* when they form only part of a complex sentence of more than one clause:

Because he was late, . . .        If it rains tomorrow, . . .

. . . when the plane arrives      . . . that you requested

Each of these expressions contains a verb and *its* subject, but you will notice that the sentence will not be complete—that is, the assertion will not be fully expressed or understood—until at least one additional clause is added.

---

* Note that prepositional phrases, which are modifiers because they function as adjectives and adverbs do, may be part of a larger participial phrase.

In these examples, one *independent* clause has been added to form a *complete sentence:*

[Because he was late], his appointment was canceled.

I will call you [when the plane arrives].

The book [that you requested] is now available.

A *sentence,* then, may be made up of a few words—a subject, and a predicate verb that establishes the action or state of being of the subject, and modifiers:

She ran.

The dog barked.

He was late.

The crowd cheered enthusiastically.

Or a sentence may be made up of more than one clause and contain several phrases as modifiers.

Because he was late, his appointment was canceled and had to be rescheduled for the following week.

The large crowd in the bleachers cheered enthusiastically as the home team took the field in the last inning.

Tests of standard usage are tests of how well you understand and can compose the many relationships of words, phrases, clauses, and sentences that make up standard written English.

Most of the problems in grammar and usage you are expected to recognize and be able to correct are considered "errors" because they result in a lack of clarity, even confusion, in the writer's expression.

Although writing that contains minor errors in standard usage may still be understood, careful writers seek expression that is precise and clear— even elegant—and that demonstrates their ability to use variety in language and structure. It is only through mastery of a wide range of expression that students may fully reveal their ideas, insights, and feelings.

# AVOIDING COMMON ERRORS IN WRITING

When we refer to errors in writing, we are referring to expressions that are illogical, inconsistent, vague, or imprecise. The elements of usage reviewed here are those that high school students should be able to recognize.

# Agreement of Subject and Verb

Agreement is a form of consistency and is one of the most basic elements of grammar. When you learn to conjugate verbs, for example, you are applying the concept of agreement. Singular subjects take singular verbs; plural subjects take plural verbs.

He speaks/they speak; One is/many are

Errors in agreement commonly occur in sentences where the subject follows the verb:

On the desk *are* my notebook, a few pencils, and the assignments for tomorrow.

"Desk" is not the subject of the verb; "notebook, pencils, assignments" is the subject, *they* are on the desk. In such inverted word order, the writer must think ahead to choose the correct form of the verb. Similarly:

There *seems* to be only *one answer*.

There *seem* to be *several ideas* worth considering.

Here *are* the *pieces* you have been looking for.

Agreement errors may also occur when a subject followed by a phrase precedes the verb:

*New York* with its many historical sites and tourist attractions *is* a fascinating city to visit.

His *many talents* in sports, academics, and student leadership *make* him a popular candidate.

Subjects may be expanded by such prepositional phrases as *along with, in addition to, as well as, together with.* These phrases, however, do not form part of the *grammatical* subject; they modify the subject:

*English,* as well as math, science, and social studies, *is* a required subject for most high school students.

*Evan,* along with several of his friends, *is* planning to visit colleges in the fall.

In some sentences, the subject may be modified by one or more clauses before the predicate verb is stated. In such sentences the writer must "remember" the actual subject before composing the correct form of the verb:

The *fact* that Americans must now compete in a global economy and must recognize the necessity for higher standards in our schools *has led* to educational reform in many states.

Many common pronouns are singular and must take a singular verb:

*Each one* of these books *is* worth reading.

*Every one* of us *is* prepared to contribute.

*None* of these solutions *is* acceptable. (No *one* is)

Note how agreement with correlatives *either/or, neither/nor* is achieved:

*Either* Susan or her brother *is* home now.

(Either Susan is . . . or her brother is)

*Neither* rain, nor sleet, nor snow *deters* us . . . .

When the correlative contains both a singular and plural expression, the verb agrees with the one closest:

Neither Susan nor her sisters *are* at home.

Either the members of the legislature or the governor *is* authorized to submit a budget.

Do not be confused when the predicate is completed with a plural expression:

His most reliable *source* of encouragement *is* friends and family.

To avoid the correct but awkward-sounding expression above, rewrite as follows:

His *friends and family are* his most reliable source of encouragement.

Collective nouns take singular verbs because all the "members" are understood to act as a single unit:

The *jury was* unanimous in its decision to acquit.

A school *board has* extensive responsibilities.

Our *family has agreed* on plans for the vacation.

The *team practices* for two hours every day.

When there is not such unity of action, you may use a plural verb:

The *jury are* not in unanimous agreement.

The *family are* expected to arrive at different times.

It is better, however, to avoid such awkward-sounding expressions by rewriting to make the plural idea clear:

*The members of the jury are* not in agreement.

*Players on the team are required* to keep their uniforms and equipment in good order.

*Family members are* expected to arrive at different times.

# Agreement of Pronoun and Antecedent

Because pronouns replace nouns or other pronouns, they must agree with their singular or plural antecedents.

*Evelyn* is very grateful to *her parents* for *their* constant support and encouragement.

Most pronoun/antecedent errors arise when we use the indefinite pronouns *anyone, anybody, everyone, everybody, someone, somebody, no one,* and so on. These pronouns are singular because they refer to *individuals:*

*Everybody* is responsible for *his* own work.

*Someone* has left *her* books on the floor.

If *anyone* calls while I am out, please tell *him* or *her* I will call back after lunch.

The common practice of replacing *him/her* with *them,* or *her/his* with *their,* solves the problem of choosing gender, but it is ungrammatical and illogical. The careful writer (and speaker) avoids these errors or rewrites:

Please tell *anyone who calls* that I will return at noon.

*Someone's books* have been left on the floor.

*Everyone* has individual responsibility for the assignments.

# Form of Pronouns

Use the subject forms when pronouns are *subjects* of verbs or identify the subject after a linking verb:

> *He and I* received the information we needed.
>
> *She* is the favorite candidate of the party.
>
> *He* is the head baseball coach.
>
> The head baseball coach is *he*.
>
> (Think of the verb *is* as an = sign.)

It is easy to avoid the awkward sound of the last sentence by choosing the preceding expression, which uses the pronoun first.

Pronouns as *objects* of verbs or prepositions must be in the object form:

> Please give *him* the information.
>
> Give the information to *them*.
>
> *Whom* did you see yesterday?

Errors often occur when we have pronouns preceded by a noun; the writer no longer "hears" the preposition and is reluctant to use the object form. But,

> Please give the information to Ellen and *him*. (to Ellen . . . to him)
>
> The host was very gracious to Ellen and *me*.
> (to Ellen . . . to me; *not* to Ellen and I)
>
> Just between you and me, this is simple.

We also use the object form with infinitives:

> We understand *her to be* the favorite candidate.
>
> We understand the favorite candidate *to be her*.

Remember to use the possessive form with *gerunds* ("-ing" verb forms that function as nouns):

> I do not approve of *your staying* out so late.
> (of your "late hours")
>
> She was concerned about *his working* too hard.
> (about his excessive work)

Note the following:

Mark's mother saw *him* [*running* after the bus].

Mark's mother encouraged [*his running* on the cross-country team].

In the first example, *running* is a participle describing *him*, which is the object of the verb *saw*. In the second example, *running* is a noun; it is the object of the verb *encouraged*.

# Parallelism

Parallelism is used for consistency and clarity. Parallel ideas and expressions in a series should be composed in the same form:

He wants to spend the summer *reading, sleeping, and traveling*.

He plans *to read, to sleep, and to travel*.

Use parallel phrases and clauses:

She is known *for* her talent and *for* her generosity.

We expect our presidents to be skilled *not only in* domestic affairs *but also in* foreign policy.

Our state senator was reelected *because* she is honest, *because* she works hard for the district, *and because* she has an important leadership position in the senate.

Use parallel construction when you use correlatives: *either, or; not only, but also:*

*Either* you will complete the work now, *or* he will complete it in the morning.

We will *either take* a train this afternoon *or take* a plane this evening.

Consistency of active and passive voice is also a form of parallelism:

The research team *formulated* its ideas and *developed* its proposal.

Ideas *were formulated* and a proposal *was developed* by the research team.

# Verbs: Using the Correct Tense

Use the simple past tense for actions completed in the past:

> The train *arrived* at 6:30.
>
> He *retired* in 1993.
>
> The Nobel prizes *were announced* in January.

Use the present perfect tense to establish facts, to assert that something *has occurred, has happened, has been done*, without reference to a specific time.

> *Have you done* your homework yet?
>
> The renovation of our house *has been completed*.
>
> I *have read* Macbeth several times.

Note the correct *sequence of tenses* in the following:

> The novelist *completed* the book in 1993, two years after he *had begun* it.
>
> She *recorded* the names of everyone who *had called* the day before.

> In the Middle Ages, most people *believed* that the earth *is* round.
>
> Copernicus *demonstrated* that the earth *orbits* the sun.

> If I *were* you, I *would accept* the offer.
>
> If the congressman *were indicted*, he *would* lose the support of many constituents.

> If we *had taken* more time to plan, our trip *would have been* more pleasant.
>
> If you *had trained* harder, you *would have* made the team.

*If you would have called earlier* is sometimes said but this is not an acceptable construction in standard English.

Finally, you are generally expected to write about works of literature in the *present tense*.

> Macbeth *is driven* by ambition.
>
> Jay Gatsby *believes* he can recreate the past.
>
> Willy Loman *dies* believing his son will achieve great success.

Aspects of character, themes, plot, and setting remain constant—they *are* what they are—regardless of how the plot concludes or when we finish reading the work.

## Logical Comparisons

My sister is *taller* than I [am].

She is *more* clever than he [is].

Josh is the *tallest* member of the team.

Among all of Miller's plays, *Death of a Salesman* is the *best* known.

Avoid incomplete comparisons in your writing:

Dreiser's novels are *more* popular now [than they were when they were first published].

Shakespeare's plays are *harder* to read [than modern works are].

The passages in brackets should be fully stated.
In informal speech we may use *so* as an intensifier:

I was *so* tired. He was *so* angry.

In writing, however, be sure every *so* is followed by a *that*, every *more* by a *than*.
Comparisons must be parallel and logical:

*The paintings of Monet are more popular than Goya* **should read**:

*The paintings* of Monet are more popular than *the paintings* of Goya.

You must compare paintings to paintings, not inadvertently compare paintings to a man.
And,

Anne is a better player than anyone on her team. **should read**:

Anne is a *better* player *than any other* [player] on her team.

or,

Anne is the *best player* on the team.

It is illogical to suggest Anne is better than she herself is.

# Clear and Logical Modification

The careful writer must also be aware of errors in modification and in the logical relationships of ideas. Many such errors are corrected simply, with commas; others may require revision or reorganization of sentences.

Introductory subordinate (dependent) clauses must be set off by a comma:

> *After the lights had come back on,* the children were no longer frightened by the thunderstorm.
>
> *When it rains,* cats and dogs prefer not to go outside.

Without the comma, such sentences would be ambiguous.

Nonrestrictive (nonessential) phrases and clauses are set off by commas:

> My aunt, *who lives in Milwaukee,* will be flying in for a weekend visit to New York.
>
> Several stranded passengers, *feeling restless and impatient,* demanded flights on another airline.

When such phrases or clauses are restrictive* (essential to the meaning of the sentence), do not set them off with commas:

> Passengers *traveling with small children* will be permitted to board the plane first.
>
> My cousin *who lives in Milwaukee* will have to fly, but the cousins *who live in the New York area* will be able to drive to my brother's wedding.

A common error occurs when we begin a sentence with a participial phrase:

> Feeling restless and impatient, seats were demanded on other airlines' flights [by many travelers].
> (The seats are not restless . . .)
>
> *Barking loudly,* we were afraid the dog would wake our neighbors.
> (We are not barking, the dog is . . .)
>
> *Tired and hungry,* even cold leftovers looked good to us.
> (The leftovers are not hungry, we are . . .)

---

*For additional examples, see *which/that/who* on page 181.

173

The *subject* of the participle must also be stated as the subject of the clause that follows:

> *Feeling restless and impatient, many stranded travelers* sought seats on other airlines' flights.
>
> *Barking loudly, the dog* wakened our neighbors.
>
> *Tired and hungry, we* were satisfied with the cold leftovers.

You may also recompose sentences to make the modification clear:

> We were afraid our dog, *barking loudly,* would wake the neighbors.
>
> *Because we were tired and hungry,* even cold leftovers looked good to us.

# EXPRESSIONS OFTEN CONFUSED, MISUSED, AND OVERUSED*

### accept/except

To **accept** is to receive, take willingly, agree to:

> I **accept** your offer, apology, invitation

To **except** is to exclude, to separate out:

> I will **except** you from the requirement.

**Except** is also a preposition:

> Everyone **except** him will be leaving on Tuesday.

### affect/effect

To **affect** (vb.) means to move, influence, or change. It also means to put on an artificial quality of personality or character; such an exaggerated or artificial person may be called **affected**.

An **effect** (n.) is a consequence or result.

To **effect** (vb.) means to put into action, to complete—a plan or a change, for example.

---

*See also Words Commonly Confused/Misspelled in Chapter 11, Spelling.

174

## aggravate

To **aggravate** means to make worse. Do not use it when you really mean to irritate or annoy.

## allusion/illusion

An **allusion** is a reference (see Glossary of Poetic Terms and Techniques, Chapter 5); an **illusion** is a false or deceptive idea or vision.

## among/between

Use **between** for two, **among** for three or more:

**between** you and me

**among** all the members of the family

## amount/number

One has an **amount** of something (the quantity as a whole) and a **number** of things (that can be counted):

an **amount** of time/a **number** of hours, days

a large **amount** of work/a **number** of tasks

See also **fewer/less** for the same distinction.

## as far as . . . is/are concerned

The expression **as far as** used by itself creates an incomplete and illogical statement; it must be completed with **is/are concerned.** The expression as **far as . . . goes/go** is also widely used and correct as completed.

*Faulty:* **As far as** plans for school construction in the future, we expect the legislature to take action in the next session.

**As far as** the weather, it will be sunny and pleasant tomorrow.

*Correct:* **As far as** plans for school construction in the future are concerned, we expect the legislature to take action in the next session

**As far as** the weather goes, it will be sunny and pleasant.

## bad/badly, good/well

Use **bad** and **good** (adjectives) to describe how one feels; use **badly** and **well** (adverbs) to describe how one does something.

He felt **bad** (sorry, regretful) because he caused the team to lose.

175

The team lost the game because he played so **badly**.

She feels **good** (in good spirits, positive) when her work is going **well**.

She is feeling **well** (no longer ill) now after a long bout with the flu.

The team lost because he did not play **well**.

### being as, being that

These expressions are not standard speech. Use *because* or *since* instead.

### compare to, compare with

Use **compare to** when you are expressing an analogy or similarity; use **compare with** when you are showing similarities and differences between two things.

He compared his small room **to** a closet.

The critics compared the movie **with** the book.

### could of/ should of

Do not make this unfortunate confusion in the way words sound! You mean **could have/should have**.

### different from (not **than**)

You should use the preposition **from** with **different** because you are making a distinction, a separation. Use **than** for comparisons, to show degrees of the same quality:

She is only slightly older **than** her sister, but her personality is very different **from** her sister's.

### due to

This expression is popularly used for almost any cause and effect relationship. Avoid its overuse in your writing:

Absence **due to** illness is excused.

Delays **due to** bad weather are common in winter.

It is more precise to say:

The road was closed **because of** an accident.

The defendant was acquitted **by reason of** insanity.

There were many landslides **caused by** the heavy rains.

176

### everybody, somebody, someone, nobody

These are *singular* forms; they may refer to many people, but they refer to *each one individually*. Singular antecedents take singular pronouns:

**Everybody** has *his/her* books, lunch, opinions.

**Someone, a person** has *his/her* opinions.

### farther/further

In general, you may use **farther** or **further** for actual or figurative distance:

The nearest town is ten miles **farther** from here.

The latest agreements move us **further** toward a full peace.

Use **further** when you mean more:

We have nothing **further** to discuss.

A final agreement requires **further** negotiations.

### fewer/less

One has **fewer** things and **less** something.

> **fewer** hours/**less** time
>
> **fewer** dollars/**less** money
>
> **fewer** ideas/**less** content

### first, second, . . .

To show transition and to enumerate examples, use these terms instead of *firstly, secondly,* . . .

### hang/hanged/hung

When we use this verb in the past tense to denote an execution, we use **hanged**; for such things as clothes and pictures, we use **hung**.

The condemned man was **hanged** at dawn.

We **hung** our winter coats in the hall closet.

### hopefully

This expression is popularly used to mean we hope, it is hoped, and so on. The careful writer should use it only as an adverb:

The cat looked **hopefully** at the leftover chicken.

But:

We **hope** the situation will improve.

**It is hoped** that research will lead to a cure.

## however

Along with its cousins *therefore, moreover,* and *consequently,* **however** should be placed *within the sentence*, close to the verb it modifies; think of it as a conjunction, not as a transition at the beginning of a sentence.

## if/whether

Use **if** to introduce conditional expressions; use **whether** (or not) for choices, decisions, questions:

**If** it rains, our game will be postponed.

**If** you work hard, you will succeed.

I do not know **whether** we will play or not.

## infer/imply

To **infer** is to conclude, to draw an inference from evidence; to **imply** is to suggest or hint.

We can **infer** from his comments that he is pleased.

She **implied** in her speech that she is planning to run for public office.

## its/it's

*it's* = a contraction* for it is.

*its* = a possessive form; do not add an apostrophe.

## if . . . were/if . . . was

Use the **if . . . were** construction for *hypothetical* conditions and situations:

**If you were** president, what would you do?

**If I were you,** I would accept the offer.

_____

*Contractions should be avoided in formal writing, unless you are quoting someone. Contractions are features of spoken language.

Use **if . . . was** for situations that *were possible*:

> **If** that really **was** Linda who called yesterday, she should have left a message.

### incredible/incredulous

**Incredible** means unbelievable, beyond belief or understanding. In formal writing, avoid using it as *hyperbole*. Use instead such terms as *astonishing* or *extraordinary*.

A person is **incredulous** when he/she utterly cannot believe what is being said.

### kind of/sort of/type of

Avoid using *a* or *an* with these expressions:

> **That type of** character is popular in children's books.
>
> **Those types of** characters are . . .
>
> **This kind of** fabric is best for the new sofa.

Also avoid using **kind of** or **sort of** when you mean *a little, rather, somewhat*.

### lie/lay

These verbs are often confused. Note their principal parts and distinctions in meaning: to **lie (down)** means to recline, be situated, rest:

> You **lie** on your bed to take a nap.
>
> The mail **has lain** on your desk since yesterday.
>
> Last winter the snow **lay** on the ground for weeks.

Note that to **lay** means to put or place something. (It is a transitive verb and always takes a direct object.):

> You can **lay** your hat and gloves on the hall table.
>
> Masons **lay bricks** and hens **lay eggs**.
>
> He cannot remember where he **laid** his car keys.

### like/as/as if

Use **like** as a preposition, use **as** and **as if** as conjunctions:

> He looks just **like** his father.
>
> A talent **like** hers is rare.

It looks **as if** it will rain this afternoon.

You should do the assignments **as** you were instructed to.

"Do **as** I say, not **as** I do!"

## only/just

These modifiers should be placed as close as possible to the expressions they actually limit:

I have **only** two dollars for lunch.

He has time for **only** a brief conversation.

I have **just** one thing to say.

## presently

This should be used to denote the immediate future; it means right *away* or in *a little while:*

I will answer your question **presently**.

He is expected to arrive **presently**.

The meeting will begin **presently**.

For current time, use **at present** or **currently**:

He is **currently** a junior at North High.

**At present**, she is working on her master's degree.

## purposely/purposefully

Use **purposely** to mean intentionally, knowingly, deliberately, that is, to describe an action done "on purpose" and not by accident.

**purposefully** is best used to mean decisively, firmly, resolutely, with determination, and with a specific purpose or goal in mind.

## so

Try to avoid the casual use of "so" just to introduce an idea or an explanation. "So" is widely used in informal speech to begin the answer to almost any question, but it should be avoided in your formal writing. Use *so* as a conjunction to show a consequence:

We were hungry, **so** we went to lunch early.

Our plane was delayed, **so** we spent several hours waiting at the airport.

**toward/towards**

Either is acceptable; **toward** is more formal.

**when/where**

These are terms of time and place; do not use them to introduce definitions.

**which/that/who**

These relative *pronouns* introduce *clauses* that describe or define. Use **that** for clauses that are *restrictive* (defining, limiting):

The books **that** you ordered will arrive tomorrow; the ones **that** Sam ordered will come next week. (those particular books . . .)

He likes the car **that** he bought last year better than any other he has owned. (that particular car )

Basketball is the game **that** he plays best.

Use **which** for clauses that are *nonrestrictive* (descriptive):

The house on the corner, **which** was built in the 1880s, will be restored to its original design.

Shakespeare's plays, **which** were written nearly 400 years ago, remain popular in theaters and movies as well as in English courses.

Use **who** for people. (**That** is sometimes used when the identification is distant or impersonal.) Do not use **which** for people:

Lady Macbeth is a character **that** (**who**) remains fascinating to many students.

Use **whom** when the pronoun is an object:

To **whom** should I give the information? (obj. of prep.)

**Whom** did you ask? (obj. of verb)

**who/whom/whoever/whomever**

When these *pronouns* introduce *clauses*, their form is determined *solely* by their function in the clause:

The new coach, **who** led the team to a county title, gave all the credit to her players.
(**Who** is the subject of the verb *led;* therefore, it is in the subject form.)

Please give the information to (**whoever** needs it.)

(**Whoever** is the subject in the clause; the *entire* clause is the object of *give to*.)

Please give the award to (**whomever** you choose.)
(**Whomever** is the object of the verb *choose;* the *entire* clause is the object of *give to*.)

Careful attention to the conventions of usage and style outlined in this chapter will enhance your ability to express ideas and discuss information clearly and persuasively. When you have command of the language you use, you have command of the relationship between thought and expression.

# Chapter 10

# PUNCTUATION: GUIDELINES AND REMINDERS

When is the semicolon or colon used? Are there any rules for commas? Do I underline titles of books and poems or put them in quotation marks? Where do I put the period when a sentence ends with quotation marks? Even experienced writers need to consult a usage handbook for the answers to some of these questions.

In conversation we use pauses, stresses, and tone of voice to make our meaning clear. The printed page, however, does not readily show what voice and gesture can reveal, so the writer uses punctuation to achieve absolute clarity. Below, you will find a review of the elements of punctuation high school students should know and use in their own writing. Featured are answers to those questions most often raised about how to punctuate. (Many of the examples from the writing of specific authors come from the passages reprinted elsewhere in the book.)

## END PUNCTUATION

The period, exclamation mark, and question mark bring statements and expressions to a close; they signal a full stop.

## The Period

Use a **period** to indicate the end of a sentence or of a group of words having the emphasis of a sentence.

*Declarative sentences* (make a statement):

Good writers are also good readers.

"Camp fires, like red, peculiar blossoms, dotted the night."
(Stephen Crane, *The Red Badge of Courage*)

*Imperative sentences* (give an order or direction):

Be sure to proofread.

Come to practice on time or leave the team.

Tell me how much I owe you.

*Fragments for emphasis:*

"No doubt my younger brother and sister were in the house and warm.
*Eating cookies.*" (William Kittredge)

"Much of their [whales'] behavior seems to be recreational: they sing,
they play. *And so on.*" (Robert Finch)

# The Exclamation Mark

Use an **exclamation mark** to show intensity and emphasis in sentences
or fragments.

Come to practice!

Be sure to proofread!

Look out!

Congratulations!

**CAUTION:** *Do not overuse the **exclamation mark** in expository writing;
use effective language and sentence structure to achieve emphasis.*

# The Question Mark

Use a **question mark** to signal interrogative forms in complete sentences, fragments, or series.

Can you explain how to do this?

Do you understand what he said?

Can you recommend a good restaurant in the theater district?

What was that all about? a joke? a mistake?

Where should we meet? at home? at school?

Ask questions as you read an essay: What is the author's purpose?
tone? conclusion? Do you agree? disagree? feel convinced?

Question marks may also be used with single words or phrases as needed:

When?

Leave the team?

You did?

What homework?

## SPECIAL CONSIDERATIONS

Periods are used in many abbreviations. For example:

| | |
|---|---|
| U.S. government | Dipl.  B.A.  M.A.  Ph.D. |
| U.N. Security Council | D.D.S.  M.D.  Esq. |
| N.Y.S. Board of Regents | A.M.  P.M. |

Some abbreviations take no periods:

| | |
|---|---|
| CIA | mph |
| MTV | rpm |
| WCBS | |

A sentence may end with more than one kind of punctuation. If it ends with an abbreviation using a period, do not add a second period.

Please report to my office promptly at 10:00 A.M.

In order to apply for a teaching position, you must have completed your M.A.

If it ends with a quotation or expression in quotation marks, place the final period *inside* the quotation marks.

Most high school students have read Poe's short story "The Cask of Amontillado."

When told his wife is dead, Macbeth remarks, "She should have died hereafter."

If the **entire sentence** requires a question mark, place it outside the quotation marks:

Have you read Poe's story "The Cask of Amontillado"?

Why does Macbeth say, "She should have died hereafter"?

If the quotation at the end of a sentence requires a question mark, keep it within the quotes. (Do not add an additional period.)

> The title of a recent editorial in *The New York Times* was "Where do we go from here?"

If a statement within the quotes is a question, the question mark within the quote is sufficient.

> Did you read the editorial entitled "Where do we go from here?"

Similarly, if an exclamation point is part of a quoted expression, place it within the quote. An additional period is not required.

> One of my favorite pieces by James Thurber is called "Excelsior!"

To make the above into a question, however:

> Have you read Thurber's story "Excelsior!"?

If a sentence ends with a passage in parentheses, put the period outside the closing parenthesis:

> We did not leave on time because Sally was late (as usual).

Even if the expression is a complete sentence, do not punctuate within the parentheses:

> We did not leave on time because Sally was late (she always is).

If, however, the expression within the parentheses requires quotation marks, a question mark, or an exclamation point, include them:

> We did not leave on time because Sally was late (isn't she always?).

In such cases, a better solution would be to separate the parenthetical statement:

> We did not leave because Sally was late. (Isn't she always?)

**What is the logic to all this?** When sentences or passages are made up of a variety of elements, punctuation should make the structure of each element clear. If the end of a sentence becomes cluttered by the need to bring several individual pieces to a close at the same time, punctuate from the inside out—smaller pieces first, then larger. But do not double the end punctuation unless it is required for accuracy. If you have a question within a question, one question mark will do. If a closing quotation ends with a "strong" piece of punctuation, don't add a modest and redundant period to the whole sentence. Close with the strength of the quote.

# INTERNAL PUNCTUATION

Internal punctuation includes the comma, the semicolon, the colon, and the dash. The single purpose of internal punctuation is to prevent confusion, to achieve clarity. The comma indicates brief pauses between separate elements in a sentence; the semicolon establishes a direct connection between two independent statements to form a single sentence; the colon serves to introduce things; and the dash permits you to digress or emphasize.

## The Comma

Use the comma in compound sentences with coordinating conjunctions *and, but, yet, so, or, for.* A compound sentence joins two or more independent clauses that could be expressed separately as simple sentences. *Note that the comma precedes the conjunction:*

"I walked slowly, *for* the detail on the beach was infinite." (Ernie Pyle)

"The luncheon hour was long past; *and* the two had their end of the vast terrace to themselves." (Edith Wharton, "Roman Fever")

"I was not going to talk about Whitewater today, *but* then I thought that if I didn't you'd think I know something about it, *and* the only way for me to prove that I don't is to talk about it at length, *so* I will." (Garrison Keillor)

In sentences where the clauses are short and the meaning is clear, you may omit a comma:

The team tied the score in the last seconds of the game and the crowd cheered wildly.

If there is any possibility of misreading, you must use a comma:

I went to the movies with Roger and Sally stayed home.

I went to the movies with Roger, and Sally stayed home.

# WHAT IS A COMMA SPLICE?

One of the most common errors in writing is the use of a comma alone to join independent clauses. This is the error familiar to students as the "run-on" sentence.

*Run on:*   The crowd cheered wildly, the game was tied in the last few seconds.

I went to the movies with Roger, Sally stayed home.

The novel was riveting, I did not want it to end.

*Correct:*   The crowd cheered wildly when the game was tied in the final seconds.

I went to the movies with Roger, and Sally stayed home.

The novel was riveting, so I did not want it to end.

# DO I USE A COMMA BEFORE THE LAST ITEM IN A SERIES?

Some editors and instructors insist that all items in a series be set off by a comma; others prefer that you omit the last one, especially in a series of single words:

You can find models of style in books, newspapers, and magazines.

You can find models of style in books, newspapers and magazines.

*SUGGESTION: For sentences like the one above, the second comma needlessly slows down the sentence and makes no contribution to clarity. In a series of longer expressions, however, or in a series without a conjunction, set off each with a comma.*

For class you are expected to bring a notebook, a pen or pencil, and the text we are reading.

"He was white-headed as a mountain, bowed in the shoulders, and faded in general aspect." (Thomas Hardy)

Writing has many purposes: personal expression, persuasion, literary effect, information.

## Use a Comma After Introductory Clauses

As the crowd cheered them on, the home team scored the winning touchdown.

If you are hungry, please help yourself to a sandwich.

"As the bell sounded the hour, there came a knocking at the street door." (Edgar Allan Poe)

Do not use a comma if the main clause is followed by a dependent clause:

Please help yourself to a sandwich whenever you get hungry.

The home team scored the winning touchdown as the crowd cheered them on.

## Use a Comma After an Introductory Phrase Only When Needed

At last, the rain began to ease, and the sun came through breaks in the clouds.

The son of a tanner, Grant was everything Lee was not.

After the Labor Day recess, Congress will reconvene.

Feeling ill and confused, he left the dinner table without speaking.

These sentences require no comma:

On the desk you will find your final check and a letter of recommendation.

"For a long time they continued to sit side by side without speaking." (Edith Wharton)

## Use Commas to Set off Descriptive and Nonessential Clauses or Phrases Within Sentences

"They were two strong men, these oddly different generals, and they represented the strengths of two conflicting currents that, through them, had come into final collision." (Bruce Catton)

The house on the corner, which was built in the 1880s, will be restored to its original design.

Shakespeare's plays, written nearly four hundred years ago, remain popular in theaters and movies as well as in English courses.

## USE COMMAS WITH SOME SINGLE WORDS AND EXPRESSIONS

"Well, Jim's habits and his jokes didn't appeal to Julie . . ." (Ring Lardner, "Haircut")

"Now, I'll read the names—heads of families first." (Shirley Jackson, "The Lottery")

## USE COMMAS WITH PARENTHETIC AND TRANSITIONAL EXPRESSIONS

Use commas to set off such expressions as *however, moreover, therefore, nevertheless, after all, by the way, of course, on the other hand, I think.*

"Yet it was not all contrast, after all . . . Furthermore, their fighting qualities were really very much alike." (Bruce Catton)

After all, what you learn is what really matters.

You must, of course, always proofread a paper before handing it in.

## COMMAS IN DATES

For expressions of day, month, and year:

July 4, 1776, marks the beginning of the American Revolution.

Registration will take place on September 9, 1994, for the fall semester and on January 12, 1995, for the spring semester.

Do not use commas for expressions of month and year only.

Joan completed graduate school in June 1987, began her legal work in September 1987, and joined our firm in January 1993.

## COMMAS WITH ADJECTIVES IN A SERIES

Use a comma when it means *and:*

The little room in Appomattox was "the scene of one of the poignant, dramatic contrasts in American history." (Bruce Catton)

The Regents examinations require you to write thoughtful, well-organized essays.

Do not use a comma if the adjective is part of the meaning of the noun:

She greeted her guests in the large sitting room.

## USE COMMAS TO SET OFF QUOTES

"I always used to think," Mrs. Slade continued, "that our mothers had a much more difficult job than our grandmothers." (Edith Wharton, "Roman Fever")

"It isn't fair, it isn't right," Mrs. Hutchinson screamed, and then they were upon her. (Shirley Jackson, "The Lottery")

## ADDITIONAL ILLUSTRATIONS OF COMMA USE

If you must sing, sing quietly.

These incidents took place a long, long time ago.

That's not what you meant, is it?

You have everything you need, don't you?

First come, first served.

Now you see it, now you don't.

Shakespeare's tragedy, *Macbeth*, is one of his best-known plays.

Verdi's only comic opera, *Falstaff,* is the last work he composed.

My sister Anne lives in Seattle; my sister Julia lives in New York.

My only sister, Anne, lives in Seattle.

## COMMON ERRORS IN COMMA USE

Do not separate compound elements or isolate essential elements with commas.

*Correct:*    "They greeted one another and exchanged bits of gossip as they went to join their husbands." (Shirley Jackson, "The Lottery")

*Faulty:*    They greeted one another, and exchanged bits of gossip as they went to join their husbands.

*Alternative:*   *They greeted* one another, and *they exchanged* bits of gossip as they went to join their husbands.

*Correct:*   "Whales possess a highly complex language and have developed sophisticated communications systems that transmit over long distances." (Robert Finch)

*Faulty:*   Whales possess a highly complex language, and have developed sophisticated communications systems, that transmit over long distances.

*Alternative:*   *Whales possess* a highly complex language, *and they have developed* sophisticated communications systems that transmit over long distances.

In the faulty examples, the first comma may *look* necessary, but it improperly separates the subject from the second verb; the final clause in each case is essential description and should not be separated from the rest of the sentence. The alternative versions are accurately punctuated and show how the original, correct sentences could be revised into compound sentences.

*SUGGESTION: In all the examples and explanations above, the commas serve one purpose: to make the expression clear on first reading. Insert commas in your own writing as you compose, as you hear the need for them. When you revise, do not be tempted to add commas simply because they look right—chances are, they do not belong.*

# The Semicolon

A comma indicates a brief pause between separate elements in a sentence, whereas a semicolon indicates a longer pause between independent statements that form a single sentence. The semicolon may replace *and* or *but* in compound sentences. Here are some of the examples used earlier now revised with semicolons.

I walked slowly; the detail on the beach was infinite.

The luncheon hour was long past; the two had their end of the vast terrace to themselves.

I was not going to talk about Whitewater today; then I thought that if I didn't, you'd think I know something about it; the only way for me to prove that I don't is to talk about it at length; so I will.

In each of these revisions, you will note that the effect of the semicolon is to indicate a cause and effect relationship or to show consequence without stating it directly. This results in forceful and emphatic sentences.

The semicolon also has a formal quality; it creates a feeling of balance and equivalence among statements.

> ". . . with a semicolon . . . you get a pleasant little feeling of expectancy; there is more to come; read on; it will get clearer." (Lewis Thomas)

## The Colon

Use the colon to introduce something: a list, the body of a letter, a quotation, or an explanation.

> "Political courage stems from a number of sources: anger, pain, love, hate." (Madeleine Kunin)

> "Mrs. Slade began again: 'I suppose I did it as a sort of joke'—" (Edith Wharton)

> "The purpose of life is to be useful. It is, above all, to *matter:* to have it make some difference that you lived at all." (Leo Rosten)

## The Dash

The dash permits you to pause without notice and insert an idea too interesting to delay and too important to put in parentheses—but don't overdo it!

> "At some gut level, the art of politics—combative, competitive, self-asserting—is sometimes difficult to integrate with our feminine selves." (Madeleine Kunin)

> "Different as they were—in background, in personality, in underlying aspiration—these two great soldiers had much in common." (Bruce Catton)

> "The wonder of ourselves, of each other, and of life—this is the true subject matter of all novels." (Sandy Asher)

## The Ellipsis

The ellipsis is used in quoted passages to show that something has been omitted.

> "The purpose of life is to be useful . . . above all, to *matter*." (Rosten)

When an ellipsis comes at the end of a sentence, the final period must be retained; that is, you will use four periods, not three. The following example shows the use of three ellipses: one in the middle of a sentence and two, each with a fourth period added, at the ends of sentences:

> Mark Van Doren asserts that "Iago's cynicism consists of believing that . . . the passions of men are toys for him to play with . . . . He likes nothing better than to make plans which other men's emotions will execute . . . ."

# The Bracket

Brackets indicate where the writer has added a word or phrase to a quoted passage. Such additions are sometimes necessary to make connections in extended quotes where you have used ellipsis.

> "The persons of the tale were long since types [to Hawthorne], as were their souls' predicaments. The broken law, the hidden guilt, the hunger for confession, the studious, cold heart that watches and does not feel . . ." (Mark Van Doren)

> Men's passions should lead them to "more and better feeling . . . ," but Iago's knowledge of men's hearts transforms those passions into destructive forces, into "toys . . . tools to use." Iago contrives malign "plans which other men's [benign] emotions will execute."

# The Apostrophe

The apostrophe has many important uses: to form contractions, to show possession, and to form the plural of numbers, symbols, and letters. Apostrophes are also easily misused. Below are examples of the most common uses.

## CONTRACTIONS

The apostrophe takes the place of a missing letter or letters in a contraction:

> It's very warm today. = It is very warm today.

> You don't have to return the book right now. = You do not . . .

Remember that contractions are characteristic of spoken language and are not generally used in formal writing.

The apostrophe is also used to abbreviate dates:

June '82

The Class of '98

## POSSESSIVE FORMS OF NOUNS AND PROPER NAMES

You form the possessive of a singular noun or name by adding an apostrophe and an *s*:

The novel's major themes (= The major themes of the novel)

My neighbor's house

Charles's notebook

Dickens's novels

In general, you form the possessive of a plural noun by adding the apostrophe alone:

My neighbors' yards

the jurors' verdict

the witnesses' statements

The Smiths' house

the Davises' horse

*NOTE: Be sure to avoid the common error of confusing the possessive form with the plural.*

Mark Twain wrote several novels; he did not write "novel's."

The local nursery sells plants; it does not sell "plant's."

## SOME PLURALS

Use the apostrophe to form the plurals of letters and some abbreviations:

There were sixteen A's on the last exam.

"Dot your *i*'s and cross your *t*'s."

Mark has earned two Ph.D.'s, each in a different discipline.

# TITLES OF WORKS OF LITERATURE

Titles of books and other full-length, separately published works should be set in italics. If you are composing on a typewriter or writing by hand, *underline* such titles. Movies and plays are also set in italics.

| | |
|---|---|
| *The Great Gatsby* | *Death of a Salesman* |
| *Huckleberry Finn* | *The Glass Menagerie* |
| *To Kill a Mockingbird* | *Macbeth* |

The names of newspapers and magazines should also be in italics.

| | | |
|---|---|---|
| *The New York Times* | *Harper's* | *Newsweek* |

Titles of poems, essays, and short stories are set off in quotes.

| | |
|---|---|
| "The Tell-Tale Heart" | "The Sleeping Giant" |
| "Roman Fever" | "The Road Not Taken" |
| "The Lottery" | "Old Photograph of the Future" |

A title should not be underlined *and* set in quotes; this is redundant and confusing.

Your own title for an essay or paper should not be underlined; use quotes only for names or phrases actually quoted within the title.

# A FINAL NOTE ON PUNCTUATION

The topics reviewed here are meant to offer fundamental guidelines and to illustrate how accurate punctuation helps make writing clear. Review some of the prose passages in other parts of the book for vivid examples of how different authors use punctuation to make their meaning and tone clear.

# Chapter 11

# SPELLING

We know how to spell many words because we recognize them from our reading and because we have, from childhood or as English language learners, developed awareness of the conventions of English spelling. Even though English spelling may seem confusing at times, most of the trouble-some sounds or patterns reflect the history of English pronunciation and the fact that the English language developed after the forces of William the Conqueror, a Frenchman from Normandy, had invaded and settled in what is now the island of Great Britain. The resulting language is a fusion of Anglo-Saxon, French, and Latin.

## SPELLING ON WRITING EXAMS

Does spelling count? The rubrics for the essays on the English Regents ELA exam include the "conventions" as a quality to be assessed. These are defined as ". . . . conventional spelling, punctuation, paragraphing, capi-talization, grammar and usage"; and on the SAT essay, frequent errors in grammar, usage, and mechanics are considered significant weaknesses in a student's writing.

If you know you have difficulties in spelling, use this chapter to review the common patterns of English spelling and to study the list of words com-monly misspelled.

A word misspelled is a word misused, and egregious spelling errors may affect the scoring of your essay. You would also be expected to observe conventional spelling in preparing a college essay, a resume, or cover letter, and would avoid the spelling "shortcuts" we sometimes find useful in com-posing e-mail or text messages.

## SPELLING RULES AND PATTERNS

As you review spelling rules and patterns, you need to be familiar with the following terms:

**vowels** The letters *a, e, i o, u,* and occasionally *y* signal the vowel, or sustained, sounds in English. The variations in these vowel sounds are spelled as combinations of more than one letter or as combinations with consonants.

**consonants** In English, the consonant letters and sounds are composed by the following: *b, c, d, f, g, h, j, k, l, m, n, p, q, r, s, t, v, w, x, z*. In contrast to vowels, consonant sounds do not sustain.

**syllable** A vowel sound or a combination of a vowel and consonant sounds that makes up a single impulse, or "beat," in a word. Words of one syllable: *think, read, act*. Words of two syllables: *reflect, insist, review*. We regularly use words of six or more syllables: *unintentionally, coincidentally*.

**endings** Single letters or syllables that indicate grammatical forms, such as noun plurals or verb conjugations. English, in contrast to other languages high school students may study, has relatively few "endings." Among them are *-s* or *-es* to form plural nouns or to indicate third-person *singular* verb forms, and the verb endings *-ing* and *-ed*.

**suffixes** Endings used to form new words and different parts of speech: *love, lovely, loveliness; occur, occurrence*. The addition of endings and suffixes to words often alters their spelling. (See next page.)

**prefixes** Units of one or two syllables that, like suffixes, are not "words" in themselves but have distinct meanings. They are placed at the beginning of existing words, or of what are called *stems* or *roots*. (See the section "Roots and Prefixes from Latin and Greek," Chapter 8, for many examples in English of Latin and Greek roots.) Words formed in this way are spelled to show their meanings: *illogical, overreact, misspell*.

Although most spelling "rules" have exceptions, there are many common patterns for spelling in English. The first group (pages 198–202) involves adding endings or suffixes.

## Words That End in Silent *e*

➤ Drop the *e* before adding a suffix or ending that begins with a vowel:

| | | | |
|---|---|---|---|
| dare + -ing | → = daring | → | + -ed = dared |
| hope + -ing | → = hoping | → | + -ed = hoped |
| amuse + -ing | → = amusing | → | + -ed = amused |
| revise + -ion | → = revision | → | + -ed = revised |
| advise + -able | → = advisable, | → | + -ed = advised |
| reverse + -ible | → = reversible | → | + -ed = reversed |

➤ When adding *s* or a suffix that begins with a consonant, retain the *e*:

| | | |
|---|---|---|
| amuse | → amuses | → amusement |
| arrange | → arranges | → arrangement |
| hope | → hopes | → hopeless |
| huge | → hugeness | → hugely |
| place | → places | → placement |
| spite | → spiteful | |
| sure | → surely | |

➤ When the word ends in *ce* or in *ge,* retain the *e* when adding *able* or *ous:*

| | | |
|---|---|---|
| change | ➤ | changeable |
| peace | ➤ | peaceable |
| service | ➤ | serviceable |
| advantage | ➤ | advantageous |
| courage | ➤ | courageous |
| outrage | ➤ | outrageous |

➤ But drop the silent *e* before adding *ing:*

| | | |
|---|---|---|
| change | ➤ | changing |
| rage | ➤ | raging |
| service | ➤ | servicing |
| trace | ➤ | tracing |

➤ Note the following **exceptions:**

| | | |
|---|---|---|
| argue | ➤ | argument |
| true | ➤ | truly |
| judge | ➤ | judgment |
| nine | ➤ | ninety |
| whole | ➤ | wholly |

## Words That End in y

➤ For words preceded by a consonant, change the *y* to an *i* before adding a suffix:

| | | | | | |
|---|---|---|---|---|---|
| accompany | ➤ | accompaniment | | | |
| busy | ➤ | business | ➤ | busily | |
| easy | ➤ | easily | | | |
| funny | ➤ | funnier | ➤ | funniest | |
| happy | ➤ | happiness | ➤ | happily | |
| lonely | ➤ | loneliness | | | |
| silly | ➤ | silliness | ➤ | sillier | ➤ silliest |

➤ The same pattern applies when we add *s* to form plural nouns or third-person-singular verb forms:

| | | |
|---|---|---|
| army | ➤ | armies |
| baby | ➤ | babies |
| city | ➤ | cities |
| marry | ➤ | marries |
| try | ➤ | tries |
| worry | ➤ | worries |

➤ But retain the y before adding *ing, ism, ish*:

| | | | |
|---|---|---|---|
| baby | ➤ | babyish | ➤ babying |
| copy | ➤ | copying | |
| crony | ➤ | cronyism | |
| marry | ➤ | marrying | |
| try | ➤ | trying | |
| worry | ➤ | worrying | |

➤ For words that end in *y* preceded by a vowel, retain *y*:

| | | | | |
|---|---|---|---|---|
| annoy | ➤ annoys | ➤ annoyance | ➤ annoyed | ➤ annoying |
| boy | ➤ boys | ➤ boyish | | |
| day | ➤ days | | | |
| destroy | ➤ destroys | ➤ destroyed | ➤ destroying | |
| monkey | ➤ monkeys | | | |
| play | ➤ plays | ➤ played | ➤ playing | ➤ player ➤ |
| playful | | | | |
| valley | ➤ valleys | | | |

➤ However:

| | | | |
|---|---|---|---|
| say | ➤ | says | ➤ **said** |
| pay | ➤ | pays | ➤ **paid** |

## Double Letters

In writing, we must often stop to think whether to double letters in adding suffixes to words. Here are guidelines to follow.

➤ For one-syllable words that end in a single consonant preceded by a single vowel, *double* the final consonant before a suffix beginning with a vowel:

| | | | | |
|---|---|---|---|---|
| bat | ➤ | batter | ➤ | batting |
| big | ➤ | bigger | ➤ | biggest |
| fit | ➤ | fitted | ➤ | fitting ➤ fittest |
| sit | ➤ | sitter | ➤ | sitting |
| spot | ➤ | spotty | ➤ | spotted |

As you look at the examples, you will notice that the effect of the double consonant is to retain the pronunciation of the base word.

➤ Words formed by adding prefixes to one-syllable words follow the same pattern:

| | | | | |
|---|---|---|---|---|
| outfit | ➤ | outfitted | ➤ | outfitter |
| unwrap | ➤ | unwrapped | | |

➤ For one-syllable words that have double vowels or that end in more than one consonant, do *not* double the final consonant:

| | | | | |
|---|---|---|---|---|
| beat | ➤ | beating | | |
| neat | ➤ | neatest | | |
| mail | ➤ | mailing | ➤ | mailed |
| read | ➤ | reading | ➤ | reader |
| fail | ➤ | failure | | |
| list | ➤ | listed | | |
| faint | ➤ | fainted | | |

➤ However:

| | | |
|---|---|---|
| quit | ➤ | quitting |

Because *u* must follow the *q*, *-ui* is considered a single vowel.

➤ Do not double the final consonant for words ending in *w*, *x*, or *y*:

| | | | | |
|---|---|---|---|---|
| draw | ➤ | drawing | | |
| mix | ➤ | mixing | | |
| play | ➤ | playing | ➤ | player |

It is when we add endings to words of more than one syllable that spelling errors commonly occur.

➤ For words of more than one syllable ending in one vowel and one consonant, double the final consonant before an ending that begins with a vowel *if the last syllable of the base word is accented*:

| | | |
|---|---|---|
| confer | ➤ | conferred |
| infer | ➤ | inferred |
| refer | ➤ | referred |
| begin | ➤ | beginning |
| deter | ➤ | deterrence |
| omit | ➤ | omitted |
| commit | ➤ | committed |
| occur | ➤ | occurrence |
| equip | ➤ | equipped |

➤ If the accent is *not* on the syllable to which the ending is added, *do not* double the final consonant:

benefit   →   benefited
credit   →   credited
open   →   opening
happen   →   happening
develop   →   developing   →   developed
deliver   →   delivered   →   delivering

➤ Note how the shift in accent determines spelling:

confer   →   conference
infer   →   inference
prefer   →   preference
refer   →   reference

Note the following exceptions:

➤ The following words double the final consonant:

program   →   programmed   →   programmer
question   →   questionnaire
excel   →   excellence   →   excellent

➤ Either form is considered acceptable for the following, but the first form, with a single *-l*, is preferred:

canceled   →   cancelled
traveled   →   travelled
traveling   →   travelling

## Adding Prefixes and Suffixes

With the exception of the patterns reviewed on the previous pages, which reflect how we pronounce the words, most words formed by adding prefixes and suffixes retain the spelling of each separate part. As a result, the full meaning of the word is reflected in its spelling:

mis + spell + ed   →   = misspelled (both *s*'s are required)
mis + understand + ing   →   = misunderstanding

dis + agree + able   →   = disagreeable
dis + taste + ful   →   = distasteful
dis + appear + ance   →   = disappearance
dis + satisfaction   →   = dissatisfaction

| un + necessary | ➤ | = unnecessary |
| un + ending | ➤ | = unending |
| | | |
| cool + ly | ➤ | = coolly |
| moral + ly | ➤ | = morally |
| | | |
| co + operate | ➤ | = cooperate |
| de + emphasize | ➤ | = de-emphasize |
| re + entry | ➤ | = reentry |
| | | |
| mean + ness | ➤ | = meanness |
| amuse + ment | ➤ | = amusement |

➤ Note that words ending in *c* add a *k* as follows:

| panic, panics | ➤ | panicky, panicked, panicking |
| mimic, mimics | ➤ | mimicked, mimicking |
| picnic, picnics | ➤ | picnicking, picnickers |

## Words That Include *ie* or *ei*

➤ Is it *i* before *e* or *e* before *i*? This is the spelling pattern everyone remembers.

*i* before *e*:

| chief | thief | relief | yield |

➤ Except after *c*:

| receive | ceiling | conceit |

➤ Or, when *ei* sounds long *a*:

| sleigh | neighbor | weigh | veil |

There are, however, several **exceptions** to this pattern. They must be memorized:

| caffeine | foreign | plebeian | sovereign |
| counterfeit | forfeit | protein | surfeit |
| either | leisure | seize | weird |
| financier | neither | sheik | |

# Noun Plurals

➤ Noun *plurals* are generally formed by adding *s*:

| | | |
|---|---|---|
| cat | ➤ | cats |
| house | ➤ | houses |
| delay | ➤ | delays |
| piano | ➤ | pianos |

➤ Nouns ending in *s*, *sh*, *ch*, *x*, and *z*, add *es* to form the plural:

| | | |
|---|---|---|
| watch | ➤ | watches |
| brush | ➤ | brushes |
| waltz | ➤ | waltzes |

➤ Nouns ending in the consonant *y*: drop the *y* and add *ies*:

| | | |
|---|---|---|
| spy | ➤ | spies |
| lady | ➤ | ladies |
| quantity | ➤ | quantities |

➤ However, do *not* alter the spelling of proper names:

There are two "Sallys" in the junior class.

Shakespeare wrote plays about the "Henrys" of England.

➤ Some words ending in *o* add *es* to form the plural:

| | | |
|---|---|---|
| echo | ➤ | echoes |
| tomato | ➤ | tomatoes |
| potato | ➤ | potatoes |
| hero | ➤ | heroes |
| veto | ➤ | vetoes |

➤ Some nouns ending in *f* or *fe* form the plural with *ves*:

| | | |
|---|---|---|
| calf | ➤ | calves |
| elf | ➤ | elves |
| knife | ➤ | knives |
| life | ➤ | lives |
| self | ➤ | selves |
| thief | ➤ | thieves |
| wife | ➤ | wives |

➤ Other nouns change their form internally:

| | | |
|---|---|---|
| man | → | men |
| woman | → | women |
| child | → | children |
| mouse | → | mice |

➤ In compound expressions, the principal noun is made plural:

sisters-in-law

passers-by

spoonsful

## Homophones

Many spelling problems occur because words have syllables whose sounds are alike but could be spelled in more than one way: for example, *cede*, *ceed*, *sede*. These are called homophones.

➤ The most common form is *cede:*

| | |
|---|---|
| precede | antecede |
| concede | intercede |

➤ A few forms are spelled *ceed:*

| | | |
|---|---|---|
| exceed | proceed | succeed |

➤ Only one form is spelled *sede:*

supersede

➤ For *able, ible,* the more common form is *able:*

| | | |
|---|---|---|
| curable | lovable | peaceable |
| imaginable | movable | |

➤ Though fewer in number, there are many common words ending in *ible:*

| | | |
|---|---|---|
| admissible | horrible | possible |
| compatible | intelligible | visible |
| credible | legible | |
| eligible | perceptible | |

➤ There are also words ending in *ance, ant,* or *ence, ent:*

| | | |
|---|---|---|
| assistant | extravagant | ignorance |
| attendant | fragrant | relevance |
| dominant | hesitance | resistance |

➤ Note, however:

| | | |
|---|---|---|
| adolescent | current | permanence |
| competent | frequent | vehemence |
| correspondent | negligence | |

➤ Many nouns end in -*er*:

| | | |
|---|---|---|
| consumer | interpreter | philosopher |
| defender | organizer | |

➤ Note, however:

| | | |
|---|---|---|
| actor | counselor | professor |
| creator | governor | tailor |

*NOTE: The careful writer must memorize the most common spellings. We cannot always use a dictionary or a spellcheck program!*

On the following pages you will find a list of words often confused and an extensive list of words commonly misspelled.

## WORDS COMMONLY CONFUSED

Many words in English sound or look very similar to one another. Such words are often "misspelled" as a result of the writer's confusion about them. Here are some of the most commonly confused words; *all are correctly spelled*. Be sure you know their respective meanings.

| | |
|---|---|
| accept/except | breath/breathe |
| access/excess | choose/chose/chosen |
| adapt/adopt | cite/sight/site |
| advice/advise | cloths/clothes |
| affect/effect | coarse/course |
| allusion/illusion | complement/compliment |
| already/all ready | desert/dessert |
| altogether/all together | device/devise |

discreet/discrete
dyeing/dying
elicit/illicit
elude/allude
envelop/envelope
formally/formerly
fourth/forth
hear/here
holy/wholly
hoping/hopping
idle/idol
imminent/eminent/emanate
its/it's
loath/loathe
local/locale
loose/lose
medal/meddle/metal/mettle
moral/morale
night/knight

principal/principle
quite/quiet
rain/reign/rein
right/rite
shone/shown
sight/site
stationary/stationery
than/then
their/there/they're
thorough/through
though/thought
threw/through
throne/thrown
to/too/two
vain/vane/vein
weather/whether
which/witch
who's/whose
your/you're

# WORDS COMMONLY MISSPELLED

You will recognize the most familiar and the most notorious spelling demons in this list.

| | | | |
|---|---|---|---|
| absence | acquire | against | analysis |
| absolutely | across | aggravate | analyze |
| academic | actually | aggravation | ancient |
| accept | address | aggressive | angrily |
| acceptance | adequately | alleviate | announcement |
| accessory | adherence | alliance | annually |
| accidentally | adjournment | ally | antagonist |
| accommodate | adjustment | almanac | antibiotic |
| accompanying | admittance | already | anticipation |
| accomplish | adolescent | altitude | antique |
| accuracy | advantage | amateur | anxious |
| achievement | advantageous | ambassador | apologetically |
| acknowledge | advertisement | amendment | apologies |
| acquaintance | advising | among | apologize |

| | | | |
|---|---|---|---|
| apology | argument | assumption | authority |
| apostrophe | arising | assurance | auxiliary |
| apparently | arrangement | atheist | availability |
| appreciate | article | athlete | avalanche |
| appropriate | artistically | athletic | average |
| approximate | ascend | attempt | awfully |
| aptitude | ascent | attendance | awkward |
| architecture | assassin | attractive | |
| Arctic | assent | audience | |
| argue | assistance | authoritative | |
| | | | |
| bachelor | before | boring | bruise |
| baggage | beginning | boundary | budget |
| banana | belief | breakfast | buoy |
| bankruptcy | believing | breath | buoyant |
| bargain | beneficial | breathe | bureau |
| barrel | benefit | bribery | burglar |
| basement | benefited | brief | burglarize |
| basically | bibliography | brilliant | business |
| beautify | bicycle | Britain | businesslike |
| becoming | biscuit | brittle | busy |
| | | | |
| cafeteria | cemetery | client | compatible |
| caffeine | censor | closet | compel |
| calculator | censure | clustered | compelled |
| calendar | century | coalition | competitive |
| calorie | certainly | coherence | competitor |
| campaign | challenge | collar | comprehensible |
| candidate | changeable | college | conceivable |
| cannibal | changing | colonel | conceive |
| canoe | channel | column | concentrate |
| capable | characterize | combustible | conception |
| capacity | chauffeur | comfortable | condemn |
| captain | chief | coming | condescend |
| career | chimney | commencement | conference |
| carrying | chivalry | commercial | conferred |
| cashier | chloride | commission | confidence |
| catastrophe | cholera | commit | confidential |
| category | choose | committee | connotation |
| caucus | choosing | communal | connote |
| carefully | choral | community | conqueror |
| cease | chose | companies | conscience |
| ceiling | chuckle | comparative | conscious |
| cellar | cite | comparison | consequence |

consequently
considerable
considerably
consistency
consistent
conspicuous
contemporary
contempt
contemptible
contemptuous
continual
continuous
contribution

controlled
controlling
controversial
convenience
convenient
convertible
convocation
cool
coolly
cooperate
corollary
corps
correlate

corrode
corrupt
counterfeit
courteous
courtesy
cousin
credible
creditor
credulous
crisis
critical
criticism
criticize

cruel
cruelly
cupola
curiosity
curious
current
curriculum
curtain
customary
customer
cyclical
cylinder

dangerous
debris
debt
debtor
deceit
deceitful
deceived
decency
decent
deception
decide
decision
default
defendant
defense
defer
deference
deferred
define
definitely
definition
deity
delegate

deliberately
deodorant
dependable
dependent
depth
deputy
descend
descendant
descent
desert
desirable
despair
despite
dessert
destroy
detriment
devastate
developed
development
deviate
device
devise
dexterity

diameter
different
difficult
dilemma
diligent
dining
disappearance
disappointment
disapprove
disaster
disastrous
discern
disciple
disciplinary
discipline
discomfort
discriminate
discriminatory
disease
disillusion
dispatch
disposal
disregard

dissatisfied
dissent
dissimilar
dissipate
divinity
divisible
division
doesn't
dominant
dominate
dormitory
dough
dramatize
drunkenness
due
dully
duly
during
dye
dyeing
dying

earnest
easily
economically
economy
ecstasy
edge

edgy
edition
editor
effect
efficiency
efficient

eight
eighth
eighty
electoral
elicit
eligible

eliminate
eloquent
elude
emanate
embarrass
embassy

| | | | |
|---|---|---|---|
| emigrant | entirely | evidently | existence |
| emigrate | envelop | exaggerate | expedite |
| emphasis | envelope | exaggeration | expedition |
| emphasize | environment | exceed | experience |
| emphatic | equality | excellence | experiment |
| empirical | equally | exceptional | explanation |
| employee | equipment | excessive | explanatory |
| encouragement | equipped | excitable | exploit |
| encouraging | equivalent | excitement | explore |
| endeavor | erroneous | exclusive | extension |
| enough | escapade | exclusively | extraordinary |
| entangle | especially | excursion | extravagant |
| enterprise | essential | exhibit | extremely |
| entertain | everything | exhibition | |

| | | | |
|---|---|---|---|
| facility | feminine | forbidden | frequently |
| fallacious | feminist | forehead | fried |
| fallacy | feud | foreign | friendless |
| familiar | fictitious | forewarn | friendliness |
| fantasy | fidelity | forgetting | friendly |
| fascinate | fiend | formally | friendship |
| fashion | fiery | formerly | fulfill |
| fatality | filial | forth | fulfillment |
| faulty | finally | forty | fundamental |
| favorable | financial | fourth | furious |
| favorite | financier | fraternity | furthermore |
| February | flair | freight | |
| felicity | fluent | frequency | |

| | | | |
|---|---|---|---|
| gaiety | genetics | governor | grievous |
| gallant | genius | gradually | grocery |
| gardener | genuine | grammar | guarantee |
| gaseous | global | grandeur | guidance |
| gasoline | glorious | graphics | guilt |
| generally | glossary | grief | gymnasium |
| generation | goddess | grievance | |
| generic | government | grieve | |

| | | | |
|---|---|---|---|
| hammer | headache | hereditary | hopeful |
| handkerchief | heard | heroes | hopeless |
| handsome | heathen | heroic | hoping |
| happiness | heavily | heroine | hopping |
| harassment | height | hindrance | humidity |
| harpoon | heir | honorable | humor |

| | | | |
|---|---|---|---|
| humorous | hybrid | hypnotize | hysteria |
| hundredth | hygiene | hypocrisy | |
| hungrily | hypnosis | hypocrite | |
| hurrying | hypnotism | hypothesis | |
| | | | |
| icicle | incidentally | infancy | interaction |
| ignorant | incompetent | inferiority | intercede |
| illegal | inconvenience | infinite | interrelated |
| illicit | incredible | ingenious | interrupt |
| illusion | indebted | ingenuity | intimate |
| illusory | indecisive | ingenuous | introduce |
| imaginary | indefinite | inhabitant | invisible |
| imagine | independence | initiative | ironic |
| immaculate | indispensable | innocence | irony |
| immediately | indivisible | inquiry | irrelevant |
| immense | indulge | insistent | irresistible |
| immigrant | interference | inspiration | irritable |
| immoderate | inertia | intelligence | island |
| impressionable | inevitable | intentionally | isle |
| | | | |
| jealousy | journey | junction | |
| jewelry | judge | justifiable | |
| journal | judgment | justify | |
| | | | |
| kerosene | knight | kowtow | |
| kindergarten | knowledge | | |
| | | | |
| laboratory | leisure | limb | losing |
| laborer | leisurely | literary | lottery |
| launch | lenient | literature | lovable |
| lawyer | library | liveliness | loveless |
| league | license | loathe | luncheon |
| legacy | lighten | loneliness | luscious |
| legible | lightning | lonely | luxurious |
| legislator | likelihood | loose | lying |
| legitimate | likely | lose | |
| | | | |
| macaroni | management | meanness | memorable |
| machinery | managing | medical | merchandise |
| magazine | maneuver | medicinal | merchant |
| magnificent | marriage | medicine | merger |
| maintenance | massacre | medieval | meteor |
| malaria | mathematics | medley | mettle |
| manageable | maximum | melancholy | miniature |

| | | | |
|---|---|---|---|
| minimum | misdemeanor | monogram | mosquitoes |
| minister | misfit | monopoly | mountain |
| miracle | missile | moral | movable |
| mirror | missionary | morale | muffle |
| mischief | misspell | mortgage | muscle |
| mischievous | monarch | mortified | mysterious |
| | | | |
| naturally | neighborly | ninth | nuisance |
| necessary | nickel | noticeable | |
| necessity | niece | notorious | |
| negligent | ninety | nuclear | |
| | | | |
| obedience | occasionally | opinion | originally |
| oblige | occur | opportunity | outrageous |
| obnoxious | occurred | opposite | overrated |
| obscure | occurrence | optimism | owing |
| observant | official | orchard | |
| obstacle | omission | ordinarily | |
| obtuse | omitted | organize | |
| | | | |
| package | pennant | pierce | predominant |
| pageant | perceive | pigeon | preference |
| paid | percentage | pillar | preferred |
| pamphlet | perception | planned | prejudice |
| parachute | perilous | plausible | preoccupied |
| paradox | permanence | playwright | preparation |
| paradoxical | permanent | pleasant | presence |
| paragraph | permissible | pledge | presidency |
| parallel | perplex | plentiful | prestige |
| paralysis | persistence | politeness | prevail |
| parcel | persistent | politician | prevalence |
| parenthesis | personally | popularity | priest |
| parliament | personnel | portable | primitive |
| partial | persuade | possess | principal |
| particle | persuasion | possession | principles |
| particularly | persuasive | possibility | priority |
| pastime | pertinent | possibly | privilege |
| patient | philosophy | potatoes | probability |
| patriotic | physical | practicality | probable |
| patriotism | physician | prairie | procedural |
| patron | pianos | prayer | procedure |
| peaceable | picnic | precede | proceed |
| peasant | picnicking | precedent | professional |
| peculiar | piece | precious | professor |

prohibitive
prologue
promenade
prominent
promising
pronunciation

propel
propeller
prophecy
proprietor
psychiatrist
psychoanalysis

psychologist
psychosomatic
publicity
punctuation
purchase
purchasing

purgatory
purity
pursue
pursuit

qualified
qualitative

quandary
quantity

query
questionable

quiet
quite

radiant
ratify
realize
really
recede
receipt
receive
recessive
recognizable
recollect
recommend

recruit
recur
reference
referred
reign
rein
reliable
relieve
reluctance
remembrance
reminisce

repetitious
requirement
requisition
residence
resistance
resolving
resourceful
responsible
restaurant
reveille
rewrite

rhapsody
rhetoric
rheumatism
rhyme
rhythm
ridiculous
rigidity
routine

sacrifice
safety
salary
satellite
satisfactory
savage
scandal
scarcely
scary
scenery
scent
schedule
schism
scissors
scold
sculptor
secede
secrecy
secretary
seize
seniority
senseless

sensible
sensitive
separate
sergeant
several
shadowy
shady
shepherd
sheriff
shield
shining
shoulder
siege
sieve
significant
simile
simultaneous
sincerely
singular
siphon
skillful
society

solemn
solicit
soliloquy
solos
sophomore
source
sovereign
spaghetti
specimen
spectacles
spectacular
spirited
sponsor
squirrel
statue
stifle
stomach
straight
strategy
strength
strenuous
stressful

studying
submission
subsidy
substantial
substitute
subtle
succeed
successful
successive
sufficient
suffix
summary
superb
surgeon
surprise
susceptible
suspense
suspicion
suspicious
sustained
syllable
syllabus

symbol
symmetrical

sympathize
symphonic

symptom
synonym

tableau
tailor
technique
temperament
temperature
temporary
tendency
terrific
terrifying
territory
testimony

thematic
theoretical
therefore
thorough
tireless
tobacco
tolerance
tomato
tomatoes
tomorrow
tournament

traction
traffic
trafficked
tragedy
tragic
transfer
transferred
transistor
transitive
transparent
traveler

treachery
treason
treasury
truant
truly
turmoil
twelfth
twilight
typical
tyranny
tyrant

umbrella
unanimous
unconscious
undoubtedly

unison
unnecessary
unprecedented
unveil

urban
urgent
usually
utensil

utterance

vacuum
valleys
valuable
variety
various

varying
vegetable
vehicle
vengeance
vengeful

vicinity
victim
village
villain
villainous

vinegar
volcano
volunteer

warrant
warrior
wary
weapon
weather

weird
whereabouts
whimsical
whistle
wholesome

wholly
woolen
wrangle
wrestle
write

writing
written

yacht

yield

# RECOMMENDED READING

The titles listed below, readily available in paperback, represent many of the classic and contemporary works most widely read and studied in comprehensive high school English courses; the emphasis is on works written in English, primarily by American writers. These titles are recommended to the student seeking to supplement regular course assignments or to prepare independently for the Regents exam. All would be suitable choices for an essay on the AP English Literature and Composition exam. These works also represent valuable additions to a student's personal library.

## NOVELS

| | |
|---|---|
| *1984* | George Orwell |
| *A Death in the Family* | James Agee |
| *A Farewell to Arms* | Ernest Hemingway |
| *A Separate Peace* | John Knowles |
| *A Star Called Henry* | Roddy Doyle |
| *A Tale of Two Cities* | Charles Dickens |
| *All the King's Men* | Robert Penn Warren |
| *Americanah* | Chimamanda Ngozi Adichie |
| *Arrowsmith* | Sinclair Lewis |
| *Babbitt* | Sinclair Lewis |
| *Beloved* | Toni Morrison |
| *Billy Budd* | Herman Melville |
| *Brave New World* | Aldous Huxley |
| *Catch-22* | Joseph Heller |
| *Catcher in the Rye* | J. D. Salinger |
| *Cold Mountain* | Charles Frazier |
| *Daisy Miller* | Henry James |
| *Deliverance* | James Dickey |
| *Ethan Frome* | Edith Wharton |
| *Farenheit 451* | Ray Bradbury |
| *Felicia's Journey* | William Trevor |
| *Great Expectations* | Charles Dickens |
| *Huckleberry Finn* | Mark Twain |
| *Invisible Man* | Ralph Ellison |
| *Light in August* | William Faulkner |
| *Lord of the Flies* | William Golding |
| *Main Street* | Sinclair Lewis |

| | |
|---|---|
| *Native Son* | Richard Wright |
| *Netherland* | Joseph O'Neill |
| *Oliver Twist* | Charles Dickens |
| *One Hundred Years of Solitude* | Gabriel Garcia Marquez |
| *Ordinary People* | Judith Guest |
| *Rabbit, Run* | John Updike |
| *Ragtime* | E. L. Doctorow |
| *Rebecca* | Daphne DuMaurier |
| *Red Badge of Courage* | Stephen Crane |
| *Rumors of Peace* | Ella Leffland |
| *Sister Carrie* | Theodore Dreiser |
| *Slaughterhouse Five* | Kurt Vonnegut |
| *So Long, See You Tomorrow* | William Maxwell |
| *Summer* | Edith Wharton |
| *That Night* | Alice McDermott |
| *The Age of Innocence* | Edith Wharton |
| *The Assistant* | Bernard Malamud |
| *The Awakening* | Kate Chopin |
| *The Bean Trees* | Barbara Kingsolver |
| *The Bonfire of the Vanities* | Tom Wolfe |
| *The Caine Mutiny* | Herman Wouk |
| *The Centaur* | John Updike |
| *The Color Purple* | Alice Walker |
| *The Crying of Lot 49* | Thomas Pynchon |
| *The Grapes of Wrath* | John Steinbeck |
| *The Great Fire* | Shirley Hazzard |
| *The Great Gatsby* | F. Scott Fitzgerald |
| *The Heart Is a Lonely Hunter* | Carson McCullers |
| *The Human Stain* | Philip Roth |
| *The Joy Luck Club* | Amy Tan |
| *The Known World* | Edward P. Jones |
| *The Natural* | Bernard Malamud |
| *The Old Man and the Sea* | Ernest Hemingway |
| *The Secret Agent* | Joseph Conrad |
| *The Scarlet Letter* | Nathaniel Hawthorne |
| *The Time Machine* | H. G. Wells |
| *Things Fall Apart* | Chinua Achebe |
| *Things Invisible to See* | Nancy Willard |
| *To Kill a Mockingbird* | Harper Lee |
| *Underworld* | Don DeLillo |
| *Washington Square* | Henry James |
| *White Teeth* | Zadie Smith |
| *Wolf Hall* | Hilary Mantel |
| *World's Fair* | E. L. Doctorow |

# AUTOBIOGRAPHY, ESSAYS, AND OTHER NONFICTION

| | |
|---|---|
| *A Civil Action* | Jonathan Harr |
| *A Hole in the Sky* | Robert Finch |
| *An American Childhood* | Annie Dillard |
| *Angela's Ashes* | Frank McCourt |
| *Black Boy* | Richard Wright |
| *Blood Dark Track* | Joseph O'Neill |
| *Cities on a Hill* | Francis Fitzgerald |
| *Dreams from My Father* | Barack Obama |
| *Growing Up* | Russell Baker |
| *Hiroshima* | John Hersey |
| *Hunger of Memory* | Richard Rodriguez |
| *I Know Why the Caged Bird Sings* | Maya Angelou |
| *Into Thin Air* | Jon Krakauer |
| *Iron and Silk* | Mark Salzman |
| *King of the World* | David Remnick |
| *Late Innings* | Roger Angell |
| *Nickel and Dimed* | Barbara Ehrenreich |
| *Night* | Elie Wiesel |
| *Notes of a Native Son* | James Baldwin |
| *Out of Africa* | Isak Dinesen |
| *Pilgrim at Tinker Creek* | Annie Dillard |
| *Stop-Time* | Frank Conroy |
| *Such, Such Were the Joys* | George Orwell |
| *The Art of Fiction* | David Lodge |
| *The Color of Water* | James McBride |
| *The Courage of Turtles* | Edward Hoagland |
| *The Crack-Up* | F. Scott Fitzgerald |
| *The Devils of Loudon* | Aldous Huxley |
| *The Duke of Deception* | Geoffrey Wolff |
| *The Last Cowboy* | Jane Kramer |
| *The Lives of a Cell* | Lewis Thomas |
| *The Mismeasure of Man* | Stephen Jay Gould |
| *The Solace of Open Spaces* | Gretel Ehrlich |
| *The Way to Rainy Mountain* | N. Scott Momaday |
| *The Warmth of Other Suns* | Isabel Wilkerson |
| *The White Album* | Joan Didion |
| *This Boy's Life* | Tobias Wolff |
| *This House of Sky* | Ivan Doig |
| *Travels with Charley* | John Steinbeck |
| *Up from Slavery* | Booker T. Washington |
| *Walden* | Henry David Thoreau |

There are many excellent collections of essays and literary nonfiction available. Here are some recommended classic and contemporary authors whose works are available in paperback editions:

| | | |
|---|---|---|
| Roger Angell | Stephen Jay Gould | Cynthia Ozick |
| Joan Didion | Garrison Keillor | David Remnick |
| Ralph Waldo | Tracy Kidder | Richard Rodriguez |
| Emerson | Verlyn Klinkenborg | Roger Rosenblatt |
| M. F. K. Fisher | Jane Kramer | Gore Vidal |
| Ian Frazier | Peter Mathiesson | Eudora Welty |
| Atul Gawande | Jane Mayer | E. B. White |
| Malcolm Gladwell | John McPhee | |
| Adam Gopnik | H. L. Mencken | |

Recommended anthologies include:

*The Art of the Personal Essay*, by Philip Lopate; Anchor Books
*The Best American Essays of the Century*, Joyce Carol Oates, ed.;
   Houghton Mifflin Co.
*The Best American Essays*, compiled from essays written for magazines
   and journals and published annually by Houghton Mifflin Co.

Other volumes in the Best American Series, also published annually, include:

*The Best American Sports Writing*
*The Best American Travel Writing*
*The Best American Science and Nature Writing*
*The Best American Nonrequired Reading*

# POETRY

Readers are urged to seek out collections of work by poets whom they encounter in class readings and whom they especially admire. *Dover Publications* offers nicely produced and very inexpensive paperback collections of poetry, including works of Shakespeare and other major British poets, as well as major American poets of the nineteenth and twentieth centuries. They are available from Dover online and in bookstores. Among the many poets introduced to high school students and whose work is widely available in paperback collections are the following:

| | | |
|---|---|---|
| W. H. Auden | Donald Hall | Adrienne Rich |
| Elizabeth Bishop | Langston Hughes | Theodore Roethke |
| Louise Bogan | Denise Levertov | Carl Sandburg |
| Gwendolyn Brooks | W. S. Merwin | Vijay Seshadri |
| Billy Collins | Edna St. Vincent | Charles Simic |
| e. e. cummings | Millay | *May Swenson |
| Emily Dickinson | Marianne Moore | William Stafford |
| *Rita Dove | Howard Nemerov | Richard Wilbur |
| T. S. Eliot | *Sharon Olds | Nancy Willard |
| Carolyn Forché | *Marge Piercy | William Carlos |
| Robert Frost | Robert Pinsky | Williams |
| Louise Glück | Sylvia Plath | |

* denotes a poet whose work has appeared on a New York State English Regents exam

Some currently available paperback anthologies of poetry include:

*Poetry 180, An Anthology of Contemporary Poems*, Billy Collins, ed.; Random House
*Good Poems*, selected and introduced by Garrison Keillor; Penguin Books
*Poetry Daily, 366 Poems,* selected from the Poetry Daily website; Sourcebooks Inc.
*The Best American Poetry*, annual series, David Lehman, ed.; Scribner
*Contemporary American Poetry*, Donald Hall, ed.; Viking
*The Mentor Book of Major American Poets*, Oscar Williams and Edwin Honig, eds.; New American Library
*The Vintage Book of Contemporary American Poetry*, J. D. McClatchy, ed.

Websites for the interested reader:

Poetry Daily: *www.poems.com*
Poetry Foundation: *www.poetryfoundation.org*
Academy of American Poets: *www.poets.org*
Poet's House: *www.poetshouse.org*
*www.poemhunter.com*

# SHORT STORIES

Some recommended authors whose stories are available in paperback:

| | | |
|---|---|---|
| Sherwood Anderson | Nathaniel Hawthorne | Edgar Allan Poe |
| John Barth | Ernest Hemingway | Isaac Bashevis Singer |
| Ambrose Bierce | Bernard Malamud | William Trevor |
| Willa Cather | Bharati Mukherjee | John Updike |
| Isak Dinesen | Alice Munro | Kurt Vonnegut |
| William Faulkner | Joyce Carol Oates | Edith Wharton |
| F. Scott Fitzgerald | Tim O'Brien | Eudora Welty |
| Mavis Gallant | Flannery O'Connor | John Edgar Wideman |

Collections available in paperback include:

Annual publications:
*The O. Henry Prize Stories*
*The Best American Short Stories*
*The Pushcart Prize: Best of the Small Presses*

Anthologies:
*American Short Story Masterpieces*, Raymond Carver and Tom Jenks, eds.
*The Norton Anthology of Short Fiction*, R. V. Cassill, ed.
*The Oxford Book of American Short Stories*, Joyce Carol Oates, ed.
*The Oxford Book of Short Stories*, V. S. Pritchett, ed.
   (includes British and American writers)
*The Vintage Book of Contemporary American Short Stories*, Tobias Wolff, ed.

# PLAYS

| | |
|---|---|
| Shakespeare | *Macbeth, Julius Caesar, Othello, As You Like It, Hamlet, King Lear, Much Ado About Nothing, The Tempest, Henry V* |
| Paddy Chayevsky | *Marty* |
| Anton Chekov | *Three Sisters, The Cherry Orchard, Uncle Vanya* |
| Henrik Ibsen | *A Doll's House, The Master Builder* |
| Edward Albee | *Who's Afraid of Virginia Woolf?, Zoo Story* |
| David Auburn | *Proof* |
| Samuel Beckett | *Waiting for Godot* |
| Robert Bolt | *A Man for All Seasons* |
| Noel Coward | *Blithe Spirit, Private Lives* |
| Mart Crowley | *The Boys in the Band* |

| | |
|---|---|
| Horton Foote | *Dividing the Estate, The Trip to Bountiful, The Young Man from Atlanta* |
| William Gibson | *The Miracle Worker* |
| Susan Glaspell | *Trifles* |
| John Guare | *Six Degrees of Separation* |
| A. R. Gurney | *The Dining Room* |
| Lorraine Hansberry | *A Raisin in the Sun* |
| Lillian Hellman | *The Little Foxes* |
| Beth Henley | *Crimes of the Heart* |
| William Inge | *Come Back, Little Sheba; Picnic; Bus Stop* |
| Eugene Ionesco | *The Lesson, The Bald Soprano, Rhinoceros* |
| George S. Kaufman/Moss Hart | *You Can't Take It With You, The Man Who Came to Dinner* |
| Jerome Lawrence/ Robert Lee | *Inherit the Wind* |
| Terrence McNally | *Master Class* |
| Arthur Miller | *All My Sons, Death of a Salesman, The Crucible, The Price, A View From the Bridge* |
| Clifford Odets | *Waiting for Lefty, The Country Girl* |
| Eugene O'Neill | *Long Day's Journey into Night* |
| Harold Pinter | *The Caretaker* |
| Terrence Rattigan | *The Winslow Boy, The Browning Version* |
| Yasmina Reza | *Art* |
| Rod Serling | *Requiem for a Heavyweight* |
| Peter Shaffer | *Equus, Black Comedy, The Royal Hunt of the Sun, Amadeus* |
| George Bernard Shaw | *Pygmalion* |
| Neil Simon | *The Odd Couple, Brighton Beach Memoirs* |
| Tom Stoppard | *Rosenkrantz and Guildenstern Are Dead, Arcadia, The Real Thing, Jumpers, The Coast of Utopia* |
| Alfred Uhry | *Driving Miss Daisy* |
| Wendy Wasserstein | *The Heidi Chronicles* |
| Oscar Wilde | *The Importance of Being Earnest* |
| Thornton Wilder | *Our Town, The Matchmaker, The Skin of Our Teeth* |
| Tennessee Williams | *The Glass Menagerie, A Streetcar Named Desire, Cat on a Hot Tin Roof, Sweet Bird of Youth* |
| August Wilson | *Fences, The Piano Lesson, Ma Rainey's Black Bottom, Jitney, Joe Turner's Come and Gone* |

# Appendices

## The New York State Common Core Learning Standards for English Language Arts

The following 11/12 grade-specific standards define end-of-year expectations and a cumulative progression designed to enable students to meet college and career readiness (CCR) expectations no later than the end of high school. The new ELA/Common Core Regents Exam is designed to assess many (but not all) of the standards in each of the categories: Reading Literature, Reading Informational Texts, Writing, and Language. Note that the 2017 Revised Standards now include reading for Literature and reading for Informational Texts in a single set of standards (RL and RI).

## 2017 REVISED ELA STANDARDS FOR READING–LITERATURE AND INFORMATIONAL TEXTS (RL AND RI)

**11-12R1:** Cite strong and thorough textual evidence to support analysis of what the text says explicitly/implicitly and make logical inferences, including determining where the text is ambiguous; develop questions for deeper understanding and for further exploration. (RI&RL)

**11-12R2:** Determine two or more themes or central ideas in a text and analyze their development, including how they emerge and are shaped and refined by specific details; objectively and accurately summarize a complex text. (RI&RL)

11-12R3: In literary texts, analyze the impact of author's choices. (RL) In informational texts, analyze a complex set of ideas or sequence of events and explain how specific individuals, ideas, or events interact and develop. (RI)

11-12R4: Determine the meaning of words and phrases as they are used in a text, including figurative and connotative meanings. Analyze the impact of specific word choices on meaning, tone, and mood, including words with multiple meanings. Analyze how an author uses and refines the meaning of technical or key term(s) over the course of a text. (RI&RL)

11-12R5: In literary texts, analyze how varied aspects of structure create meaning and affect the reader. (RL) In informational texts, analyze the impact and evaluate the effect structure has on exposition or argument in terms of clarity, persuasive/rhetorical technique, and audience appeal. (RI)

11-12R6: Analyze how authors employ point of view, perspective, and purpose to shape explicit and implicit messages (e.g., persuasiveness, aesthetic quality, satire, sarcasm, irony, or understatement). (RI&RL)

11-12R7: In literary texts, analyze multiple adaptations of a source text as presented in different formats (e.g., works of art, graphic novels, music, film, etc.), specifically evaluating how each version interprets the source. (RL) In informational texts, integrate and evaluate sources on the same topic or argument in order to address a question or solve a problem. (RI)

11-12R8: Delineate and evaluate an argument in applicable texts, applying a lens (e.g., constitutional principles, logical fallacy, legal reasoning, belief systems, codes of ethics, philosophies, etc.) to assess the validity or fallacy of key arguments, determining whether the supporting evidence is relevant and sufficient. (RI&RL)

11-12R9: Choose and develop criteria to evaluate the quality of texts. Make connections to other texts, ideas, cultural perspectives, eras, and personal experiences. (RI&RL)

# WRITING STANDARDS
## GRADES 11/12   (W)

1. Write arguments to support claims in an analysis of substantive topics or texts, using valid reasoning and relevant and sufficient evidence.

2. Write informative/explanatory texts to examine and convey complex ideas and information clearly and accurately through the effective selection, organization, and analysis of content.

3. Write narratives to develop real or imagined experiences or events using effective technique, well-chosen details, and well-structured event sequences.

4. Produce clear and coherent writing in which the development, organization, and style are appropriate to task, purpose, and audience.

5. Develop and strengthen writing as needed by planning, revising, editing, rewriting, or trying a new approach.

6. Use technology, including the Internet, to produce and publish writing and to interact and collaborate with others.

7. Conduct short as well as more sustained research projects based on focused questions, demonstrating understanding of the subject under investigation.

8. Gather relevant information from multiple print and digital sources, assess the credibility and accuracy of each source, and integrate the information while avoiding plagiarism.

9. Draw evidence from literary or informational texts to support analysis, reflection, and research.

10. Write routinely over extended time frames (time for research, reflection, and revision) and shorter time frames (a single sitting or a day or two) for a range of tasks, purposes, and audiences.

11. Develop personal, cultural, textual, and thematic connections within and across genres as they respond to texts through written, digital, and oral presentations, employing a variety of media and genres.

# LANGUAGE STANDARDS
# GRADES 11/12   (L)

*Conventions of Standard English*

1. Demonstrate command of the conventions of standard English grammar and usage when writing or speaking.

2. Demonstrate command of the conventions of standard English capitalization, punctuation, and spelling when writing.

*Knowledge of Language*

3. Apply knowledge of language to understand how language functions in different contexts, to make effective choices for meaning or style, and to comprehend more fully when reading or listening.

*Vocabulary Acquisition and Use*

4. Determine or clarify the meaning of unknown and multiple meaning words and phrases by using context clues, analyzing meaningful word parts, and consulting general and specialized reference materials, as appropriate.

5. Demonstrate understanding of figurative language, word relationships, and nuances in word meanings.

6. Acquire and use accurately a range of general academic and domain-specific words and phrases sufficient for reading, writing, speaking, and listening at the college and career readiness level; demonstrate independence in gathering vocabulary knowledge when considering a word or phrase important to comprehension or expression.

# HOW IS THE REGENTS ELA
# (COMMON CORE) EXAM SCORED?

## WEIGHTING OF PARTS

Each of the three parts of the Regents Examination in English Language Arts (Common Core) has a number of raw score credits associated with the questions/tasks within that part. In order to ensure an appropriate distribution of credits across the test, each part is weighted.

For Part 1, each multiple-choice question is worth one point. The Part 2 essay is scored on a 6-point rubric and then weighted $\times$ 4. The Part 3 Text Analysis is scored on a 4-point rubric and then weighted $\times$ 2.

As you will notice, the Part 2 Argument Essay is the most heavily weighted section.

The table below shows the raw score credits, weighting factor, and weighted score credits for each part of the test. This information will be used to determine each student's scale score (final exam score) through the use of a conversion chart provided by NYSED.

| Part | Maximum Raw Score Credits | Weighting Factor | Maximum Weighted Score Credits |
|------|---------------------------|------------------|--------------------------------|
| Part 1 | 24 | 1 | 24 |
| Part 2 | 6 | 4 | 24 |
| Part 3 | 4 | 2 | 8 |
| | | | Total 56 |

The conversion table is determined independently for each administration of the exam. You can find the conversion tables for both forms of the Regents English Exams at *http://www.nysedregents.org*.

## SCORING RUBRICS FOR THE REGENTS ELA (COMMON CORE) EXAM

Parts 2 and 3 of the Regents Examination in English Language Arts (Common Core) will be scored using new holistic rubrics. Part 2 will be scored using a 6-credit rubric, and Part 3 will be scored using a 4-credit rubric. Both rubrics reflect the new demands called for by the Common Core Learning Standards for English Language Arts and Literacy through the end of Grade 11.

## New York State Regents Examination in English Language Arts (Common Core)
### Part 2 Rubric
### Writing from Sources: Argument

| Criteria | 6 — Essays at this Level | 5 — Essays at this Level | 4 — Essays at this Level | 3 — Essays at this Level | 2 — Essays at this Level | 1 — Essays at this Level |
|---|---|---|---|---|---|---|
| **Content and Analysis: the extent to which the essay conveys complex ideas and information clearly and accurately in order to support claims in an analysis of the texts** | -introduce a precise and insightful claim, as directed by the task<br><br>-demonstrate in-depth and insightful analysis of the texts, as necessary to support the claim and to distinguish the claim from alternate or opposing claims | -introduce a precise and thoughtful claim, as directed by the task<br><br>-demonstrate thorough analysis of the texts, as necessary to support the claim and to distinguish the claim from alternate or opposing claims | -introduce a precise claim, as directed by the task<br><br>-demonstrate appropriate and accurate analysis of the texts, as necessary to support the claim and to distinguish the claim from alternate or opposing claims | -introduce a reasonable claim, as directed by the task<br><br>-demonstrate some analysis of the texts, but insufficiently distinguish the claim from alternate or opposing claims | -introduce a claim<br><br>-demonstrate confused or unclear analysis of the texts, failing to distinguish the claim from alternate or opposing claims | -do not introduce a claim<br><br>-do not demonstrate analysis of the texts |
| **Command of Evidence: the extent to which the essay presents evidence from the provided texts to support analysis** | -present ideas fully and thoughtfully, making highly effective use of a wide range of specific and relevant evidence to support analysis<br><br>-demonstrate proper citation of sources to avoid plagiarism when dealing with direct quotes and paraphrased material | -present ideas clearly and accurately, making effective use of specific and relevant evidence to support analysis<br><br>-demonstrate proper citation of sources to avoid plagiarism when dealing with direct quotes and paraphrased material | -present ideas sufficiently, making adequate use of specific and relevant evidence to support analysis<br><br>-demonstrate proper citation of sources to avoid plagiarism when dealing with direct quotes and paraphrased material | -present ideas briefly, making use of some specific and relevant evidence to support analysis<br><br>-demonstrate inconsistent citation of sources to avoid plagiarism when dealing with direct quotes and paraphrased material | -present ideas inconsistently and/or inaccurately, in an attempt to support analysis, making use of some evidence that may be irrelevant<br><br>-demonstrate little use of citations to avoid plagiarism when dealing with direct quotes and paraphrased material | -present little or no evidence from the texts<br><br>-do not make use of citations |

| Criteria | 6 | 5 | 4 | 3 | 2 | 1 |
|---|---|---|---|---|---|---|
| **Coherence, Organization, and Style:** the extent to which the essay logically organizes complex ideas, concepts, and information using formal style and precise language | -exhibit skillful organization of ideas and information to create a cohesive and coherent essay<br><br>-establish and maintain a formal style, using sophisticated language and structure | -exhibit logical organization of ideas and information to create a cohesive and coherent essay<br><br>-establish and maintain a formal style, using fluent and precise language and sound structure | -exhibit acceptable organization of ideas and information to create a coherent essay<br><br>-establish and maintain a formal style, using precise and appropriate language and structure | -exhibit some organization of ideas and information to create a mostly coherent essay<br><br>-establish but fail to maintain a formal style, using primarily basic language and structure | -exhibit inconsistent organization of ideas and information, failing to create a coherent essay<br><br>-lack a formal style, using some language that is inappropriate or imprecise | -exhibit little organization of ideas and information<br><br>-are minimal, making assessment unreliable<br><br>-use language that is predominantly incoherent, inappropriate, or copied directly from the task or texts |
| **Control of Conventions:** the extent to which the essay demonstrates command of standard English grammar, usage, capitalization, punctuation, and spelling | -demonstrate control of conventions with essentially no errors, even with sophisticated language | -demonstrate control of the conventions, exhibiting occasional errors only when using sophisticated language | -demonstrate partial control, exhibiting occasional errors that do not hinder comprehension | -demonstrate emerging control, exhibiting occasional errors that hinder comprehension | -demonstrate a lack of control, exhibiting frequent errors that make comprehension difficult | -are minimal, making assessment of conventions unreliable |

- An essay that addresses fewer texts than required by the task can be scored no higher than a 3.
- An essay that is a personal response and makes little or no reference to the task or texts can be scored no higher than a 1.
- An essay that is totally copied from the task and/or texts with no original student writing must be scored a 0.
- An essay that is totally unrelated to the task, illegible, incoherent, blank, or unrecognizable as English must be scored as a 0.

New York State Regents Examination in English Language Arts (Common Core)
Part 3 Rubric
Text Analysis: Exposition

| Criteria | 4 Responses at this Level | 3 Responses at this Level | 2 Responses at this Level | 1 Responses at this Level |
|---|---|---|---|---|
| **Content and Analysis: the extent to which the response conveys complex ideas and information clearly and accurately in order to respond to the task and support an analysis of the text** | -introduce a well-reasoned central idea and a writing strategy that clearly establish the criteria for analysis<br><br>-demonstrate a thoughtful analysis of the author's use of the writing strategy to develop the central idea | -introduce a clear central idea and a writing strategy that establish the criteria for analysis<br><br>-demonstrate an appropriate analysis of the author's use of the writing strategy to develop the central idea | -introduce a central idea and/or a writing strategy<br><br>-demonstrate a superficial analysis of the author's use of the writing strategy to develop the central idea | -introduce a confused or incomplete central idea or writing strategy and/or<br><br>-demonstrate a minimal analysis of the author's use of the writing strategy to develop the central idea |
| **Command of Evidence: the extent to which the response presents evidence from the provided text to support analysis** | -present ideas clearly and consistently, making effective use of specific and relevant evidence to support analysis | -present ideas sufficiently, making adequate use of relevant evidence to support analysis | -present ideas inconsistently, inadequately, and/or inaccurately in an attempt to support analysis, making use of some evidence that may be irrelevant | -present little or no evidence from the text |
| **Coherence, Organization, and Style: the extent to which the response logically organizes complex ideas, concepts, and information using formal style and precise language** | -exhibit logical organization of ideas and information to create a cohesive and coherent response<br><br>-establish and maintain a formal style, using precise language and sound structure | -exhibit acceptable organization of ideas and information to create a coherent response<br><br>-establish and maintain a formal style, using appropriate language and structure | -exhibit inconsistent organization of ideas and information, failing to create a coherent response<br><br>-lack a formal style, using language that is basic, inappropriate, or imprecise | -exhibit little or no organization of ideas and information<br><br>-use language that is predominantly incoherent, inappropriate, or copied directly from the task or text<br><br>-are minimal, making assessment unreliable |

| Control of Conventions: the extent to which the response demonstrates command of conventions of standard English grammar, usage, capitalization, punctuation, and spelling | -demonstrate control of the conventions with infrequent errors | -demonstrate partial control of conventions with occasional errors that do not hinder comprehension | -demonstrate emerging control of conventions with some errors that hinder comprehension | -demonstrate a lack of control of conventions with frequent errors that make comprehension difficult<br>-are minimal, making assessment of conventions unreliable |

- A response that is a personal response and makes little or no reference to the task or text can be scored no higher than a 1.
- A response that is totally copied from the text with no original writing must be given a 0.
- A response that is totally unrelated to the task, illegible, incoherent, blank, or unrecognizable as English must be scored as a 0.

231

# Examination
# June 2019
## English Language Arts

## PART 1—Reading Comprehension

**Directions** (1–24): Closely read each of the three passages below. After each passage, there are several multiple-choice questions. Select the best suggested answer to each question and write its number in the space provided. You may use the margins to take notes as you read.

### Reading Comprehension Passage A

When Marvin was ten years old, his father took him through the long, echoing corridors that led up through Administration and Power, until at last they came to the uppermost levels of all and were among the swiftly growing vegetation of the Farmlands. Marvin liked it here: it was fun
(5)  watching the great, slender plants creeping with almost visible eagerness towards the sunlight as it filtered down through the plastic domes to meet them. The smell of life was everywhere, awakening inexpressible longings in his heart: no longer was he breathing the dry, cool air of the residential levels, purged of all smells but the faint tang of ozone. He wished he could
(10) stay here for a little while, but Father would not let him. They went onwards until they had reached the entrance to the Observatory, which he had never visited: but they did not stop, and Marvin knew with a sense of rising excitement that there could be only one goal left. For the first time in his life, he was going Outside.[1]

---

[1]Outside—the part of the Moon outside of Marvin's space habitat

(15)    There were a dozen of the surface vehicles, with their wide balloon tyres [tires] and pressurized cabins, in the great servicing chamber. His father must have been expected, for they were led at once to the little scout car waiting by the huge circular door of the airlock. Tense with expectancy, Marvin settled himself down in the cramped cabin while his father started

(20)    the motor and checked the controls. The inner door of the lock slid open and then closed behind them: he heard the roar of the great air-pumps fade slowly away as the pressure dropped to zero. Then the 'Vacuum' sign flashed on, the outer door parted, and before Marvin lay the land which he had never yet entered.

(25)    He had seen it in photographs, of course: he had watched it imaged on television screens a hundred times. But now it was lying all around him, burning beneath the fierce sun that crawled so slowly across the jet-black sky. He stared into the west, away from the blinding splendour of the sun— and there were the stars, as he had been told but had never quite believed.

(30)    He gazed at them for a long time, marvelling that anything could be so bright and yet so tiny. They were intense unscintillating[2] points, and suddenly he remembered a rhyme he had once read in one of his father's books:

    Twinkle, twinkle, little star,
    How I wonder what you are.

(35)    Well, he knew what the stars were. Whoever asked that question must have been very stupid. And what did they mean by 'twinkle'? You could see at a glance that all the stars shone with the same steady, unwavering light. He abandoned the puzzle and turned his attention to the landscape around him.

(40)    They were racing across a level plain at almost a hundred miles an hour, the great balloon tyres sending up little spurts of dust behind them. There was no sign of the Colony: in the few minutes while he had been gazing at the stars, its domes and radio towers had fallen below the horizon. Yet there were other indications of man's presence, for about a mile ahead

(45)    Marvin could see the curiously shaped structures clustering round the head of a mine. Now and then a puff of vapour would emerge from a squat smoke-stack and would instantly disperse.

    They were past the mine in a moment: Father was driving with a reckless and exhilarating skill as if—it was a strange thought to come into a child's

(50)    mind—he was trying to escape from something. In a few minutes they had reached the edge of the plateau on which the Colony had been built. The ground fell sharply away beneath them in a dizzying slope whose lower

---

[2]unscintillating—not sparkling

stretches were lost in shadow. Ahead, as far as the eye could reach, was a jumbled wasteland of craters, mountain ranges, and ravines. The crests of

(55) the mountains, catching the low sun, burned like islands of fire in a sea of darkness: and above them the stars still shone as steadfastly as ever. . . .

And now on the right was a wrinkled, dusty plain, and on the left, its ramparts and terraces rising mile after mile into the sky, was a wall of mountains that marched into the distance until its peaks sank from sight

(60) below the rim of the world. There was no sign that men had ever explored this land, but once they passed the skeleton of a crashed rocket, and beside it a stone cairn[3] surmounted by a metal cross. . . .

The sun was now low behind the hills on the right: the valley before them should be in total darkness. Yet it was awash with a cold white radiance

(65) that came spilling over the crags beneath which they were driving. Then, suddenly, they were out in the open plain, and the source of the light lay before them in all its glory.

It was very quiet in the little cabin now that the motors had stopped. The only sound was the faint whisper of the oxygen feed and an occasional

(70) metallic crepitation[4] as the outer walls of the vehicle radiated away their heat. For no warmth at all came from the great silver crescent that floated low above the far horizon and flooded all this land with pearly light. It was so brilliant that minutes passed before Marvin could accept its challenge and look steadfastly into its glare, but at last he could discern the outlines

(75) of continents, the hazy border of the atmosphere, and the white islands of cloud. And even at this distance, he could see the glitter of sunlight on the polar ice.

It was beautiful, and it called to his heart across the abyss of space. There in that shining crescent were all the wonders that he had never known—the

(80) hues of sunset skies, the moaning of the sea on pebbled shores, the patter of falling rain, the unhurried benison[5] of snow. These and a thousand others should have been his rightful heritage, but he knew them only from the books and ancient records, and the thought filled him with the anguish of exile.

(85) Why could they not return? It seemed so peaceful beneath those lines of marching cloud. Then Marvin, his eyes no longer blinded by the glare, saw that the portion of the disk that should have been in darkness was gleaming faintly with an evil phosphorescence: and he remembered.

---

[3]cairn—memorial
[4]crepitation—crackling sound
[5]benison—blessing

He was looking upon the funeral pyre[6] of a world—upon the radioactive
(90)  aftermath of Armageddon.[7] Across a quarter of a million miles of space,
the glow of dying atoms was still visible, a perennial reminder of the ruined
past. It would be centuries yet before that deadly glow died from the rocks
and life could return again to fill that silent, empty world. . . .

So, at last, Marvin understood the purpose of this pilgrimage. He [his
(95)  father] would never walk beside the rivers of that lost and legendary world,
or listen to the thunder raging above its softly rounded hills. Yet one day—
how far ahead?—his children's children would return to claim their heritage. The winds and the rains would scour the poisons from the burning
lands and carry them to the sea, and in the depths of the sea they would
(100)  waste their venom until they could harm no living things. Then the great
ships that were still waiting here on the silent, dusty plains could lift once
more into space, along the road that led to home. . . .

—Arthur C. Clarke
excerpted and adapted from "If I Forget Thee, Oh Earth. . ."
*Expedition to Earth*, 1999
Orbit

---

[6]pyre—bonfire
[7]Armageddon—a catastrophic battle

1 The images in the first paragraph serve to

   (1) create a sense of solitude
   (2) illustrate the randomness of nature
   (3) create a feeling of anticipation
   (4) illustrate the importance of family     1____

2 Lines 15 through 24 establish

   (1) Marvin's misgivings about going Outside
   (2) the inhospitable conditions of Outside
   (3) Father's fears about traveling Outside
   (4) the unpleasant sensations of Outside    2____

3 The statement "it was a strange thought to come into a child's mind" (lines 49 and 50) signals

   (1) a change in Marvin's understanding
   (2) Marvin's growing embrace of the unknown
   (3) Marvin's objection to his father's behavior
   (4) a chance for Marvin's rescue    3____

4 The phrase "jumbled wasteland of craters, mountain ranges, and ravines" (line 54) reveals the

   (1) futility of the Colony
   (2) desolation of the Outside
   (3) uncertainty of Marvin's future
   (4) loneliness of Marvin's past    4____

5 The "glare" described in lines 74 and 86 represents Marvin's

   (1) romantic vision of the Earth
   (2) obsession with the Earth's past
   (3) vague memory of the Earth
   (4) faith in the Earth's restoration    5____

6 Lines 81 through 84 emphasize Marvin's

   (1) sense of deprivation
   (2) appreciation of his situation
   (3) fear of destruction
   (4) recollection of his childhood    6____

7 The details in lines 86 through 90 confirm the
Earth has been damaged by

    (1)  climate change
    (2)  cosmic instability
    (3)  human actions
    (4)  natural occurences          7____

8 The images in lines 98 through 100 convey
feelings of

    (1)  fear and disappointment
    (2)  cleansing and renewal
    (3)  preservation and protection
    (4)  confusion and impatience      8____

9 Which lines best capture Marvin's understanding
of his father's perspective?

    (1)  "Tense with expectancy, Marvin settled him-
self down in the cramped cabin while his
father started the motor and checked the
controls" (lines 18 through 20)
    (2)  "They were intense unscintillating points,
and suddenly he remembered a rhyme he
had once read in one of his father's books"
(lines 31 and 32)
    (3)  "In a few minutes they had reached the edge
of the plateau on which the Colony had been
built" (lines 50 and 51)
    (4)  "He [his father] would never walk beside the
rivers of that lost and legendary world, or
listen to the thunder raging above its softly
rounded hills" (lines 94 through 96)    9____

## Reading Comprehension Passage B

### This Life

My grandmother told me there'd be good days
to counter the dark ones,
with blue skies in the heart as far
as the soul could see. She said
(5)    you could measure a life in as many ways
as there were to bake a pound cake,
but you still needed real butter and eggs
for a good one—pound cake, that is,
but I knew what she meant. She was always
(10)   talking around corners like that;
she knew words carried their treasures
like a grape clusters around its own juice.
She loved words; she thought a book
was a monument to the glory of creation
(15)   and a library . . . well, sometimes
just trying to describe Jubilation
will get you a bit tongue, so let's
leave it at that. But my grandmother
was nobody's fool, and she'd tell anybody
(20)   smart enough to listen. Don't let a little pain
stop you; try as hard as you can
every minute you're given or else
sit down and shut-up—though in her opinion,
keeping quiet in noisy times was a sin
(25)   against everything God and democracy
intended us for. I know she'd like
where I'm standing right now. She'd say
a man who could measure his life in deeds
was larger inside than the vessel that carried him;
(30)   she'd say he was a cluster of grapes.
My grandmother was only four feet ten
but when she entered a room, even the books
came to attention. Giants come in all sizes:

239

Sometimes a moment is a monument;
*(35)*  sometimes an institution breathes—
like a library. Like this halcyon[1] day.

—Rita Dove
from *The Poets Laureate Anthology*, 2010
W. W. Norton & Company, Inc.

---

[1]halcyon—peaceful

10 Lines 1 through 4 establish the grandmother's

    (1) questioning nature
    (2) vivid imagination
    (3) cautious attitude
    (4) optimistic outlook          10____

11 The figurative language in lines 9 and 10 highlights the grandmother's

    (1) desire to avoid conflicts
    (2) tendency to keep secrets
    (3) strategy to impart wisdom
    (4) ability to create humor      11____

12 Which phrase from the poem clarifies the narrator's statement in line 30?

    (1) "there'd be good days" (line 1)
    (2) "smart enough to listen" (line 20)
    (3) "measure his life in deeds" (line 28)
    (4) "sometimes an institution breathes" (line 35)    12____

13 The personification in lines 32 and 33 emphasizes
the grandmother's

    (1) small size
    (2) commanding presence
    (3) family history
    (4) successful career      13____

14 The overall tone of the poem can best be described as

    (1) objective      (3) respectful
    (2) skeptical      (4) critical    14____

# Reading Comprehension Passage C

*Texting isn't the first new technology blamed for ruining communication and common courtesy.*

Is text-messaging driving us apart? These days, we talk to each other a lot with our thumbs—mashing out over six billion text messages a day in the United States, and likely a few billion more on services like WhatsApp and Facebook Messenger.

(5)　But some worry that so much messaging leads, paradoxically, to less communication. When Sherry Turkle, the MIT clinical psychologist and author, interviewed college students, they said texting was causing friction in their face-to-face interactions. While hanging out with friends they'd be texting surreptitiously at the same time, pretending to maintain eye con-
(10)　tact but mentally somewhere else. The new form of communication was fun, sure, but it was colliding with—and eroding—the old one.

"Our texts are fine," as one student said. "It's what texting does to our conversations when we are together that's the problem." . . .

New technologies often unsettle the way we relate to one another,
(15)　of course. But social ruptures caused by texting have a strong echo in the arguments we had a hundred years ago. That's when a newfangled appliance gave us a strange new way to contact one another en masse:[1] the telephone. . . .

At first, the telephone was marketed mainly as a tool for business. Physi-
(20)　cians and drugstores bought them to process orders, and business owners installed them at home so they could be quickly reached. The phone, pro-claimed early ad copy, gave business leaders an ESP-like "sixth sense"[2] of their far-flung operations. . . .

Nonetheless, the telephone quickly gave birth to curious new forms
(25)　of socializing. Callers arranged regular weekly "visiting" calls, dialing remote family to catch up on news. "Distance rolls away and for a few minutes every Thursday night the familiar voices tell the little family gossip that both are so eager to hear," a Bell ad cooed in 1921.

Phone companies even boasted that the phone was an improvement over
(30)　that stodgy, low-fi communication, the letter. "Correspondence will help for a time, but friendships do not flourish for long on letters alone," a 1931 Bell sales manual noted. "When you can't visit in person, telephone periodically. Telephone calls will keep up the whole intimacy remarkably well."

---

[1]en masse—in a group at the same time
[2]ESP-like "sixth sense"—heightened intuition

Soon, though, social critics began to wonder: Was all this phone chatter
(35)   good for us? Was it somehow a lesser form of communication than what had
come before? "Does the telephone make men more active or more lazy?"
wondered the Knights of Columbus in a 1926 meeting. "Does the telephone
break up home life and the old practice of visiting friends?"

Others worried that the inverse would occur—that it would be so easy
(40)   to talk that we'd never leave each other alone. "Thanks to the telephone,
motor-car and such-like inventions, our neighbors have it in their power
to turn our leisure into a series of interruptions," complained an American
professor in 1929. And surely it couldn't be healthy to talk to each other so
much. Wouldn't it create Too Much Information [TMI]?

(45)   "We shall soon be nothing but transparent heaps of jelly to each
other," a London writer moaned in 1897. Others fretted that the
telephone sped up life, demanding instant reactions. "The use of the
telephone gives little room for reflection," wrote a British newspaper in
1899. "It does not improve the temper, and it engenders a feverishness in
(50)   the ordinary concerns of life which does not make for domestic happiness
and comfort."

Perhaps the strangest thing was being in the room while a friend talked
to someone else—someone outside the room. In 1880, Mark Twain wrote
"A Telephonic Conversation," transcribing the half-a-conversation as he lis-
(55)   tened to his wife on the phone. To the observer, as the skit pointed out, a telephone call sounded like disjointed nonsense. Even phone companies worried
about whether the device created new forms of rude behavior; a 1910 Bell ad
warned about "Dr. Jekyll and Mr. Hyde at the Telephone." . . .

Indeed, some believed the phone improved our social behavior, because it
(60)   forced a listener to pay closer attention to a speaker. Devoid of visual signals,
we must be "all ears and memory," a pundit[3] wrote in 1915: "The mind cannot wander." Plus, by eradicating distance, wouldn't the phone reduce misunderstanding? War, even? "Someday we will build up a world telephone system
making necessary to all peoples the use of a common language, or common
(65)   understanding of languages, which will join all the people of the earth into one
brotherhood," gushed John J. Carty, AT&T chief engineer, in 1907.

These utopian[4] views, of course, were wildly optimistic. But the
gloomy views of pessimists, as [author, Claude] Fischer notes, didn't come
true either. Even Emily Post, the etiquette expert, came around to the
(70)   telephone. By the 1920s, she'd accepted "Hello" as a suitable greeting, and
even thought it was acceptable to invite someone to dinner with a call.

---

[3]pundit—an expert who shares opinions with the public
[4]utopian—idealistic

"Custom which has altered many ways and manners has taken away all opprobrium[5] from the message," she shrugged.

(75) Nowadays, the telephone call seems like a quaint throwback to a gentler era. When Jenna Birch, the journalist, started dating a man who insisted on calling her on the phone, she found it warm and delightful—though her friends thought the behavior odd. Phone calls now seem retro.[6]

Academics have observed this shift, too. "My students just do not think of the phone as a mechanism of vocal interaction—they think of that as
(80) very rare," says John Durham Peters, a communication professor at the University of Iowa, and author of Speaking Into the Air. He doesn't think the shift to texting has degraded our interactions, though. By the middle of the 20th century, studies found that the telephone appeared not to have eroded social contact—indeed, some research found those with phones
(85) wrote more old-fashioned letters than those without. Similarly, modern surveys by the Pew Research Center have found that teenagers who text the most are also those who spend the most time face to face with friends. Communication, it seems, begets more communication, and—as Peters argues—just because talk happens in text doesn't mean it's not meaningful.
(90) "Media scholars," he notes, "have this long romance with 'conversation' as the cure to the disease of media."

Still, it's not hard to be dispirited[7] by the divided attention so many of Turkle's subjects bemoaned in their lives. Indeed, Michéle Martin, of Carleton, thinks we're living through a replay of the telephone, where the
(95) things that made it valuable—instant communications—are the same that made it annoying. "People believe they are liberated because they can bring the mobile phone everywhere," Martin says. "But at the same time they are slaves to it."

The poet Carl Sandburg captured that dissonance in a 1916 poem about
(100) the telephone. He imagined a telephone wire being aware of the disparate[8] uses to which it was being put—coursing with conversations both deep and frivolous. "It is love and war and money; it is the fighting and the tears, the work and want / Death and laughter of men and women passing through me, carrier of your speech."

—Clive Thompson
excerpted and adapted from "OMG! We've Been Here B4"
*Smithsonian*, March 2016

[5]opprobrium—disgrace
[6]retro—dated
[7]dispirited—discouraged
[8]disparate—varying

15 The first paragraph of the text serves to

    (1)  highlight the prevalence of texting
    (2)  stress the benefits of texting
    (3)  explain the origins of texting
    (4)  support the abolition of texting        15____

16 As used in line 9, the word "surreptitiously" most
nearly means

    (1)  politely               (3)  secretively
    (2)  boldly                (4)  earnestly     16____

17 The details in lines 19 through 23 reveal that the
telephone was initially

    (1)  associated with the supernatural
    (2)  not considered very useful
    (3)  often blamed for worker illness
    (4)  not used for social purposes       17____

18 The use of the word "cooed" (line 28) implies that
telephone advertisers were

    (1)  helpful and patient
    (2)  strategic and persuasive
    (3)  childish and inconsiderate
    (4)  sarcastic and relentless         18____

19 Lines 34 through 44 illustrate society's

    (1)  enthusiasm about using new technology
    (2)  dependence on those proficient in new
         technology
    (3)  grasp of the significance of new technology
    (4)  concern about the impact of new technology   19____

20 The figurative language in lines 45 and 46 implies that telephone use would cause people to

(1) lose self-confidence and motivation
(2) lack substance and individuality
(3) attract danger and adversity
(4) become narrow-minded and uninformed          20____

21 The statements from a Bell ad (lines 57 and 58) and the AT&T chief engineer (lines 64 through 66) offer

(1) contrasting perspectives on the potential effects of the telephone
(2) strong support for the growing popularity of the telephone
(3) alternative options for communicating with family members
(4) insightful evaluation of the importance of long-distance conversations          21____

22 The "utopian views" of the early 1900s (line 67) suggested that telephone use could

(1) improve local commerce
(2) encourage language studies
(3) promote global unity
(4) influence community values          22____

23 The information about Emily Post (lines 69 through 73) contributes to a central idea that

(1) rules of proper behavior can be confusing
(2) norms of good conduct are universal
(3) concepts of politeness can evolve over time
(4) conventions of salutation depend on status          23____

24 The quotations in lines 96 through 98 reflect a sense of

(1) bias                    (3) suspense
(2) irony                   (4) resolution          24____

246

# PART 2—Argument Response

**Directions:** Closely read each of the *four* texts provided on pages 248 through 255 and write a source-based argument on the topic below. You may use the margins to take notes as you read and scrap paper to plan your response. Write your argument on a separate sheet of paper.

---

**Topic:** Should pets be allowed in the workplace?

---

**Your Task:** Carefully read each of the *four* texts provided. Then, using evidence from at least *three* of the texts, write a well-developed argument regarding whether or not pets should be allowed in the workplace. Clearly establish your claim, distinguish your claim from alternate or opposing claims, and use specific, relevant, and sufficient evidence from at least *three* of the texts to develop your argument. Do *not* simply summarize each text.

**Guidelines:**

**Be sure to**

- Establish your claim regarding whether or not pets should be allowed in the workplace.
- Distinguish your claim from alternate or opposing claims.
- Use specific, relevant, and sufficient evidence from at least three of the texts to develop your argument.
- Identify each source that you reference by text number and line number(s) or graphic (for example: Text 1, line 4 or Text 2, graphic).
- Organize your ideas in a cohesive and coherent manner.
- Maintain a formal style of writing.
- Follow the conventions of standard written English.

**Texts:**

Text 1—Do Pets in the Workplace Improve Morale?
Text 2—Why Pets in the Workplace May Not Be As Great As You Thought
Text 3—Why a Pet-Friendly Office May Be the Key to Employee Satisfaction
Text 4—Don't Bring Your Dog to Work

## Text 1

## Do Pets in the Workplace Improve Morale?

Human resource managers are always looking for ways to improve morale and create a more appealing workplace culture. The popularity of the recent film release "The Secret Life of Pets" [2016] underscores the love we Americans have for our pets. In fact, around 65 percent of U.S. households are home
(5)  to at least one pet. The majority of these are dogs and cats. . . .

The benefits of being around animals have inspired human resource personnel and other business decision makers to allow pets in the workplace. The top motive for making this allowance is the stress-reducing effect that animals bring. Employees who are less stressed at work are more
(10)  productive and miss fewer days due to being sick.

Pet-friendly businesses usually focus mainly on allowing dogs in the workplace. However, some allow cats, birds and reptiles. A retail business might have "shop cats" that live on the premises, or smaller animals kept in cages that can become company mascots and offer a source of stress relief for workers.

**An Internet giant paves the way with pets in the workplace.**
(15)  . . .These days, about 2,000 dogs accompany their owners to Amazon each day. Workers and management have embraced the culture, and the pet-friendly policy benefits both owners and those who don't own pets. No matter what the workday brings, Amazon staff members are never far away from a coworker's terrier or spaniel poking its head around a corner.
(20)  Any stress they were feeling melts away. . . .

**Pet-friendly workplaces rate higher.**
Banfield Pet Hospital recently surveyed over 1,000 employees and 200 human resource decision makers for its Pets At Work barometer called "Pet-Friendly Workplace PAWrometer." The goal was to measure worker opinions about pets in the workplace. Those who worked in pet-friendly offices were
(25)  found to believe it improves the atmosphere in the workplace significantly.

The majority of workers in pet-friendly workplaces consider the policy to be positive. A full 91 percent of managers and 82 percent of employees felt workers become more loyal to the company with this policy. A large majority felt it made the workplace more productive,
(30)  and 86 percent of workers and 92 percent of management reported decreased worker stress levels. Not only do pets in the workplace make the environment less stressful, workers are also less burdened with guilt about leaving a pet at home alone while they are at work. They are then more likely to work longer hours if required.

(35)   While pet-friendly businesses improve existing employees' lives, they are also appealing to new applicants. It's a benefit that millennials[1] find appealing and offers a way to draw in a larger talent pool.

So, how do pet-friendly workplaces stack up in terms of pros and cons? Let's take a look:

**The benefits of pets in the workplace.**

(40)   • **Happier, more productive workers.** Both pet owners and non-pet owning employees report lowered stress levels and a higher level of job satisfaction with pets on the premises. This naturally leads to increased productivity.

• **Healthier workers.** In addition to reduced stress levels, being around
(45)   animals has documented positive effects on blood pressure, cholesterol levels and the immune system.

• **Increased loyalty.** Over half of employees in non-pet-friendly workplaces report they'd be more likely to continue working for a company if they could bring their pet to work.

**Potential problems you may encounter by allowing pets in the workplace.**

(50)   • **Not everyone is an animal lover.** There are people who dislike animals for one reason or another. Allergies, phobias, or a general dislike of animals could cause pets in the workplace to encroach[2] upon productivity and quality of life for these individuals.

• **Hygiene and cleanliness issues.** Even potty-trained pets can have an
(55)   accident now and then. There is no guarantee this won't happen in the workplace, especially with a high volume of animals brought to work.

• **Interoffice squabbles.** Not all animals get along, so there is the potential for fights between dogs and cats brought to work.

While worker distraction is a concern for some human resource
(60)   managers considering a pet-friendly policy, the vast majority report that the benefits to morale and overall productivity far outweigh time spent "distracted" by pets in the workplace.

Advocates of allowing pets in the workplace insist that there are ways around the "cons" or risks of pet-friendly workplaces. The key to a success-
(65)   ful pet policy is a clear structure. . . .

—excerpted and adapted from "Do Pets in the Workplace Improve Morale?"
*https://online.arbor.edu*, August 8, 2016

---

[1]millennials—the generation born in the 1980s or 1990s, especially in the U.S.
[2]encroach—intrude

## Text 2

## Why Pets in the Workplace May Not Be
## As Great As You Thought

. . .Study after study has proven how pets have a calming effect on
our bodies and minds, how they help children with A.D.D. [Attention
Deficit Disorder] focus better, how they reduce blood pressure and
lower stress, how pets at the workplace make employees more creative,
*(5)* productive, and cordial to each other, and how they're such awesome
additions to our lives overall.

So it would seem that if we spend the best parts of our waking hours at
work, there's no better way to carry forward these wonderful benefits that
pets bring into our work lives too, right? Well, unfortunately there are no
*(10)* simple answers here.

While there is a growing wave of companies led by the usual suspects—
Google, Zynga, Ben & Jerry's, and others—that allow employees to take
their pets along to the workplace, there's also a growing debate about the
practicality of the whole idea. And these voices of concern are not just com-
*(15)* ing from the minority of pet-haters or pet-neutral folks around. Even pet
owners have reservations about bringing their beloved pooch to the office
with them on a daily basis. Here's why:

**Not in the Pink of Health**

. . .Spare a thought for the millions of your fellow Americans who suffer
from pet related allergies. The Asthma and Allergy Foundation of America
*(20)* pegs the figure of Americans with one form of pet allergy or another at
15% to 30% of the total population. Some of these allergies are so severe
that they cause rashes, temporary breathlessness, panic attacks, and even
severe respiratory disorders.

In addition to a physical reaction to the presence of pets around them,
*(25)* you could have coworkers who are genuinely scared of animals and feel
stressed out around them. For such individuals a pet in their workplace
is not a calming presence, but rather a constant threat to their wellbeing
and safety.

**Safety First**

. . .Many industries by their very nature are not conducive[1] to having
*(30)* pets sauntering around. Medical facilities, pharmaceutical companies,
chemical laboratories, and food businesses are all sectors where a pet can

---

[1]conducive—favorable

be a serious threat to the quality of the final product or service. In such environments, pets pose a genuine contamination hazard and are best kept out, no questions asked.

(35)    In some cases, it's in your pet's best interest to chill out at home and skip the trip to the workplace. Industries like construction, mining, refineries, and more can be dangerous for your pet's health and well-being. You wouldn't want to put your pet at risk just so you can be happy at work, would you? . . .

### Real Costs to the Company

(40)    As any pet owner will tell you, owning their bundle of joy is not cheap. From $1570 for a large dog to $575 for a parakeet per year, pet ownership comes at an ever-increasing price tag. When you turn your office into a pet friendly zone, you are in turn taking on some of the expenses of owning a pet upon yourself. Be prepared to stock your workplace with at least basic

(45)    pet supplies like snacks, water bowls, kitty litter, and chew toys.

If you think your costs end there (or are tangible), you are mistaken. Pets at the workplace also bring with them a built-in deterrent[2] for employees seeking career opportunities at your organization. With the market for talented and qualified workers already so scarce, adding an extra filter to

(50)    your recruitment process may not be the smartest idea from a competitive perspective. . . .

While the benefits that pets bring with them are numerous and the pro-pet lobby gets louder with every passing day, organizations need to also give credence[3] to the real issues that four-legged and feathered guests at work

(55)    bring along with them. . . .

—Rohan Ayyar
excerpted and adapted from "Why Pets in the Workplace
May Not Be As Great As You Thought"
*www.fastcompany.com*, November 14, 2014

---

[2]deterrent—obstacle
[3]credence—support

## Text 3

## Why a Pet-Friendly Office May Be the Key
## to Employee Satisfaction

...The pet-friendly office is transforming our current idea of the typical nine-to-five workspace. Although the primary allure appears to be 24/7 cuddles with man's best friend, the actual benefits of a pet-friendly office go much deeper.

(5)    Some of the world's biggest companies have proudly joined the ranks of pet-friendly businesses, from Googleplex,[1] to Build-A-Bear Workshop, to hospitals in New Jersey. This shift in office culture has shown that pet-friendly offices can provide unexpected (and positive) results to all varieties of businesses. ...

### Employee Satisfaction and Stress

(10)    Employee satisfaction is a constant concern for an engaging and exciting place. Studies have shown that unhappy workers can cause businesses to lose thousands of dollars over time due to sick leave, mediocre work, and destructive behavior. Keeping the office engaging and exciting can be a struggle, and combating organizational stress may be key to improving (15) a company's profits. ...

Giving employees the option to bring their pet to work could also save them the worry associated with leaving a pet at home. Instead of scrambling through the end of the day to go home and let the dog out, they have the dog with them and can continue to work without rushing. Instead of (20) spending money on a pet daycare on a regular basis, workers can watch their furry friend while in the office.

Pets are also known to be great stress-relievers in general. It's no wonder that Animal-Assisted Therapy is recognized as one of the leading treatments for post-war PTSD [Post-Traumatic Stress Disorder] and is gaining ground (25) as a popular solution for social workers. Multiple studies have shown that simply petting cats or dogs can be extremely beneficial for our health; from lowering blood pressure to increasing bone density.

### Attract Millennials

As a millennial, I can assure you: I would choose a pet-friendly office over the majority of other job offers out there. The benefit of bringing my pup to (30) work is a much stronger pull than a larger paycheck or fancy corner office.

Millennials love their pets, and millennials love pet-friendly offices. In fact, you could even argue that millennials are the reason pet-friendly offices

---

[1]Googleplex—Google headquarters

are taking the business world by storm. Being the largest demographic to enter the workforce, they have already brought with them a demand for a
(35)    new form of workplace flexibility and a break from the traditional office culture of our predecessors. . . .

### Improve Communication

If you've ever walked your dog through a park or downtown area, there's a significant chance that you've received more waves, 'hellos', and acknowl- edgements than if you had been walking by yourself. Walking or even being
(40)    near a dog is an excellent ice-breaker.

Shifting to a pet-friendly workspace can bring that same level of open and enthusiastic communication into the office. Water cooler conversa- tions[2] will lose some of their awkward chatter, and employees will have the added encouragement of meeting new people in the building through their
(45)    pets. This can lead to some inspiring brainstorm conversations as well as an increase in camaraderie[3] and trust among workers.

A 2012 study by the Virginia Commonwealth University found that employees that brought their dogs to work were not only less stressed than their pet-free predecessors, but those employees believed they were
(50)    50 percent more productive with the presence of their pets. The public relations manager of the company that participated, Lisa Conklin of Replacements Dinnerware, stated after the conclusion of the study:

"The study proved what we always thought: having dogs around leads to a more productive work environment, and people get to know each oth-
(55)    er through the pets. If you are in a position where something is stressful, seeing that wagging tail and puppy smile brightens the day—it can turn around the whole environment."

### Promote Employee Activity

On top of all these benefits, pets can also improve employee activity. Dog owners in the office will most likely have to walk their dog at least once a
(60)    day, allowing them the opportunity to get away from their computer and into the open air. Workplace wellness has received considerable attention lately and more companies are making this a priority. Pet-friendly offices can inspire a smooth transition to a more 'mobile' office. . . .

—Katie McBeth
excerpted and adapted from "Why a Pet-Friendly Office May Be the Key to
Employee Satisfaction"
*https://thebossmagazine.com,* September 28, 2016

---

[2]water cooler conversations—informal conversation
[3]camaraderie—fellowship

## Text 4

## Don't Bring Your Dog to Work

If there's a dog in the cubicle next to you, you're hardly alone: About 7 percent of employers now allow pets in the workplace, reports NPR [National Public Radio]. Five years ago, that figure stood at 5 percent. That might not seem like a big jump, but once you remove jobs that don't have
(5)   offices from the equation—manufacturing and agriculture, for instance— that's about a 50 percent increase. That rise is a victory for people who tout the benefits of inviting dogs and other furry friends into the office: It lowers the stress of employees, increases morale, produces tangible health benefits, and reduces turnover, all at no cost to the company.
(10)   But how do the dogs feel about it?

"Most people do not understand dog body language," said E'Lise Christensen, a board-certified veterinary behaviorist in Colorado. One major concern she has with the rise of pet-friendly work environments is the corresponding increased risk for behavioral problems, especially dog bites.
(15)   Since almost no one, not even many dog trainers, knows how to properly interpret dog body language, co-workers might interpret the panting of a dog in the office as a friendly smile, rather than a sign of nervousness. And in dogs, nervousness can lead to bites. "[People] can identify abject[1] fear, and they can identify extreme aggression, but they cannot reliably identify
(20)   things in between," said Christensen. It's in that wide middle area where we may not recognize pet discomfort.

Bonnie Beaver, executive director of the American College of Veterinary Behaviorists and a professor at Texas A&M University, said in an email that dog bites are not the only behavioral issues that might present problems.
(25)   Generally, dogs are expected to sit still in an office setting, which can be difficult for active dogs, leading to boredom (which, in turn, leads to problem behaviors like chewing up desk legs). These policies are also particularly hard on dogs if they're taken to the office only occasionally, instead of regularly; dogs are big on routines, and uncertainty adds to their
(30)   fear and stress.

Once you expand the conversation beyond our most domesticated companion, the prospects get even iffier. "Not all animals are comfortable with a very social setting," said Christensen. Each new animal, like cats or pot-bellied pigs, brings its own social complexities, not to mention the
(35)   possibility of contagious disease (it's rare that employers require proof of

---

[1]abject—severe

254

vaccination). Rabies, ringworm, and parasitic infections like scabies are all potential health risks for humans that come into contact with pets that haven't been properly vetted.[2]

(40)  Of course there's obvious appeal. Many people love dogs. They write whole articles gushing about a furrier workplace. (Dog skeptics, at least vocal ones, are harder to find.) When an employer is on board, the policy is often as informal as a person in charge saying, "Yeah, sure, whatever. Bring your dogs. It'll be great." Little or no oversight is applied to a matter that needs it in order to ensure the environment is conducive[3] to pets in the
(45)  workplace.

Christensen said companies should ideally hire an in-house behavioral expert to oversee a pet-at-work policy, especially in the initial stages, "but unless you're Google, I don't see that happening." More realistically, she said, better awareness will go a long way. Employers should take care to
(50)  craft a policy that works for dogs' well-being as well as humans'. This can include requiring proof of vaccinations, as well as providing training for offices on dog behavior (which can be as basic as watching videos).

"It's critical that people with dogs get special education, in at least body language, even if they think they know normal body language," said
(55)  Christensen. Given that most people can't even tell the difference between a relaxed and anxious dog, this advice seems prudent. Before more offices throw open their doors to dogs willy-nilly[4] and more pets start tagging along on the morning commute, we should learn how better to listen to them. They might be asking to stay at home.

—Matt Miller
excerpted and adapted from "Don't Bring Your Dog to Work"
*www.slate.com*, August 15, 2016

---

[2]vetted—examined
[3]conducive—favorable
[4]willy-nilly—in an unplanned manner

# PART 3—Text-Analysis Response

**Directions:** Closely read the text provided on pages 257 through 259 and write a well-developed, text-based response of two to three paragraphs. In your response, identify a central idea in the text and analyze how the author's use of *one* writing strategy (literary element or literary technique or rhetorical device) develops this central idea. Use strong and thorough evidence from the text to support your analysis. Do *not* simply summarize the text. You may use the margins to take notes as you read and scrap paper to plan your response. Write your response on a separate sheet of paper.

**Guidelines:**

**Be sure to**

- Identify a central idea in the text.
- Analyze how the author's use of *one* writing strategy (literary element or literary technique or rhetorical device) develops this central idea. Examples include: characterization, conflict, denotation/connotation, metaphor, simile, irony, language use, point-of-view, setting, structure, symbolism, theme, tone, etc.
- Use strong and thorough evidence from the text to support your analysis.
- Organize your ideas in a cohesive and coherent manner.
- Maintain a formal style of writing.
- Follow the conventions of standard written English.

## Text

...There were a number of people out this afternoon, far more than last Sunday. And the band sounded louder and gayer. That was because the Season had begun. For although the band played all the year round on Sundays, out of season it was never the same. It was like some one
*(5)* playing with only the family to listen; it didn't care how it played if there weren't any strangers present. Wasn't the conductor wearing a new coat, too? She was sure it was new. He scraped with his foot and flapped his arms like a rooster about to crow, and the bandsmen sitting in the green rotunda blew out their cheeks and glared at the music.
*(10)* Now there came a little "flutey" bit—very pretty!—a little chain of bright drops. She was sure it would be repeated. It was; she lifted her head and smiled.

Only two people shared her "special" seat: a fine old man in a velvet coat, his hands clasped over a huge carved walking-stick, and a big old
*(15)* woman, sitting upright, with a roll of knitting on her embroidered apron. They did not speak. This was disappointing, for Miss Brill always looked forward to the conversation. She had become really quite expert, she thought, at listening as though she didn't listen, at sitting in other people's lives just for a minute while they talked
*(20)* round her.

She glanced, sideways, at the old couple. Perhaps they would go soon. Last Sunday, too, hadn't been as interesting as usual. An Englishman and his wife, he wearing a dreadful Panama hat and she button boots. And she'd gone on the whole time about how she ought to wear
*(25)* spectacles;[1] she knew she needed them; but that it was no good getting any; they'd be sure to break and they'd never keep on. And he'd been so patient. He'd suggested everything—gold rims, the kind that curved round your ears, little pads inside the bridge. No, nothing would please her. "They'll always be sliding down my nose!" Miss Brill had wanted to
*(30)* shake her.

The old people sat on the bench, still as statues. Never mind, there was always the crowd to watch. To and fro, in front of the flower-beds and the band rotunda, the couples and groups paraded, stopped to talk, to greet, to buy a handful of flowers from the old beggar who had his

---

[1]spectacles—glasses

(35)  tray fixed to the railings. Little children ran among them, swooping and
laughing; little boys with big white silk bows under their chins, little
girls, little French dolls, dressed up in velvet and lace. And sometimes
a tiny staggerer came suddenly rocking into the open from under the
trees, stopped, stared, as suddenly sat down "flop," until its small high-
(40)  stepping mother, like a young hen, rushed scolding to its rescue. Other
people sat on the benches and green chairs, but they were nearly always
the same, Sunday after Sunday, and—Miss Brill had often noticed—
there was something funny about nearly all of them. They were odd,
silent, nearly all old, and from the way they stared they looked as though
(45)  they'd just come from dark little rooms or even—even cupboards!

Behind the rotunda the slender trees with yellow leaves down droop-
ing, and through them just a line of sea, and beyond the blue sky with
gold-veined clouds.

Tum-tum-tum tiddle-um! tiddle-um! tum tiddley-um tum ta! blew the
(50)  band. . . .

Oh, how fascinating it was! How she enjoyed it! How she loved sitting here, watching it all! It was like a play. It was exactly like a play.
Who could believe the sky at the back wasn't painted? But it wasn't till
a little brown dog trotted on solemn and then slowly trotted off, like a
(55)  little "theatre" dog, a little dog that had been drugged, that Miss Brill
discovered what it was that made it so exciting. They were all on the
stage. They weren't only the audience, not only looking on; they were
acting. Even she had a part and came every Sunday. No doubt somebody would have noticed if she hadn't been there; she was part of the
(60)  performance after all. How strange she'd never thought of it like that
before! And yet it explained why she made such a point of starting from
home at just the same time each week—so as not to be late for the performance—and it also explained why she had quite a queer, shy feeling
at telling her English pupils how she spent her Sunday afternoons. No
(65)  wonder! Miss Brill nearly laughed out loud. She was on the stage. She
thought of the old invalid gentleman to whom she read the newspaper
four afternoons a week while he slept in the garden. She had got quite
used to the frail head on the cotton pillow, the hollowed eyes, the open
mouth and the high pinched nose. If he'd been dead she mightn't have
(70)  noticed for weeks; she wouldn't have minded. But suddenly he knew he
was having the paper read to him by an actress! "An actress!" The old
head lifted; two points of light quivered in the old eyes. "An actress—

are ye?" And Miss Brill smoothed the newspaper as though it were the manuscript of her part and said gently; "Yes, I have been an actress for
(75)   a long time."...

—Katherine Mansfield
excerpted from "Miss Brill"
*The Garden Party and Other Stories*, 1922
Alfred A. Knopf, Inc.

# Examination June 2019
## English Language Arts

## Answer Key

**Part 1**

| | | |
|---|---|---|
| 1. 3 | 9. 4 | 17. 4 |
| 2. 2 | 10. 4 | 18. 2 |
| 3. 1 | 11. 3 | 19. 4 |
| 4. 2 | 12. 3 | 20. 2 |
| 5. 1 | 13. 2 | 21. 1 |
| 6. 1 | 14. 3 | 22. 3 |
| 7. 3 | 15. 1 | 23. 3 |
| 8. 2 | 16. 3 | 24. 2 |

# INDEX

Abbreviations, 185
Abstract, 66
  to concrete, 66
Academic language, 128–132
Accept/except, 174
Active voice, 170
Adjectives, 162
  academic language, 130–132
  archaic, 135
  in a series, 190–191
  vocabulary study, 147–148
Adverb, 163
Affect/effect, 174
Aggravate, 175
Allegory, 94
Alliteration, 83, 94
Allusion, 94
Allusion/illusion, 175
Ambiguity, 77, 94
Among/between, 175
Amount/number, 175
Analogy, 66
Analysis, 103
Anecdote, 66, 124
Antecedent, 162
Antecedent-pronoun agreement, 168
Antithesis, 66
Apostrophe, 194–195
  with contractions, 194–195
  with possessive forms of nouns, 195
  with possessive forms of proper names, 195
  with some plurals, 195
Archaic language, 133–135
Argument, 66, 124
As far as . . . is/are concerned, 175
As/if/like, 179–180
Assonance, 81, 94
Atmosphere, 51, 66
Attitude of speaker, 86
Audience, 108, 124
Autobiography. See also Biography
  definition of, 66–67
  recommended, 217–218

Bad/badly, 122, 175–176
Ballad, 78, 94
Being as/being that, 176
Biography, 67. See also Autobiography

Blank verse, 94
Bracket, 194

Caring, 123
Cause and effect, 59, 103–104
Character, 67, 101
  focus, 106–107
  reading, 51–52
Characterization, 67
Chronological order, 58
Chronology and plot, 48–49
Claim, 3, 32–33
Classification, 62–63, 103
Clauses, 164–165
  comma after introduction, 189
  dependent, 164, 189
  descriptive, 189
  independent, 165, 188
  nonessential, 189
  parallel, 172
  restrictive, 173
  subordinate (dependent), 173
Close reading, 5–6
Coherence, 124
Collective nouns, 168
Colon, 193
Comma, 187
  with adjectives in a series, 190–191
  after introduction clause, 189
  after introductory phrase only when needed, 189
  in dates, 190
  descriptive and nonessential clauses or phrases set off using, 189
  errors involving, 191–192
  before the last item in a series, 188
  with parenthetic and transitional expressions, 190
  quotes set off using, 191
  with some single words and expression, 190
  splice, 188
Common Core Learning Standards, 2
Compare to/compare with, 176
Comparison and contrast, 59–61, 102–103
Composition evaluation, 118
Compound
  elements, 191

expressions, 205
 sentences, 187, 192
Conclusions, 108
Concrete, 67
 to abstract, 55–56
Conflict, 67
 external, 48, 67
 internal, 48, 67
 plot and, 47–48
Conjunctions, 163, 187
 coordinating, 163, 187
 subordinating, 163
Connotation, 95, 145–146
Consonants, 198–204
Contractions, 194–195
Controlling idea, 124
Conventions, 124
Coordinating conjunction, 163, 187
Correlatives, 167, 170
Could of/should of (could have/should have),
 176
Couplet, 83, 95

Dash, 193
Dates, 190, 195
Declarative sentences, 183
Definition in nonfiction, 62–63
Denotation, 95
Denouement, 67–68
Dependent clauses, 164, 189
Describe/description, 104, 124–125
Descriptive clauses or phrases, 189
Details, 102
Determinism, 68
Development, 125
Diction, 125
Different from (not than), 176
Direct objects, 144
Dramatic monologue, 95
Due to, 123, 176

Effective, 122
Either/or, 167, 170
Elegy, 86, 95
Elements and techniques, 107–108
Ellipsis, 193–194
Emphatic sentences, 192
Endings, 198
End punctuation, 183–187
Epic, 78, 95
Episode, 68

Essay
 definition of, 68
 exam preparation, 119
 formal, 69
 informal, 69
 planning of, 32
 recommended, 217–218
 topics for. See Topics for essay
Everybody, somebody, someone, nobody,
 177
Examinations. See also Regents exams
 compose, 120
 composition evaluation, 118
 edit as you go, 120–121
 essay exams, preparing, 119
 ideas, gathering your, 119–120
 learning standards, 223–227
 organize, 120
 poetry on, 87
 prompt, writing from a, 115
 scoring rubrics, 227–232
 writing on timed, 119–121
Exclamation mark, 184
Exemplification, 104
Explain/show/discuss, 104
Explication, 86
Exposition, 35–38, 68, 125
Extended metaphor, 61–62
External conflict, 48, 67

Farther/further, 177
Fewer/less, 177
Fiction reading, 46–53
Figurative language, 77, 95
First, second..., 177
Flashback, 68
Focus, 125
 character, 106–107
 topic and, 102
Foreshadowing, 68
Form, 69
Formal essay, 69
Fragments for emphasis, 184
Free verse, 95

General to specific, 66
Genre, 69, 103
Gerunds, 169
Good/well, 175–176
Greek prefixes, 141–142
Greek roots, 139

Hang/hanged/hung, 177
Hard/difficult, 123
Him/her/them, 168
Homophones, 205–206
Hopefully, 177–178
However, 178
Hyperbole, 95–96

Iambic pentameter, 96
Identify, 104
If . . . were/if . . . was, 178–179
If/like/as, 179–180
If/whether, 178
Image, 69, 107
Imagery, 77, 96
Imperative sentences, 184
Incredible/incredulous, 179
Independent clauses, 165, 187–188
Infer/imply, 178
Informal essay, 69
Intensifiers (adverbs), 163
Interjection, 163
Internal conflict, 48, 67
Internal punctuation, 187–195
Internal rhyme, 81, 96
Intransitive verbs, 144
Introductory phrase, 189
Ironic, 50, 72
Irony, 69, 82, 88, 96
Italics
   for quotes, 196
   for titles of works of literature, 196
Its/it's, 178

Journal, 69
Just/only, 180

Kind of/sort of/ type of, 179

Language
   academic, 128–132
   archaic, 133–135
   figurative, 95
   fluent and precise, 104–105
   of poetry, 78–83
   unfamiliar, 133–135
Latin prefixes, 140–142
Latin roots, 137–139
Learning standards, 223–227
Lie/lay, 179
Like/as/if, 179–180

Limited omniscient point of view, 50, 70–71
Literacy, 2
Literature. *See also* Reading
   punctuation of titles of works, 196
   on Regents exam, 101–159
   writing about, 101–108
Logical
   comparisons, 172
   modification, 173–174
Lyric, 96
   poetry, 78

Melodrama, 69
Memoir, 69
Metaphor, 77, 96–97
Meter, 75, 97
Monologue, 69
Motivation, 51, 70

Narration in nonfiction, 58
Narrative, 125
   poetry, 78
   point of view, 70
Narrator, 49, 70
Naturalism, 70, 103
Neither/nor, 167
New York State Standards in Literacy
   guide to, 1
   terms for understanding, 2–3
Nobody, everybody, somebody, someone, 177
Nonessential clauses or phrases, 189
Nonfiction. *See also* Reading
   abstract to concrete, 55
   cause and effect, 59
   chronological order, 58
   comparison and contrast, 59–61
   concrete to abstract, 55–56
   definition or classification, 62–63
   extended metaphor, 61–62
   general to specific, 55
   narration, 58
   order of importance, 63–65
   patterns and organization, 54–65
   purpose, 54
   question to answer, 56–58
   reading, 53–66
   recommended, 217–218
   tone, 65–66
Nonrestrictive (nonessential) phrases, 173
Not only/but also, 170
Noun(s), 162

academic language, 130–132
archaic, 134
collective, 168
modifiers of, 164
plurals, 204–205
possessive forms of, 195
vocabulary study, 146–147
Novels, recommended, 215–216

Objective, 50
point of view, 70
Object of verb, 169–170
Ode, 97
Omniscient, limited, 50
Omniscient narration, 49
Omniscient point of view, 70–71
Only/just, 180
Onomatopoeia, 83, 97
Order of importance, 63–65
Oxymoron, 97

Paradox, 97
Parallelism, 170
Parentheses, 186
Parenthetic expressions, 190
Participial phrase, 173
Participle, 164, 174
Passive voice, 170
Patterns and rules, 197–206
Period, 183–184
Persona, 49, 70–71
Personal narrative, 109
Personification, 82, 97
Persuasive writing, 53, 66, 112
Phrases, 164–165
descriptive, 189
nonessential, 189
nonrestrictive (nonessential), 173
parallel, 170
participial, 173
restrictive, 173
Plays, recommended, 220–221
Plot
chronology and, 48–49
conflict and, 47–48
definition, 71, 104
story and, 47
time and, 49
Plurals, 195, 204–205
Poem(s)/poetry
on examinations, 87

for further reading, 87–93
internal rhyme of, 81
lyric, 78
narrative, 78
prose, 86–87, 97
reading, 75–99
recommended, 218–219
structure and language of, 78–83
theme in, 83–85
tone in, 80, 86
writing about, 86
Poetic justice, 71
Point of view, 49, 71
limited omniscient, 50, 71
narrative, 49–51, 70
objective, 70
omniscient, 70–71
Position paper, 125
Possessive form, 195
Prefixes, 136, 198, 202–203
Preposition, 163
Presently, 180
Present perfect tense, 171
Present tense, 171
Prologue, 71
Prompt, 115, 125
Pronoun(s), 162, 169–170
Pronoun-antecedent agreement, 168
Proper names, 195
Prose, 71, 86, 97
Protagonist, 71
Punctuation
end, 183–187
internal, 187–195
Purpose in nonfiction, 54
Purposely/purposefully, 180

Quatrains, 80, 83, 97
Question, 56–58
Question mark, 184–185
Quotation marks, 185–186
Quotes, 191, 196

Reading. See also Literature; Nonfiction
autobiography, recommended, 217–218
character, 51–52
close, 5–6
essays, recommended, 217–218
fiction, 46–53
for information and understanding, 23–30
narrative point of view, 49–51

nonfiction, 53–66, 217–218
novels, recommended, 215–216
plays, recommended, 220–221
plot
   chronology and, 48–49
   conflict and, 47–48
   story and, 47
   time and, 49
poetry, 75–99, 218–219
setting, 51
short stories, 220
for text analysis, 35–43
theme, 52–53
useful terms, 45–46
Reading comprehension
   close reading, 5–6
   informational passage, 16–21
   poem, 12–15
   questions used in, 6
   sample passages for, 7–21
Realism, 71
Regents exams. *See also* Examinations
   description of, 3
   samples, 233–292
   vocabulary study, 127–159
Restrictive clauses, 173
Restrictive phrases, 173
Rhetoric, 72
Rhetorical question, 72
Rhyme, 80–81, 98
Rhyme scheme, 83, 98
Rhythm, 75, 97
Romance, 72, 103
Roots. *See also* Spelling
   Greek, 136, 139
   Latin, 140–142
   prefixes and, 136–142, 198
Rules and patterns, 197
Run-on sentence, 188

Sad/depressing, 123
Same, 124
Satire, 72, 98
Semicolon, 192–193
Sentence(s)
   complete, 165
   compound, 187, 192
   declarative, 183
   emphatic, 192
   entire, 185–186
   exclamation mark, 184

imperative, 184
period, 183–184
question mark, 184–185
run-on, 188
Series, 188
Setting, 51
Short stories, 72, 220
Significant details, 102
Simile, 77, 98
Simple past tense, 171
So, 180
Soliloquy, 52, 72, 98
Somebody, someone, nobody, everybody, 177
Sonnet, 83, 98
Sort of/type of/kind of, 179
Source-based argument, 31
Speaker, 72, 79–80, 86, 98
Specific to general, 55–56
Spelling. *See also* Roots
   homophones, 205–206
   noun plurals, 204–205
   prefixes and suffixes, 202–203
   rules and patterns, 197–198
   on writing exams, 197
Spelling words
   commonly confused, 206–207
   commonly misspelled, 207–214
   with double letters, 200–202
   ending in silent *e*, 198–199
   ending in *y*, 199–200
   including *ie* or *ei*, 203
Standards, 223
Stanza, 98–99
Story and plot, 47
Structure of poetry, 78–83
Subject and themes, 105
Subject of the participle, 174
Subject of verb, 166, 181–182
Subject-verb agreement, 166–168
Subordinate (dependent) clauses, 173
Subordinating conjunctions, 163
Suffixes, 198, 200, 202–203
Syllable, 198
Symbol, 72, 99
Synonymies, 121–124
Synonyms, 142–143

Tense of verb, 171
Text analysis
   exposition, 35–38
   reading and writing for, 35–43

That/who/which, 181
Themes, 73, 80
  in poetry, 83–85
  reading, 52–53
  subject and, 105
Them/him/her, 168
Thesaurus, 142–143
Thesis, 73
Thesis statement, 3
Time and plot, 49
To cause, 121
To change, 121
To look down upon someone/something, 122
To look upon someone/something, 121
Tone, 73, 125
  definition of, 99
  in poetry, 80, 86
  in writing, 65–66
Topics for essay
  analysis, 103
  classification, 103
  comparison and contrast, 102–103
  details, selecting significant, 102
  developing the, 102–104
  exemplification, 104
  topic and focus, 102
Toward/towards, 181
Tragedy, 103
Transition, 73, 125
Transitional expressions, 190
Transitive verbs, 144–145
Turning point, 73
Type of/kind of/sort of, 179

Underline, 196
Understanding, 101, 107
Understatement, 99
Unity, 125

Verb(s)
  academic language, 128–130
  archaic, 133–134
  definition, 162
  intransitive, 144–145
  object of, 169–170
  subject and, agreement between, 166–168
  subject of, 166, 181–182
  tense of, 171–172
  transitive, 144–145
  vocabulary study of, 143–144

Verisimilitude, 73
Verse
  blank, 94
  free, 95
Vocabulary study, 127–159
  adjectives, 147–148
  from book reviews, 156–159
  nouns, 146–147
  from Op-Ed pages, 152–156
  from Regents exams, 149–152
  verbs, 143–146
Vowels, 197, 200–201, 204–205

When/where, 181
Whether/if, 178
Which/that/who, 181
Who/whom/whoever/whomever, 181–182
Words
  commonly confused, 206–207
  commonly misspelled, 207–214
  with double letters, 200–202
  ending in silent e, 198–199
  ending in y, 199–200
  Greek prefixes, 141–142
  Greek roots, 136, 139
  including ie or ei, 203
  Latin prefixes, 140–142
  Latin roots, 137–139
  learning in context, 135
  from Regents exams, 149–159
  roots and prefixes, 136–142, 198
Writing
  audience, 108
  character focus, 106–107
  conclusions, 108
  elements and techniques, 107–108
  essay topics, 101
  on examinations, 109–125
  explication, 86
  fluent and precise, 104–105
  to inform or persuade, 109–115
  literature as focus of, 101–108, 101–159
  personal narrative, 109–111
  persuasive, 109–115
  poetry as focus of, 86
  from prompt, 115–118
  subject and themes, 105
  for text analysis, 35–43
  tone, 65–66